SCULTHORPE: MAN OF STEEL

SCULTHORPE: MAN OF STEEL

PAUL SCULTHORPE

C

Century · London

Published by Century 2007

2 4 6 8 10 9 7 5 3 1

First published in Great Britain in 2007 by
Century
Random House, 20 Vauxhall Bridge Road,
London SW1V 2SA

www.rbooks.co.uk

Addresses for companies within The Random House Group Limited can be
found at: www.randomhouse.co.uk/offices.htm

The Random House Group Limited Reg. No. 954009

A CIP catalogue record for this book
is available from the British Library

ISBN 9781846051623

The Random House Group Limited makes every effort to ensure that the
papers used in its books are made from trees that have been legally sourced
from well-managed and credibly certified forests. Our paper procurement
policy can be found at: www.randomhouse.co.uk/paper.htm

Typeset by SX Composing DTP, Rayleigh, Essex
Printed and bound in Great Britain by
Clays Ltd, St Ives PLC

Dedication

To Lindsay: For staying by me through thick and thin. I don't know what I've done to deserve you. I will never be able to thank you enough.

To Mum and Dad: For all the support and loving. If I can do half the job you did with my kids, I know I'll have raised them well.

To Jake and Lucy-Jo: You are my world. For making the darkest days seem sunny and for leaving me with a constant smile on my face.

To Danny and Lee: I told you all those games of knee rugby in the lounge would pay off. Maybe that's what caused my injuries!

To Ian and Eileen: They say you can't choose your relatives. If you could, I would have picked you two.

To Lisa: I grew up with two brothers, but have had a sister ever since I met you.

To Paula: For the endless support, reassurance and help – and especially for putting up with all those bad moods!

To Mum and Dad: For all the advice, backing and belief . . . and the hours of checking the facts!

To Hannah: For being the most fantastic daughter any dad could ever wish for.

Contents

Foreword by Eric Ashton,
   Former St Helens chairman   ix
Introduction by Ricky 'The Hitman' Hatton, IBF and IBO
   world light-welterweight boxing champion   xi

1 On Top of the World   1
2 Early Days   14
3 Now the Wire!   30
4 From Dorahy to Darryl   44
5 Time to Move On   51
6 To Ell and Back   67
7 Basil's Brush – A New Broom   83
8 Bronco Busting   94
9 Grabbing the Bulls by the Horns   112
10 Down to Earth   127
11 Gambling Fever   138
12 Dan and Dusted   149
13 Bye, Bye Basil   157
14 Final Misery   166

15 Tour de Farce   175
16 Tough Cookies   192
17 Jokers Wild   201
18 Nearest and Dearest   210
19 Under the Influence   231
20 Places to Go, People to Meet   243
21 Heroes and Heartbreakers   257
22 The Times They Are A Changing   266

Foreword
By Eric Ashton

Former St Helens champion

Of all the memories I have of St Helens' double-winning season of 1996, one of the brightest was a moment of sheer class against us – the moment which convinced me we simply had to sign Paul Sculthorpe.

In May of that year we won a spectacular game 25-24 at Warrington, but it was Paul's all-round display and one superb piece of skill which left a lasting impression. He came away from the back of a scrum deep in his own half, took a defender with him, and then turned the ball inside to send winger Richard Henare racing away for a long-range try.

At the time Paul was still a teenager, yet playing with so much maturity. I have never seen anyone so outstanding. We made inquiries as soon as possible, and Warrington told us they would not take less than £250,000. In the end he cost another £100,000 on top, but what a signing!

I spoke to an agent and asked him if he knew of any club

looking for a couple of players who we were prepared to let go. He came back to me and asked who we would sell to Hull.

Alan Hunte wanted to leave at that time, and he was joined by Simon Booth, who was going to university over there, and Steve Prescott left as well. Those sales brought in £350,000 and that went straight to Warrington for Paul – and I never had any doubt about the decision, even though some of our directors questioned why we had spent so much.

It is true that he did take time to settle in, but I had no doubts once that period was over that he would be worth every penny – and more.

Paul is big, he is powerful, he is dominant and he has a presence about him. He is so gifted, has good hands, and is so nicely balanced. Then there is the bonus of his kicking game, for field position or goal kicking. Both are top class.

All that before you come to his leadership qualities, which are tremendous as well. He can tell people in his way, a nice way, to get the players to do things. Everything seems to revolve around him. I hear the players say, 'Scully said this, Scully said that'. The players respect him.

When he won the Man of Steel two years running everyone could witness what a great player Paul had become – and off the field he is such a marvellous ambassador for the sport.

There was one time when we needed someone at very short notice to be available at a major supermarket in Prescot, where a car was being raffled. I phoned Paul; it was not a problem. He went to the supermarket and was friendly, approachable and helpful. And he never asked for a penny.

He is the complete player in all respects – I have signed plenty of players for St Helens over the years and Paul Sculthorpe goes down as one of the best.

Introduction
By Ricky 'The Hitman' Hatton

IBF and IBO world light-welterweight boxing champion

A lot of people call boxing the toughest sport in the world, and after some of the bruises I've woken up with over the years I'm not about to disagree.

But if there is anything to push it close, it's rugby league – and I am speaking with a bit of experience there, as well.

Don't get me wrong: I've never been in the middle of a scrum with some big prop forward trying to rearrange my ears. I'm not that stupid, despite what Scully may tell you.

My experience of exactly how tough these guys really are came when Scully visited my gym for a sparring session a couple of years ago. Fair enough, it was pretty much a staged event for a TV feature of some kind, but I still got enough of a taste to realise how hard these blokes are.

There were never going to be any serious punches thrown – would you fancy someone of his size catching you round the head? – but it was still quite a vigorous workout. Certainly more than I expected, anyway.

And although it was only knockabout stuff, it was obvious how fit these lads really are. I know Scully has a close interest in boxing, and from the way he handled himself it's not just from watching the odd match on the telly either.

Everyone knows I'm a big Manchester City fan, and, aside from boxing, my great love is football and particularly watching them. But I think most sportsmen take an interest in most sports – it's just in the nature – and so I knew about Scully's exploits even before we met.

I must admit, though, that ever since he was swinging punches at me I've followed his career that little bit closer than anyone else's, and I was cheering as loudly as anyone when he came back from his injury at the start of the season.

When you're as active as Scully, not being able to play must have been hell for him, and I take my hat off to him for the way he kept at it, refused to give in and came back in such brilliant fashion.

Simply getting back on to the field was an achievement in itself, but to do it in the way he did was mind-blowing – in the World Club Challenge, against the top Aussie side, the Brisbane Broncos, who were at full strength, and not having played a serious game for six months. You wouldn't have thought it possible.

But he didn't just come back, he won the man of the match trophy and turned the game around to the point where St Helens ended the night as world champions.

Having said that, you know what the really annoying thing is? The fact that Scully has been at the top level for ten years, won just about everything there is to win personally and with his team, yet still hasn't a mark on his face.

Makes you sick – he's possibly even better looking than me! Perhaps I should get him back in the ring after all, and put that matter straight!

Only joking, Scully. It's a pleasure to contribute to your book, mate, and may we both stay at the top for years to come. But if you think I'm returning the favour and going through some tackling practice with you, there's more chance of me wearing a United shirt and getting a season ticket to Old Trafford!

1

On Top of the World

The Reebok Stadium is only about sixteen miles from St Helens. It is a journey that, given a decent run, shouldn't take more than half an hour. When I walked out at Bolton Wanderers' impressive ground on 23 February 2007, it had taken me precisely 175 days. But just for a few seconds, when the final whistle blew on Saints' World Club Challenge success over Brisbane Broncos, I suddenly felt the whole agonising process had been well worth the wait.

Actually, that's not exactly true. There were times over the last Christmas period when I felt in anything but a festive mood. I don't think there were too many around who would really blame me, either. After all, when you're a professional sportsman there can't be many worse positions to be in than having to spend all night and most of the day with your right knee locked in a brace.

Yet that's just what I had to endure because of the biggest nightmare of my career, and one in which there seemed to be a steadily growing band who were convinced I was finished. So forgive me if I wallow in the memory a little, but could you really imagine a better scene for a comeback game, one that proved so many people wrong, and ended up with my team as world champions to boot?

My problems had been going on for the best part of three years before that memorable night at the Reebok. Back, hamstring, knee . . . you name it, I seemed to have problems with it, and the most worrying thing was that there was no obvious end to the bloody things either.

I had reached the stage where it seemed I would just have to put up with the pain and discomfort if I wanted to carry on playing. But then, fifteen minutes into our Super League game against Wakefield on 1 September, I knew it was all over for me as far as that season went. There would be no Grand Final, no skippering Great Britain in Australia on the Tri-Nations tour. Just endless hours of what little fitness work I could do, and a hefty dose of finger-crossing that I would come back better than before.

Even now I wince at the thought of that Wakefield game. We kicked off, I chased the ball downfield with the rest of the lads, and realised I had absolutely no power in my right knee. I think I knew then that my season was over, but with the prospect of Old Trafford around the corner, I certainly wasn't about to admit it while there was still a glimmer.

I had given it a rest for three weeks, specifically because I had my eyes on the qualifying semi-final against Hull, who had finished runners-up to us in the regular Super League season. But when I ran out for our usual training session on the Tuesday, traditionally our biggest of the week, something just wasn't quite right. I knew I had to come through it if I was to have any chance of playing against Hull. But within five minutes those hopes were dead and buried.

I've never really been one for throwing a paddy and like to think I can keep my emotions in check as well as anyone, although Ando will no doubt say I have my moments. But that day I just blew my top, and walked off the training field on my own with all the lads wondering what was going on. Daniel Anderson, our coach, obviously needed an explanation, and it was terrible having to tell him I had no chance of playing again that season, never mind the bloody Hull game.

Ando was as good as gold, as was everyone at the club, and in fact before I'd even got showered after that all too brief session, physio Matt Viljoen had arranged for a surgeon called Andrew Williams to have a look at me at the Chelsea and Westminster Hospital. St Helens had promised they would scour the country for the best man to sort my knee out once and for all, and they wasted no time in proving true to their word.

I'd been under the knife because of my knee before, back in 2004, because of all the wear and tear over the years, which had left me unable to straighten my leg properly. But when I'd had that exploratory op it didn't show anything. There was no floating bone, no cartilage displaced, no obvious reason why my leg wouldn't lock out, so it had basically just been left.

When you talk about decisions you wished you had made differently, that is a mile in front of anything! I must admit that when my knee went this time, I was asking myself all sorts of questions. Things like why no one had spotted anything before, why no one had suggested a closer look at the problem until a solution was found. All sorts of things went through my mind, but unfortunately none that would provide a short cut back to the pitch.

So there I was, season over, and a revolutionary – so I discovered – new operation to get me back into action. In basic terms what Andrew did was to cut the tendons from my calf that were joined to my femur and leave them separated, so that I could extend my leg again. Everything on that right side had shortened up because my body had just grown used to it. The scar tissue under my knee had been causing a problem, the other muscles had been overcompensating and I was effectively playing with a bent leg.

Rob Harris, the Manchester City physio, had taken a look at me during the Tri-Nations in 2004, when my back had collapsed on me. He immediately said it was all linked to me being unable to extend my knee properly, and because rugby league players take a pounding more than probably any other sport, the problem had grown fourfold. But, as I say, an exploratory op back then had found nothing, and, boy, was I about to pay the price now!

So while the rest of the Saints lads were celebrating last season's Grand Final win, I was already pinning my hopes on being ready for the World Club Challenge in four months time, when the English and Aussie champions would go head to head. I'd asked Mr Williams, the surgeon, about it as soon as I'd had my operation back in September, and he told me that although I might have an outside chance at best, April was a more realistic time to be coming back. With the game being in February, that was *not* what I wanted to hear.

The temptation, as I say, had been there initially just to try and keep playing. But I had no power in the knee, and knew I would have seriously regretted it later in my career. At least I knew I would get a bit of a head start on the lads when it came to pre-season. Basically I didn't really have a close season, because I was back in action a month before the rest of the lads, desperately working towards that goal of facing Brisbane.

Obviously I couldn't do a full-scale workout, but I did what I could and just didn't have a break. I'd had a date in my mind from the day I walked off the training ground before the Hull play-off game, even though I don't think there were too many at Saints who seriously thought I'd make it. When I'd mention it to Matt he'd laugh along with me and say 'we'll see', but deep down I think he was probably just trying to humour me.

But I was determined to get myself back, even though it hardly looked likely when they strapped my knee in a brace after surgery. I slept in the bloody thing for three months, and they didn't actually take it off until a few weeks before the World Challenge itself. I had gone so long without being able to straighten my leg that I needed help to do so.

Naturally I took it off when I was doing my exercises in the daytime, but any time I relaxed I'd whack it back on, simply because it made it easier to keep the leg straight. Fortunately it did the job because when I went down to see Mr Williams again for the assessment that would determine if I did indeed have any chance of playing, he was amazed at the progress I'd made.

He admitted then that I would have a chance of making the start of the season – and seeing as Super League kicked off a week before the Brisbane game suddenly I felt I was flying again. Obviously the knee was a lot weaker at first, simply through a lack of use, but just walking felt great, being able to lock my leg out – I didn't fully realise the restrictions I'd been training and playing under in the past.

All of a sudden I could put my full weight on my legs again without feeling any pain. It was only really then that the rest of the Saints lads told me that I'd been running with a limp for the past two years without really realising it. From then on things got better and better, until the week before the game, when I was running so much more freely. It was only looking back that I realised how bad it had been – like the game at Castleford the previous season when I'd basically limped my way to the line for a try.

Even so, despite the fact that I was well on the road to recovery, I had still done no contact work at all just a week before we were due to face the Broncos. In fact, the only bash-up I had between the Wakefield game on 1 September and the World Challenge final in February was a mocked-up session seventy-two hours before kickoff.

My final check-up came on the Monday of game week, and it meant I missed a training session, which was hardly the best because Ando said I'd have to do the same work as the others if I was to be considered. That suddenly had me very worried – but he came through for me. The lads were supposed to have the Tuesday off, but a few came in for optional work and in the afternoon Daniel set up a special match just for my benefit.

He had arranged a three-on-three game in a ten-metre corridor on the pitch outside, with five of the younger lads like Ste Tyrer, Gary Wheeler, Ste Bannister and a couple more under 21s to help. Basically it was just a 'bash 'em' game, to give me at least some experience of getting hammered again. To be honest, that was the most nervous I was. You can do all the training in the world, but until you're in anything resembling a game situation, you don't know for certain how things are going to go. It didn't help that all the lads who'd come in for extra training were standing around the outside of the pitch to watch me. But I needn't have worried because the session was absolutely brilliant. Coming off in one piece was a fantastic feeling, and having the chance to take out some aggression instead of skulking around the house gave me a right buzz.

In fact it was only after it that I realised how down I had been for the past few months, albeit subconsciously. Not being able to do your job isn't the best feeling in the world, but I'd basically had to like it or lump it. And because I didn't like it, I'd been bloody lumping it for the best part of six months.

After that, the rest of the week was a breeze – I even did the full wrestling session with the lads on the Wednesday, went through the 'captain's run', which is always a bit light-hearted anyway, and then it was just a case of running through the game plan and various plays.

The funny thing was that for all the earlier speculation that I might have a chance, there had been nothing in the press. Funny how all those people who were quick to write me off as a has-been weren't so sharpish to take a punt that I'd be back. Maybe it was because they'd realise how stupid they would all look – although that doesn't seem to have stopped them in the past. And they've made a pretty good job of it, too.

But I couldn't have given a toss about whether anyone else thought I would be playing. I knew I was – half an hour on the bench and then out there, back into the action. Fantastic! Friday couldn't come quickly enough for me. There were, of course, still the formalities to go through – like officially telling Ando I was fit and ready. Although when he asked me 'are you up for it?' I don't really know what else he expected me to say.

He only actually named his side after the last session on the Thursday, but by then the lads knew I was in because I'd come through everything alongside them. I don't think I have ever been so desperate to play a game, and the fact it was the World Club Challenge made it even better. And the fact that we'd managed to keep it such a secret from all those people who thought I'd struggle to come back again in any form was just the icing on the cake for me.

The lads were all really up for it, but personally I was looking forward to running out for the warm-up as much as the match itself. Just the chance to be out there, getting ready for a serious game after so long, was absolutely brilliant. And I have to thank everyone who was at the Reebok that night for the great reception I received. Obviously they were largely Saints fans, but the great thing about rugby league is that fans from all clubs go to the big games, and they seemed just as pleased to see me again as those from my own club. I had nothing but good wishes and support from the lot of them, and I was determined not to let them down.

I must admit there was a slight temptation to run out of the tunnel with two fingers up at the press box, but in the end I thought, 'sod you lot, I've got more important things on my mind.' I knew I was fit, probably as fit as I've ever been, and I knew that being injured didn't affect your level of ability, so why shouldn't I do the business again? It was the same story when I did my Achilles in June 2007. People had formed the wrong impression of me because they'd only seen me the previous year, when I knew I was nowhere near my best fitness-wise. This was my chance to show everyone – just as I plan to again.

Unfortunately on the pitch things weren't going too well for the lads, and we were 8–0 down pretty early on, when Corey Parker scored a try, which he converted himself, and then added another penalty. If you'd had to stake your life on the outcome then, I don't think too many in the ground would have backed a Saints win. So twenty minutes in – some ten minutes ahead of his original plan, Ando said the words I was desperate to hear: You're on!

I think he knew that the team and the crowd both needed a lift, and he obviously felt that throwing me back into action would get it. Given how things went afterwards, I suppose it would be hard to argue with him. There was never any chance of me going into it not fully warmed up, either. From the moment we'd gone for a run on the pitch before kickoff, I'd gone straight back on the bike in the dressing room. And when the game started, I was on the bike by the side of the dugout. I had probably pedalled the distance from St Helens to Bolton and back by the time I got on.

I was determined that when my call came to play I wasn't going to blow it by being too stiff, or pull a muscle while cooling down from my earlier preparations. In fact when I went back in at half-time I was straight back on the bike for another fifteen minutes, so all in all I must have done more than two and a half hours without a break. I don't suppose anyone could seriously doubt my fitness after that. Mind you, I'd been on the bloody bike most days for six months, so I reckon I could have taken on the Tour de France, never mind the World Club Challenge, by then.

My first touch filled me with confidence as well, taking a short ball, hitting a bit of space and just pushing through. I felt big and strong, and was absolutely delighted when I got a big hit but bounced straight back to my feet. That proved to me I was 100 per cent again, if a little rusty just through lack of match practice.

Then, out of nothing, we got a try just before half-time when Adey Gardner scored in the right corner. I knew what was coming now, even if none of the fans did. Ando had asked me the day before if I fancied taking the goal kicks. Again, it was a question to which I think he knew the answer before I opened my mouth.

Clearly not too many around that part of the Reebok realised I'd be kicking, though, judging from the looks on a few faces as I lined up the conversion. But I felt confident and just smoked it, straight through the middle, and all of a sudden the Brisbane lead was down to only two points. Talk about a psychological boost coming at just the right time.

Actually, when Ando had mentioned taking the kicks I'd done a bit of a session before the game, but was still a little wary of doing too much. So I only took three kicks at goal because I didn't want to load my knee – and I got them all, from varying angles as well, so I was full of confidence as I lined up that first kick.

The mood in the dressing room at the break was totally different from how it would've been had the hooter gone two or three minutes earlier. There's a big difference between going in two points down or four points down in a game of that intensity, and we knew we were right in there fighting again. After all, we'd come back from 18–6 down to beat Brisbane in the World Challenge once before, in 2001, and we'd had a couple more pre-season games than them, so we had every reason to be full of confidence.

To be honest, the second half is a bit of a blur – but I can still remember the relevant bits! They scored after a kick across the field, which made our half-time confidence seem a bit misplaced, but still the gap was only one converted try. And my big moment was just around the corner.

One thing I had really missed was running off Keiron Cunningham, the Saints hooker and the best in the world at his position. Over the years Kez has put me in for more tries than I can remember, and, bloody hell, he came up trumps this time. If you had to pick anyone to put it on a plate for you, it would be him. There is simply no one better.

I remember running the line, Shane Perry coming out to block, but stepping past him and when Kez popped the ball out I was in for a try. Just to cap it all, I got up and kicked the conversion as well, and we were level. They got another penalty to go 14–12 in front again, but there was no way we were going to blow it now and when Adey went in for his second, I kicked another goal and we were champions.

That final whistle was a massive relief on so many levels – obviously because of what we had won but personally because I had come through unscathed, no reaction to the leg and everything to look forward to once more. But there was one more surprise to come, when Andrew Whitelam, the Super League media boss, told me I'd been voted man of the match. I'd been so caught up in the occasion that I hadn't even heard the announcement. Talk about a night to end them all – try scorer, successful goalkicker, man of the match in the World Challenge, against the champion Aussie team. It doesn't come much better than that.

Funnily enough, I had absolutely no problem with the knee during the game, but as soon as the whistle went it began killing me. I'd got a couple of bangs on it throughout the course of the match, but afterwards it felt as if someone had been jumping on it. And when I woke up the next morning I couldn't put any serious weight on it at all.

I had learned enough over the years to know that if I'd gone out that night with the rest of the lads and had a few drinks, it wouldn't have done me any good, because I needed to rest the leg after six months of not playing. You don't think about it so much when you're a kid, but, as you get older, you realise that if you have a few pints when you've got a bit of a knock, it makes it ten times worse. And I'd spent enough time on the sidelines without helping to put myself back there – even though

I was to suffer another blow just three months later when my Achilles went in a routine training session.

So when I got up the next day in real pain I wasn't unduly worried, because I knew it wasn't a recurrence of the same problem, just a reaction to my first game in six months, and there was always going to be some sort of kickback. The bang I'd received in the match had loosened some debris in the knee, which was catching a bit, so within a couple of days I was back down to London to have a scan, and the shit scraped out of my knee. It was totally different from before, so there was no sense of trepidation this time, either, because I knew it wasn't anything serious, like damaged ligaments or cartilage.

But to be honest, I didn't need any alcohol to put me on cloud nine after that game. I was managing to get up there perfectly well by myself, thank you. I knew I'd played better games and made far more influential contributions, but, for the first one, this would do very nicely.

Yet for all I enjoyed it, I never bothered watching a rerun on Sky when I got in. In fact I never watch any of my games, unless it's during a video session with Ando and the lads at Saints. I've since seen little snatches of it on various sports programmes, but I'm not one for sitting down and going through the whole thing again. Anyway, my dad made up for it by watching it about ten times the following day.

I'm just not interested in seeing things again, whether I've played the game of my life or had a nightmare. A player knows how he's done and doesn't need any ex-pros or so-called experts pointing things out. It's like the Challenge Cup final we played against Wigan a couple of years ago, when we and my brother Danny made history by lining up on opposite sides. I've never watched that either, even though we won. Maybe I should sneak a copy into the house and stick it on the next time he's round!

Besides, I had everything I needed from the game inside my own head, and the lads were absolutely brilliant, all getting in touch to tell me how made up they were for me as much as for themselves. It seemed a few others were of the same opinion. When we had got back to the changing rooms after the lap of honour I showed Wello – full back Paul Wellens – my mobile: there were already loads of missed calls and texts from people wishing me well. Over the course of the night I got another thirty-odd as well. It was absolutely mad, but I made sure I replied to every one – the way I went, it's just surprising I wasn't out for another six months with pulled finger muscles.

I've never really been one for displaying my medals, either. I've got a lot of framed shirts in my pool room, but there is no showy cabinet full of things I've won. I've got a couple of things up, but most of my medals just go in a drawer in my house, and I think a few are at Mum and Dad's in Oldham. I don't wear any of my Super League Grand Final winners' rings either. I gave the first one to my son, Jake, and that's safely stashed in his special drawer in his bedroom. Woe betide anyone who tries to have a look in there, I tell you.

But just because they're not on show doesn't mean I don't love picking up winners' medals and trophies. I plan to collect a whole load more before I finally hang up my boots. Maybe then I'll dust them down and put them on show to remind me of the great times I've had – but for now I'm going to be too busy concentrating on winning a few more. I want to win now as much as I did when I was first starting, and it's just a pity it does not include an Ashes winning series against the Aussies.

2

Early Days

It's funny to look back on now, but the first time I ever picked up a rugby ball was only under the threat of a bollocking off my dad! At the time I was more into football, even though I was anything but the new Gazza, and loved nothing more than a kickabout with our Lee, who is three years older.

I trained with him at Failsworth Tigers, and although I knew even then that I wasn't the most talented youngster Oldham had ever seen, I loved every minute of it. I suppose you could say that as far as football was concerned I was born to play rugby! Finesse? I was more Ronald McDonald than Ronaldo!

As with most boys with older brothers, I tended to follow Lee around, and because he only ever played football that was the sport for me back then. But when I was eight, my dad spotted an advert in the *Oldham Chronicle* about a new rugby team that was being formed, and asked me and our Dan if we fancied it.

Dan was really up for it, and I suppose I was sent along as his older brother to look after him – as if he's ever needed that! And when I say I was told to go, that's exactly what happened. I wasn't that bothered, to be honest, but I was bothered about getting a roasting off my old fella, so off I went – with Lee along as minder!

I'd watched my dad, who was always rugby league mad, play a few amateur games for Shaw and St Anne's, but had never considered it myself. That changed after the first training session for Royton Tigers, as the new club was called. It was back in 1985, and was run by a couple called Steve and Marilyn Bithell, and I owe a hell of a lot to them. If they and Tony 'Tiger' Finnan, the ex-Huddersfield hooker who was helping them, hadn't got Royton off the ground and got them into the newly formed Greater Manchester League, who knows what I'd be doing.

That first session was hardly the most organised, or tactically in-depth, but I absolutely loved the collision side of things and was hooked from the off. I can still remember walking home totally filthy and freezing.

We had about eight games in that first season at Under 9s and it really set the tone for the whole of my younger career – I hardly ever played in a side of my own age, and I was a year above in this one as well. For some reason in the very first game I got the goal-kicking duties too. They obviously hadn't seen me playing football!

Mind you, I got two goals in the first game against Hollinwood, and then got four tries in the next one against Tameside. I think that was my first man of the match award – a little trophy and a Mars bar! I ended up winning quite a few of them over the coming months, so it's a surprise I didn't end up as big as a house.

I was also captain in that first season, and when they came to pick a representative side from the league I was in that as well.

That was quite a big thing, because a lot of the other lads around had been playing the game for a couple of years, so you can imagine how made up my mum and dad were.

I have always been quite tall, and loved ripping the ball in, so I actually started off at prop forward. Thank God that all bloody changed when I started playing seriously! Mind you, I still took a few bashes when we played a representative team from the Barrow league at Oldham Edge, on the coldest day ever.

They had a kid – this was Under 9 remember – who had virtually a full beard, and he just ran right through us all game. Absolutely demolished us. It turned out to be a kid called Paul Gardner, the brother of Adey, the winger in the St Helens team now. And he wonders why I always put a bit extra in when I'm tackling him in training! Actually Paul became a good mate; he ended up signing for Warrington at the same time as myself, and obviously I get on a treat with his brother.

One thing that had to stop because of my new interest in rugby was my scrambling. On my seventh birthday, my mum and dad had bought me a little 50cc bike, and me and Lee were always out at every opportunity. We used to go up to the local ATC trials track and razz about up and down the hills. We'd go off all over the place watching stock car racing as well, but it was biking that was the real attraction. We'd be out scrambling, or doing a bit of the old moto-cross, and I suppose if you'd asked which sport I fancied back then it would have been something to do with bikes. As I grew a bit older, Lee had a bigger bike and I got his.

I remember one time when Lee was showing us how good he was, and he went flying over the top of this hill. Only when he didn't come up again on the other side did we realise that something was wrong. Me and Dan shot up to see what had gone on – he was stuck in a bloody tree!

I don't think I actually ever came off to any great extent, and I was pretty good at it to be honest. And when we got home before Mum and Dad came back from work, we'd sneak a few rides in the street as well. They never actually caught us, but I think one of the neighbours grassed us up because they found out somehow!

But then my rugby came along, and I didn't really have much time to be doing both, so the bikes had to take a back seat, even though I'm still really into them. My mum was particularly pleased to see the back of that, although she worried more over the past few years, when I had a real beast of a bike. In fact I only got rid of it recently to keep her happy.

Having said that, Mum had enough to worry about with rugby playing a bigger and bigger part. She gets really nervous before games, and when I was a kid she'd be running on the pitch every time I went down, to make sure I was okay. Maybe that's why I always made a point of getting back up as quickly as possible, however bad I felt, to keep her on the sidelines with the other parents!

So, all in all, that first season with Royton went really well, and pretty early into the next one I was involved in my first transfer and I joined Oldham Juniors. They were actually coached by an Italian, the marvellously named Tony Piano, who was helped by stalwarts like Laurie Dawson and Phil McLean, who – along with wife Pauline – became a really close family friend. A lot of the lads were my future team mates from Counthill Secondary School, although I really only joined because Paul Highton, the future Salford forward, asked me to go along.

That was when I got my first real taste of tactics and proper structured training, and we had a great time until I eventually left. I also got my first taste of a cup final in 1987, even though I had to sit that one out and watch from the sidelines, because I was cup tied.

Oldham played Ince St Williams at Naughton Park, Widnes' old ground, and got torn apart by another lad who went on to become a future team-mate, Rob Smyth. In a nutshell, he was just too bloody fast for anyone to get near! That was still hugely disappointing, even though I was only watching from the sidelines, mainly because I couldn't do a thing to help the lads out.

By now I had become big mates with Ian Knott, who was to play alongside me at Warrington, and when he went to Mayfield I went along with him. Mayfield was coached by Howard Leach, a man held in total respect by players, parents and fellow coaches alike.

Also in 1988 we moved house to Waterhead and I went to Watersheddings School. Watersheddings had the best name for sport among Oldham's junior schools, thanks to the efforts of teacher Brian Whitworth, a lifelong Oldham RL fan and the town's premier chess coach. In fact he once told me that to play competitive chess needs more mental toughness than rugby league. Around about that time I also got into the North Lancashire Schools Under 11s side, which was my first real step up the representative ladder, and from there it was to the full Lancashire Schools Under 11s side and North West Counties League Under 11s.

Then in 1989 I moved to Counthill Secondary School. I had started actually watching rugby league now as well, because I'd decided that was what I was going to do for a living.

Whenever it was on the box I'd be watching, trying to pick up what the pros did, and got hold of as many videos as possible of the great games in Australia. My favourite player was the Parramatta loose forward Ray Price, known as 'Mr Perpetual Motion'. He was skilful, totally committed – and as hard as nails. The particular video I watched didn't, unfortunately, include too many Great Britain wins. Not too much has changed there, sadly, although I do think there's not a great deal between us now in terms of actual talent.

But the thing I really looked forward to was going to Watersheddings on a Sunday afternoon after Mayfield played, to watch the pros. I was there in February 1987, when Paddy Kirwan scored under the posts and Mick Burke booted the conversion to give them a famous 10–8 Challenge Cup win over Wigan, who were on their way to becoming the most dominant side in world rugby. I actually ended up as a ball boy at Watersheddings, in the days when the likes of Mike Ford, Richard Russell and John Henderson were playing, and got my first injury courtesy of that. I jumped over a fence to go and fetch the ball, and landed on a nail, which went right through the bottom of my foot and the cut became infected. I was sitting at home feeling pretty fed up with myself, when all three of them turned up to see me, because they'd found out about my accident while working as a ball boy.

I had my picture taken with them all, but the best bit was that they'd sent John Watkins, the physio, into town to buy me a new pair of trainers for my pains. They'd paid for them out of their own pockets, and even as a kid I realised what a fantastic gesture it was. That's something I've always tried to remember when people are asking for autographs, or want a quick word. I know how much it meant to me when I was a youngster, so I always try to make time when I get stopped now.

I made some really close friends during my days with Mayfield as well, although I got a first-hand taste of how cruel fate can be through one of them. My pal John Power eventually went on to sign for Oldham, and in one game against Dewsbury, when he was still looking to force his way into the senior side, he broke his neck. He's still in a wheelchair to this day, but it hasn't stopped him living life to the full and he's fighting it all the way. He was taken to Wakefield's Pinderfields Hospital, but then another tragedy struck. Danny Navesey, an Oldham Juniors team-mate, and Steven Charlesworth, a schoolmate of mine, used to visit him a hell of a lot. One night they were travelling back down the M62 when they hit one of the motorway lights, which fell on the car and killed them both. They were smashing lads with loving families and the tragedy brought the RL public of Oldham together in mourning.

On the playing side, I also got my first chance to rub shoulders with the top stars at Carnegie College. On those days the top 20 players in each age group from all around the country were invited over for a training week, where pros like Phil Clarke, Denis Betts and Gary Price would come along. Funnily enough, I came up against Gary in one game after I'd gone to Saints and we ended up having a real scrap – and I'm sure I won on points. But it was quite a bizarre twist, the pupil having a dust-up with the man who had been teaching him the game as a kid.

Phil in particular seemed to take a shine to me, and even gave me his phone number in case he could ever help out. A little while later I actually rang him over something and he was really good in passing on advice. That was something else for the memory bank when I was to get a bit older.

By now I was going full-steam ahead with my rugby, and was so excited when we reached the final of the North West Counties with Mayfield. This time there were no problems about being cup tied, and I felt like a real pro when we walked out to play Orrell St James, who were coached by Andy Farrell's dad, Peter, with Howard Leach, probably the best junior coaches in the country.

They were the top side around the area at the time, and we got stuffed. Personally I played okay, but the disappointment wasn't something I particularly wanted to go through again. Unfortunately it doesn't always work out like that, does it?

Playing for Mayfield also led to my first overseas 'tour'. A weekend trip to the Isle of Man, staying in a hotel in Port Erin, was hardly the same as playing in the heat of Port Moresby, or strolling out in Sydney or Brisbane, but for us youngsters it was the dog's. They were looking for a team from Rochdale to play Wigan's youngsters in the curtain raiser to the Charity Shield, and, because they didn't have a school town team, we got invited. If meeting Fordy and Co. at Oldham was great, this was something else besides.

All the big names were there – Martin Offiah, Andy Goodway, Kurt Sorensen, Joe Lydon – and for a kid it was hard not to get starry-eyed just looking at them. Kurt in particular was great with the amount of time he spent with us, giving us all loads of encouragement and stuff.

Unfortunately we lost again, largely because they had a certain Sean Long in their side, or Stan as he was called by Malcolm Lord, the MC at the post-match function. Unlike a lot of curtain raisers, it had been on the full pitch, twenty minutes a side. To be honest, we could have done with it being across the field, at half-time, because we might not have lost as heavily! I also did my first ever interview at the post-match function at the Tower Ballroom, Douglas. Keith Macklin, a well-known northern commentator, had me on stage firing a few questions at me, and, although I can't remember what I said, I know I'm a lot more comfortable being interviewed now than I was back then.

It's funny, but one thing I remember about that trip is polishing my boots until you could see your face in them. That's something I do even now. A lot of the Saints lads will leave their gear to get cleaned up at the club, but I've never felt totally comfortable unless I'm doing my own boots. I always get my own bag ready for the game, sort out my own stuff, because if anything's missing or not done correctly, it's down to me.

My dad had always told me, virtually from day one, that part of the preparation if you wanted to do things properly was playing with clean boots. It seems pretty obvious now, but when you're a kid it is a bit of a ball-acher. I'm glad he drummed it into me, though, I have to say.

I also remember Kevin Tamati, a New Zealand international who had a great career at Warrington, giving us a fantastic motivational speech at an awards evening at the King's Hall, in Widnes. He told us all about the places in the world he'd visited and the great people he'd met, all through being involved in rugby league. To a young lad like myself that really captured my imagination and made me doubly determined to make a career out of the sport.

After that trip to the Isle of Man we all came back feeling ten feet tall, even though we'd lost. I suppose it was a little taste of the big time and we all wanted a bit more. We got it in 1991 when Mayfield got to the final again, this time against Orrell, but lost to a side which proved to be our nemesis in those days.

We played a team from York at Central Park before a Wigan game, and it was a full house, as it tended to be most of the time back then. It was a pretty good season all round, because I also played for the Oldham Town team, and we beat a bloody good Castleford side at North Chadderton in the English Schools Under 13 final.

The Oldham supreme was Iain McCorquodale, who held iconic status among Oldham's rugby league-playing kids. Iain was an ex-Oldham and Workington goal-kicking winger, who played for Fulham in their first ever game, beating Wigan. Iain also loved schmoozing the players' mums as well, and assisted by teacher Fred Laughton, a lovely guy who sadly died last year. A man whose passion was his work, rugby league and music, he'd also do anything to help the Oldham schoolkids.

Unfortunately that was that as far as Mayfield was concerned, because the team finished at the end of that season and I moved on to Waterhead Under 14s and ended up having such a good year that I got picked for Oldham Schools Under 16s, where I played with Iestyn Harris. By now I was playing in the second row, and we won the National Schools Cup against St Helens Under 16s at Watersheddings.

Waterhead were coached by Ian Ogden, a former Oldham scrum half, and club stalwart Peter Byrne, and we won the North Western Counties league and cup double that year. The Waterhead club gym was run by Ken 'Tug' Wilson, another ex-Oldham player, and a man to whom I owe a great deal for instilling the proper attitude to discipline and training. Tug was mentor to countless future pros, including the likes of Barrie McDermott, Kevin Sinfield and Paul Highton. Sadly Tug died a few years ago, but he will never be forgotten.

By now I also had a taste of the biggest stage of all – Wembley, walking out as one of the ball boys before the Wigan– Warrington Challenge Cup final in 1990. We went down the day before and, listening to us on the way there, you'd have thought we were playing in the big match itself. On the day of the match I was walking around the outside of the pitch beforehand and someone shouted 'Scully' from the crowd. I couldn't believe it – there were thirty thousand or whatever in the stand and one of our Lee's mates was right near the front waving at me. I felt like a real star!

We paid for another night and stayed down on the Sunday as well, because Oldham Athletic were playing Nottingham Forest in the League Cup final; sadly, the weekend finished on a bit of a sour note because Latics lost. Having said that, it didn't end on half as sour a note for us as for Paul Highton and Jon Farrell, a couple of the players who'd come down with us. Unfortunately for them they didn't come back with us as there was a cock-up with the head count and we left them in London. They eventually managed to get a lift back off one of the supporters' coaches, and although we have a good laugh about it now it wasn't too funny at the time.

The following year, 1991, I became involved in a project run by Haydn Walker, the coach of Orrell St James' amateur side. He was taking a squad to Australia, to be assembled from players in the North West Counties League, but which needed £120,000 raising to help fund it. I was picked for the squad but after a few months I pulled out because it was becoming obvious that selection for the final party had changed from ability to play to ability to pay, and as such I wanted nothing to do with it.

But it was never going to dim my enthusiasm for the game,

especially because things were starting to take off with Counthill as well around then, and we twice reached the final of the English Schools Cup. Head of PE was Bill Hainsworth; a lovely bloke whose first love was cricket, he also loved having an RL team to carry on the traditions of the school, and his assistant was the great Sam Shephard, international referee and a fantastic character. When he died most of Oldham turned out for his funeral. They were a huge success: reaching that final was almost unheard of, because the teams from Wigan, Leigh and the top Yorkshire sides had enjoyed a virtual monopoly of it until then. We lost one of the finals, but won the other one when I kicked a goal off the touchline in the last couple of minutes, against a St Helens side with Lee Briers as the star man. I remind him of that every now and again, and all in all we only lost one game in a year and a half.

The next season I joined Rose Bridge, in Wigan, and we built a virtually unbeatable team. In my time there we lost only once in two seasons, against a Briers-inspired St Helens Crusaders. We won all the trophies going, including the National Under 16 Cup, at Central Park against Hunslet Boys Club. We had players from all regions, including current Barrow star Mike Whitehead, ex-Leigh player Phil Kendrick, and Paul Wingfield and Carl Roden, who went on to join Warrington. But then the British Amateur Rugby League Association (BARLA) decided that no player could join clubs outside their district league, in order to get rid of 'super-teams'.

Rose Bridge were coached by former Wigan enforcer Denis Boyd, and Billy Halliwell. They were also managed by Ian McCulloch; he was to become my father-in-law, but I will expand on that elsewhere.

While I was with Rose Bridge Under 16s I also got picked for

BARLA's Under 18 side. Everyone seemed huge compared to me, especially Adrian Morley, who was like a real giant.

The first game against the Junior Kiwis was for BARLA Presidents' XIII in Sheffield, and I also played for the BARLA Young Lions in two games against France in Workington and Marseille, when we were coached by a great bloke, Phil Kitchin, and managed by the late Mike Morrissey.

I did well against the Kiwis, just missing out on the man-of-the-match award in the first and winning it in the second. New Zealand legend Frank Endacott presented me with my award, and once again I was struck by how much time he took to have a chat and encourage me.

There was no time to enjoy things, though, because I had to dash straight from playing them in Whitehaven for the England Schools Under 16s trials. After playing that Kiwi side, which included the likes of Henry Paul, Tevita Vaikona and Joe Vagana, it seemed a hell of a lot easier!

That led to huge controversy, although a lot of the politics really went over my head. England Schools had written a letter to BARLA complaining that I was too young to be involved at that level. I don't know if any laws were passed about that, but it gave you a taste of how red tape can affect the actual game – it's something that still really bloody annoys me to this day, especially when it meant I couldn't go on the BARLA tour of Morocco.

I made some great friends at BARLA, including Cumbrians Lee Prest, Chris McKinney and Craig 'Butch' Barker, for whom I had the honour of opening his sports shop, which was a great occasion and one which was absolutely mobbed. Missing that BARLA tour was offset somewhat when I was picked to captain England Schools against France, coached by Dennis McHugh.

We won 40–0 and I was made man of the match again, winning the Gilbert Dautant Trophy.

Incidentally, if you think that all my rugby meant I was neglecting my school work, nothing could have been further from the truth. Yes, I would do the same as many other kids and wish I was out on the rugby field rather than sitting through double maths, but I kept my head down and got on with things.

I got on well with most of the teachers, although Mr Broadfoot, the geography teacher, did think I was too laid back. And of course I got the usual advice at the careers evenings, when they'd tell me how I could never expect to make a living out of playing rugby league. I thought about that when I moved into my new house near Orrell a couple of years ago. If I hadn't made it as a pro, I might have ended up as one of the blokes building it!

And there was no way Mum and Dad would ever have let me drop off with my schooling, even though they both loved seeing me play and do well. The pair of them have always been very supportive, just like Lindsay, my wife, has – although when she sees me moping around after a defeat, or injury, I'm sure there are times she'd have wished I had done a 'normal' job!

As it was, I left school at sixteen with all my GCSEs. I got six A–C grades and two Ds – needless to say one of those was in geography and the other was in home economics, so I don't think Vivienne Westwood had anything to worry about. Anyway, I passed all the major subjects, like English language and literature, maths and sciences. I was always pretty good with numbers, which came in handy when making sure I wasn't being diddled on contract payments! Just joking, Eamonn.

Together with a load of mates, I moved on to Oldham Sixth Form College to do my A levels, and was suddenly having to think about what I would do for a career if I didn't make it as a rugby player. I decided I wanted to go into some form of sports psychology, although it never got close to the stage where I sat exams or went too far down that road.

By now I was also at Warrington, and it was hugely embarrassing turning up at college in a sponsored car with my name all over the side, as a seventeen-year-old. It had been given to me courtesy of Dave Twiss, a fellow who was manager of Hall Motors in the town and a real character. By now my rugby was beginning to take up so much time that I asked the teachers if I could do just two A levels. They tried to convince me my marks were good, and it would be a pretty daft move to take, but my mind had been made up and I did a course in PE and psychology in Oldham.

We did more of that at Warrington for a while, when we were taught by Bill Beswick, who used to be the English basketball coach and went on to work as Steve McClaren's sidekick with Middlesbrough, but although I enjoyed the work, and didn't find it too much of a problem, I was struggling to fit it all in alongside my training, which was beginning to take up more and more of my time. So when Warrington called me in to discuss things, there was only ever going to be one decision for me. Assuming, that is, they were about to offer me a serious contract, because up to that point I had always believed I would get one. As it was, I had nothing to worry about.

They sat me down, came straight to the point, and told me they wanted me to go full time with them. The way they put it, that was hardly a question which needed too much consideration – stay at college trying to get the qualifications and hunt for work, or start immediately on your perfect job. Suddenly I could see a whole new world opening up in front of me. I didn't need asking twice – I was on the road to professional rugby league and, as far as I was concerned, no one was going to stand in my way.

3
Now the Wire!

When I packed my bags at Wilderspool and headed to St Helens, the transfer fee of a then world record £370,000 for a forward made headlines all over the world. It didn't seem a good time to mention that they could have had me for the price of a decent second-hand car when I was just a kid!

By the time I was fourteen, word had gone around among the rugby league clubs that there was a half-decent youngster playing in the Oldham area, and there was invariably a scout or two at most of our games. Obviously I got wind of that, and quite a few of them made themselves known to my dad, but no one seemed prepared to take the plunge and come up with a firm offer. It didn't get to the stage where I was wondering if the big break would ever come; I was only just in my teens, for God's sake, but I did begin to wonder if maybe they were looking for something a bit different. Fortunately those doubts didn't last too long.

Eventually Widnes were the ones to set the ball rolling, when Dennis McHugh sauntered over to my dad after one school game against Leigh and said they were keen for me to go to

Naughton Park. I knew Jimmy Reader, Warrington's 'star-finder', had been one of the more regular visitors to see me play, and that finally sparked him into making a definite move. The following week Waterhead were playing St Jude's at home, and Jimmy brought Wire chairman Peter Higham along to watch. He was obviously pretty impressed because they told my dad they wanted me at Wilderspool, as well as my team-mate Paul Gardner, as mentioned earlier the brother of Saints winger Adey.

Peter invited me and Dad round to his house in Appleton, a couple of miles from the Warrington ground, to discuss things in more detail, and I was like a kid waiting for Christmas in the days before we were due to see him. I'd never been paid a penny for playing rugby before – that sort of thing doesn't even cross your mind when you're that age, does it? – so I was pretty much in the dark as to what they'd come up with. When Peter produced a contract worth £16,000 over the next four years, I nearly fell off my chair. I think I'd signed it before he'd finished talking! It might seem like chicken feed now, given some of the money flying around, but back then I thought I was a bloody millionaire.

It was only when I looked back that I realised that, had I been a couple of years older, I would probably have walked away with a deal about five times that amount. About fifteen years ago clubs were paying stupid money to sign kids, I think to make sure they didn't miss out on anyone decent. Whatever the reason, most of those clubs were in the fast lane to the poor-house and something had to stop. It was nothing out of the ordinary to hear of lads getting £50–£70,000, and Warrington were as bad as the rest in doing this. For example, on one occasion I heard that they had offered absolute fortunes to get a couple of kids who never went close to justifying that money, but that was the way things were going back then, and you were never going to find someone turning it down.

That was still a couple of years before the game was turned on its head by the advent of Super League, and there were plenty of clubs – bloody big names as well – which were sliding dangerously close to bankruptcy. Mind you, I didn't really sit there with my chin on the floor at missing out on an even bigger payday. Sixteen grand would do very nicely, thank you very much. After all, in my mind I knew that if all went to plan and I made the grade, there would be plenty of money in the future. And, let's be honest, it wasn't about the cash back then. My expenses didn't extend much beyond wanting a few quid if I was nipping into town with my mates; mortgages and bills were something for the grown-ups. Certainly nothing for a youngster like me to be worrying about.

I'm sure that when I eventually went to Saints there were a few questions asked – albeit a little tongue in cheek – about the money they could have saved had they been a bit quicker off the mark all those years earlier. Mind you, they can all point to a few of them, can't they? We all know about Leeds turning down a knobbly-kneed winger called Brian Bevan because they didn't think he had the physique or the talent to make it at Headingley; and I've heard he didn't make too bad a job of things at Warrington!

In hindsight the only thing that upset me a little was that, despite all the clubs that were interested in me, I never got so much as a tentative offer from my hometown Oldham – and I'd been bloody training with them for two years! I'm not saying it was my dream to play for them, but I would have liked the offer. Maybe it was just a case of the Sculthorpe pride – but I don't suppose things turned out too badly in the end. Looking back, they probably didn't think they could compete with some of the clubs which were interested, so it was off to Wilderspool for me – and the chance to work with some of the biggest names in the business.

There was another important bit of business for me to concentrate on as well – getting a bank account. For a lad who'd only ever had pin money in the past, there had never been a need to have one, but I didn't fancy stashing thousands under my bed – Mum and Dad certainly didn't! – so it was down to see the men in suits. They got the shock of their lives when this kid walked in to open an account and proudly presented them with a hefty cheque. I think they were expecting me to come up with a tenner, and wait for my half-price rail card or a couple of HMV tokens! I was half tempted to go berserk and splash out on a load of new stuff, but I'd been well educated about the value of money by Mum and Dad; most of it sat in the bank until I eventually bought myself a car a couple of years later.

My dad was bloody glad when I did pass my test as well, because he made that many trips taking me to training I think his car could have done it without a driver in the end. But it was an absolute delight to be mixing with professionals at Warrington, superstars like Jonathan Davies, Mike Gregory, Paul Cullen, Bob Jackson . . . the list seemed endless. And my big mate Ian Knott was on the books as well, so Dad used to share the driving with his dad, Phil, while having a close pal in the same boat made it a hell of a lot easier for me to settle in straight away.

Training was three times a week after school – or, in the case of many of the players, after a hard day's graft – because Wigan was the only full-time club in the game back then. There was no such thing as a regular training ground either. We'd be all over the place, running around Lymm Dam or Morley Common, spending as much time avoiding the dog crap as anything. We'd do a lot of the skills work on the all-weather pitch at Broomfields – it must have been the only all-weather pitch in the country that got waterlogged if it rained for more than half an hour. The best facilities were at Priestley College, just down the road from Wilderspool, and it always went down well with the lads when Phil Chadwick told us that's where we were heading. Chaddy was a real character, with his long hair and moustache; he was more like a roadie for Black Sabbath than our fitness conditioner. He worked on the bins by day and he was bloody fit – I never saw anyone beat him at chins or dips – and after a few sessions under his watchful eye I'd taken my fitness to another level.

There was no team bus or anything to get us to these places like Lymm Dam and the like. We'd just head to Wilderspool, get changed and then jump in our cars and make our own way there, or, in the case of me, Knotty and some of the other young lads, rely on our parents to ferry us around. Not that Dad or Phil Knott were too concerned about it. Warrington really used to include the parents as much as they could, and there were countless dos for the whole family. They weren't exactly black-tie bashes – more pie and peas evenings – but you were really made to feel wanted. Although I don't think Paul Williamson ever used to look forward to them. They used to have a Prick of the Month award, given for all sorts of reasons – poor performances in training, dodgy kit, whatever – and Paul seemed to get it more than anyone. Fortunately that was one trophy I was never too bothered about not winning, and luckily I never did. Boomer, as we called him, seemed to have a monopoly on it, anyway. I think they may even have given it to him for keeps in the end!

Back then Warrington was a really homely club and I absolutely loved it, and the senior pros were very good at making us feel part of it. Gary Sanderson, who I bumped into recently, was particularly good to me and I have never forgotten the time he took to help me settle in. I also became close to Clarrie Owen, the club president – a really lovely guy and a good friend.

It was just a fantastic place to be, and I used to love it when we'd all head down to Sue's Diner, a little truckers' café in Warrington, after training. All the lads would go down to this greasy spoon, and it really helped foster a great team spirit. In fact the only thing missing was taking part in a serious game, because there wasn't a team for kids our age, even though I was training with the seniors. I had to content myself with playing for Rose Bridge and the Oldham town team, but at least working with the pros at Warrington got me into good habits. Well, off most of them, at least, but I'll come to that in a while!

It was only after I'd left school and turned sixteen that I was eligible for the Academy, and, boy, was I champing at the bit by then. I was working with legends like Jiffy, Greg Mackey, Mike Greg and Jacko, but never really had a chance to prove it on the stage I wanted – a professional pitch, in a Warrington shirt. But before I was to get my chance with the Academy, I also had my first date with the surgeon – on my nose. I'd been having a bit of trouble with my breathing during games for a while, mainly because of the knocks I'd taken on my conk at various levels. So everyone decided enough was enough, and sent me off to BUPA at Stretton for rhinoplasty. Thanks very much!

If anyone ever tells you it's a simple operation, that you'll hardly know a thing until it's done, give them a smack: they're bloody lying! When I came round, if that's the word, I was bleeding through my nose, my ears, my mouth. If it had a hole, it seemed to have blood coming out of it! But the most worrying thing was when I started bleeding through my eye sockets. To a teenage lad it was incredibly frightening, especially when I lost a hell of a lot of strength as a result. By the time I got my chance in the Academy, I was well off the pace, and finding it a lot harder than I know I should have done. But Warrington were really good about things, and after only half a dozen games I was thrown into the A team.

After waiting for so long for a game of any kind with them, it all suddenly seemed to be happening at a real pace now. Clive Griffiths, the A-team coach, dropped it on me out of the blue. St Helens – it had to be, really, didn't it? – at Wilderspool. And if I thought I was on the way to making the big time, Bernard Dwyer soon brought me crashing down to earth with an almighty bump. Literally. Bernard, in case you didn't know, looked like he'd been carved out of granite. If they'd tried they'd probably have broken the bloody chisel, he was that hard – and I was up against him at loose forward. Even so, I was doing pretty well and it was nip and tuck in the twenty minutes or so I'd had since coming off the bench. Bernard was probably not best pleased at some young kid trying to give him the runaround, so it didn't take long for him to decide that I needed to be taught a lesson. I couldn't get enough of the ball and thought I could take on the world, but Dwyer's stiff arm soon put me right on that one. I went down like a lead balloon and when I came round in the dressing room was feeling a little bit dazed, to say the least. I couldn't remember a thing about what had happened; it was only when Dad and the rest of the lads came in that it started to come back to me. It should have been a harsh warning and kept me on my guard. Unfortunately not – as the following week proved.

This time we were up against Hull at The Boulevard, never the most welcoming of places even for a reserve match with not a great deal riding on it. This time I was up against Rob Wilson and was on from the start – once again I came nowhere near finishing the game. It was almost a replica of the Saints game, as Wilson laid me out with a stiff arm. This time I was sparked, out cold, and I got the mandatory two weeks on the sidelines because of concussion. So that was two games, and a total of about three-quarters or an hour's actual action. It also signalled the start of me wearing a headguard!

You'd have thought that it could have left a few doubts in my mind when I came back, but nothing could have been further from the truth. I was absolutely loving my new life, and did pretty well in the few games that were left when I returned to action. It was all still relatively new to me and I was desperate to take in all the advice I could – although when someone suggested I should start dishing it out a bit myself to prove I was no soft touch, I think I took things a little too far, as I got sent off twice.

The first sending off came at The Willows against Salford, when I was accused of using my elbow by dropping on someone in the tackle, even though the video showed I was clearly innocent, but that was nothing to what I wanted to do to the touch judge who came on, pointed me out to the ref and left me facing that horrible walk back to the dressing room. That was my first trip to Rugby League HQ – fortunately I haven't been too frequent a visitor over the years – and the disciplinary panel found me not guilty. It must have been the quickest decision the disciplinary panel had ever reached as it was so obvious.

I was doubly relieved at that because I was due to play for Great Britain Academy against France the following week, my first 'proper' trip away. Dad and Danny had already booked their tickets for Carcassonne, and I think I'd have sooner faced Dwyer and Wilson combined than the trouble back home if they'd had their trip ruined because I was stuck back in England! Maybe the disciplinary panel saw the size of my dad and couldn't face explaining it to him, either. Whatever their reasoning, I wasn't about to argue and it was a bloody relief to be cleared.

But what is it they say about learning your lesson? I obviously hadn't because when Warrington played Oldham in the semi-final of the A-team cup, I was off again. There were extenuating circumstances again, but knew I was in bother and would be lucky to escape with a sending off being sufficient punishment this time. I'd been playing bloody well, if I say it myself, and it was a cracking game, when Craig Booth came round the blind side and gouged me.

Unfortunately as he was helped off I passed him on the way to the sheds, the victim of another referee not seeing the full picture. I felt terrible at letting the rest of the lads down, especially because the game was really tight. Luckily Francis Maloney popped over a fifty-yard drop goal in extra time to get me off the hook. I wasn't quite so lucky when I got back in the car to RLHQ as this time I landed a one-match ban – the first suspension of my career.

There was an amusing conclusion to the tale a week or so later, when we were all in the players' bar at Wilderspool. A couple of reporters had suggested that my indiscipline could end up wrecking a hugely promising career, and, unfortunately for one of them, our Lee spotted him having a drink, and threatened to put him through the wall if he wrote anything like that again. Cheers for that, Lee. Nothing like getting the media on your side from the off! Having said that it must have worked, because I got the best write-up of my life after that!

Warrington themselves were pretty good about it all, because they'd seen the video and knew exactly what had gone on. It didn't stop me getting a bollocking, but fortunately didn't stop my progress either. I had vowed to take a deep breath before getting involved in any further trouble and it seemed to work, because I came back in the form of my life and first-team coach Brian Johnson had told me if I carried on that way a chance with the seniors was just around the corner.

I'd been in the squad a few times, just as eighteenth man to get some experience, when Jonno called me in and said I was on the bench against Salford. Fantastic! All I'd worked for was about to come true. Okay, maybe it wasn't the most glamorous game in the world, but to me it was the Challenge Cup final and Grand Final rolled into one. That Sunday I couldn't get to Wilderspool quickly enough. I didn't have long to wait for my chance, either, as Warrington quickly took command and Jonno decided this was the ideal opportunity to blood the new boy.

I couldn't have dreamed of a much better start either, as I took a ball off Kelly Shelford, ducked under a couple of tackles – I was getting wise to those swinging arms by now – and put Jason Lee in for a try. It didn't exactly knock Manchester United and Liverpool off the back pages, but as my team-mates rushed over to congratulate me it was the best feeling in the world. I was on the march; Sculthorpe had arrived at last, and after despatching Castleford the following week, I couldn't wait for the next game, against Leeds at home, and the prospect of being in direct competition with one of my heroes, Ellery Hanley. Some hope!

If Bernard Dwyer had brought me down to earth on my A-team debut, Jonno managed a similar job when he named the side to play Leeds and I wasn't in it. What made it even worse was the fact that I'd already been told I'd be one of the substitutes again, but then Paul Darbyshire, who had been struggling with a knock, declared himself fit and I was down to eighteenth man. Talk about being gutted. Hadn't I sat correctly on the bench? Had there been something wrong with my celebrations after setting up Jason? I've never wished an injury on anyone, but at that moment I admit I was hoping Darby's knock would take another week to clear up!

Not that I had too long to wait for another chance. And talk about throwing you into the lion's den – Widnes, away, the following week. No one in rugby league needs telling about the rivalry between Wire and Widnes. In a nutshell they bloody hate each other, and the talk of a possible merger between the clubs as part of the newly planned Super League had only intensified that. In the end it was a strange old day, because before the game it was announced that the two wouldn't be joining forces, respective chairmen Peter Higham and Jim Mills were photo-graphed shaking hands, all smiles, and the game almost became a bit of a sideshow to the main event.

Just to make it extra special for Warrington fans, they won the game as well and I celebrated my first points for the first team with a drop goal. Not a bad afternoon's work! Once again it was back to the Village Hotel for a couple of drinks before I headed back home in Dad's car, leaving the rest of the lads to rampage – sorry, celebrate – around town.

It was at about this time that I decided I should have my own car – Dad wasn't about to argue – and I spent some of that initial contract money on an old Astra, which I loved. I was studying PE psychology at Oldham College by then, and felt like the mutt's nuts when I could drive myself there. I didn't know it then, but the sport was set to undergo the biggest trans-formation of its history, and my schooling days were about to come to an abrupt end. Not that I was too concerned about that.

Don't forget, just about every club was still part-time, but we were soon to become fully-fledged professionals in every sense. That left some of the older players in a bit of a dilemma. Did they shelve their careers for another couple of years playing the sport they loved, or was it just too big a risk for those with kids and mortgages? Fortunately that wasn't an issue for me, and it opened up a whole new world.

Before Super League kicked off in the spring of 1996, we had that shortened Centenary season when I began to establish myself as something of a first-team regular. I'd ended that previous year with six appearances to my name, all of them off the bench, but this time I was in from the off. I played just about every game in the 1995 season, most of them for the whole eighty minutes, and was attracting some pretty pleasing head-lines. In fact only Iestyn Harris and Mark Hilton featured in more games than me, and I really began to feel like I was on my way.

Warrington clearly thought so as well, because before too long Jonno pulled my dad, who – as ever – had come to watch training, as he did all the time. The first contract had been for three years and had little more than a season to go, and although I had no intention of packing my bags, Warrington had no way of knowing that and wanted to make sure I was tied up on a 'proper' deal. They asked me what I was after, but I had no idea what to say. As a seventeen-year-old you might think you know everything, but you're hardly well versed in contract negotiations. Even so, I knew I wanted more than the £12,000 a year Warrington were willing to give me, and Dad didn't waste much time in telling them so. One Saturday morning at training he told Jonno I could make more than that if I was part-time and had a nine to five career. I fully agreed with what Dad had done, but it did leave part of me wondering what would happen if Warrington told me to stuff it.

Needless to say Jonno was a bit put out by my response, and on the face of it you could hardly blame him. Here was some kid, still wet behind the ears in rugby terms, knocking back a full-time offer because he felt he was worth more. I needn't have worried. As soon as Peter Higham got wind of it, he bumped the offer up to twenty grand a year for the next three seasons, and that was me sorted. Big time here I come! On the pitch, fortunately for me, I was justifying that money as well. In fact after one game at Sheffield I was awarded ten out of ten by one of the trade papers. I don't exactly see eye to eye with what some of the reporters have written about me all the time – that's putting it mildly! – but on this occasion I reckon they got it spot on! That was the first time I played stand off as well, and I had a field day, setting up a bagful of tries as we ran riot.

But if that was a good day, there was no doubting the blackest, as that shortened season didn't so much grind to a halt as hit the buffers full on. We had enjoyed some memorable clashes with St Helens over the years, but 4 January 1996 went into the history books for all the wrong reasons. Personally I will never forget it, and I wasn't even playing in the game.

We had been drawn away to Saints in the semi-finals of the Regal Trophy, and although we expected a tough game no one had the faintest idea what lay ahead. I was watching from the stands with a niggling injury (I can't remember exactly what), and couldn't believe it as they hammered us 80–0. Eighty bloody points to nil! Everyone was just shell-shocked, couldn't take it in. And what made it worse was hearing those St Helens fans really ripping the piss out of my club. It was obvious something had to change, and I think all the players knew what to expect when Jonno sat us down and told us he was jacking it in. Personally I was gutted for him. He was the one who'd given me my big break in the first team, and was a genuinely nice fellow to boot.

Clive Griffiths stepped up for the rest of the season, starting with – nice one, fixture planners – an immediate return to St Helens. It says everything about how poor our display had been in that game that, even though we got done 54–14, people said we'd gained a bit of respectability. If being on the wrong end of a half-century of points was respectability, you could stuff it!

But the tone had been set for the rest of the season by that eighty-point humiliation, and we lost our last three games against Halifax, Oldham and Workington. The close season couldn't come quickly enough for us. Surely things could only get better . . .

4

From Dorahy to Darryl

Before the Super League could roar into action I was in for another surprise – and it was a hell of a lot more pleasant than the one I'd sat through and suffered at Knowsley Road a couple of months earlier.

The announcement about Rupert Murdoch's rugby revolution had sent shockwaves throughout the game over here, and there were protests all over the place, first at the suggested mergers and then from the clubs which didn't make it into the Super League. Fans of Huddersfield, Hull, Widnes and, strange as it may seem now, Keighley in particular, were fuming at missing out – and they didn't miss a chance to let their feelings be known.

But that was nothing to the bitter arguments Down Under, as the Australian Rugby League (ARL) dug their heels in and tried to make a stand by signing up the biggest names. Obviously the English bosses didn't want the cream of their talent to be forced out of the game when the revolution arrived, and all of a sudden silly money started to get thrown around, in the form of loyalty payments. Basically this meant a nice hefty cheque for carrying on doing what you intended to do in the first place.

Iestyn Harris was an obvious candidate for a loyalty payment at Warrington, while Lee Penny, Jon Roper, Mark Hilton and Mike Wainwright pocketed the same wedge as well. And the other name on the list? Yours truly! A cheque for £20,000 fitted very nicely in the back pocket, thank you very much Mr Murdoch, and all for something I loved doing.

Things started in pretty promising fashion on the pitch as well, despite going out of the Challenge Cup at Leeds in the game before our first ever Super League fixture. It came a couple of weeks after we'd lost in the cup at Wilderspool, and I don't think too many people gave us a serious chance when we walked out at Headingley. But with Warrington, as I was growing to realise, you expected the unexpected, and once more we didn't disappoint, coming away with a thrilling 22–18 victory, courtesy of me setting up my big mate Knotty for the winner.

But the one match that really sticks in my memory from that first season was when St Helens came to Wilderspool. Saints were unbeaten at the time and beginning to overhaul their deadly rivals Wigan in terms of serious challengers for honours, but they came within a whisker of losing that record to us. Unfortunately Ian Pickavance scored the winner for them in the final minute, but I really came off feeling I'd had a stormer.

I was up against Adam Fogerty, who went on to play Gorgeous George in the film *Snatch*, and he spent most of the afternoon trying to soften me up. Every time I had the ball he seemed to be there, either with a sly dig or a huge shot, but I acquitted myself well, he shook my hand and congratulated me afterwards and we became very close mates. That was the day I took the ball towards the touchline straight from a scrum, in a move we'd worked on all week, passed it inside and sent Richard Henare seventy metres to the line. It was a fantastic moment, one of those instances when it goes exactly as you've planned it in training – it was just a pity it didn't earn us both points. John Dorahy, our coach, had arrived a couple of months before the season and was still desperate to prove a point to English fans after a bitter departure from Wigan a couple of years earlier. JD had brought some great ideas with him, and when they come off in a game – like that Henare try – there's a real buzz about the team.

Under Dorahy we didn't do too badly in that first Super League campaign, finishing in fifth place, albeit sixteen points off St Helens. Personally it had been something of a triumph, as I started twenty-four games that year and got five tries as well. After seven in the Centenary season, I was in danger of being referred to as the prolific Sculthorpe! Actually, calling it 'something of a triumph' was a bit of an understatement, as I also got my first taste of senior international honours.

I knew I'd been playing well, but it was still the most pleasant of surprises when Phil Larder named me in his England side for the European Championship game against France. Now I know the French are hardly the biggest draw in world rugby for supporters, but, believe me, that June night at the Gateshead International Stadium was a bloody big one for me. There might only have been six thousand-odd fans up in the Northeast, but it really was a night to remember for yours truly. Okay, on the face of it going over for a try thirteen minutes from the end when your side is already 63–0 in front isn't exactly a score which caused too much of a ripple in the record books. But it did in our house!

We ended up winning 73–6 and, boy, did it feel good! Two weeks later I was in the side again, as we went to Cardiff Arms Park for the decider against Wales. It was bizarre lining up against Gareth Davies, Mark Jones and especially Iestyn, all of whom I played alongside every week, but there was no way I expected any favours – especially in their own back yard. This time I was moved up to second row – couldn't complain at that one when it was Andy Farrell coming in as loose forward – and although I didn't score I managed another eighty minutes and we won 26–12. Not bad going for your first two internationals – two wins, and a total of ninety-nine points scored. Bring on the Aussies, eh!

Surely those two performances had to put me in contention for Great Britain's tour of Papua New Guinea, Fiji and New Zealand at the end of the first Super League season, especially with Phil Larder in charge once again. I wasn't disappointed, although that particular trip turned out to be one of the most infamous of all time – and certainly the biggest shambles.

It had begun as something of a fiasco, as the ARL pulled Lee Jackson, Gary Connolly and Jason Robinson out because they had signed contracts Down Under. That was bad enough – but when you consider we were also without the likes of Shaun Edwards, Paul Newlove, Martin Offiah, John Bentley and Steve McNamara, it's a wonder we managed to find enough to make up the touring party in the first place. Even so, we set off intent on winning all our ten matches – some hope! It started well enough, with a comfortable win over the PNG President's XIII, but when we went to Lae for a full Test against them it was like something out of a Tarzan film. I've never played in such unbearable heat and thank God they allowed unlimited sub- stitutions – we ended up making twenty-six replacements and won by two points. Alarm bells suddenly started to ring somewhat, although we got back on track a little with an easy midweek win in Fiji, and then a seventy-two-point stroll in the

Test, to leave us in high spirits as we arrived in New Zealand.

It didn't take long for that confidence to be blown away, however, as we drew with the Lion Red Cup XIII and then got done by the NZ President's XIII. No matter, it was the Test matches themselves which really counted, and by the time I came off in the first game at Auckland we were 12–4 up and looking good. Cue referee Bill Harrigan to stamp his own style on proceedings when he sent Adrian Morley, who had come on for his debut in place of me, to the sin bin for holding down Sean Hoppe. We all thought it was desperately harsh, but once Harrigan's got a whiff of the headlines and publicity, there is no stopping him – as we found to our cost.

Within eight minutes the Kiwis had run in three tries and we had lost 17–12 to leave that dressing room like a morgue. A midweek defeat to the Maoris didn't improve things – but that was nothing compared to what lay around the corner. None of us expected it to be the most successful trip ever in terms of finances, as if you ever really consider that anyway as a player. But without an Australian leg to the tour, it didn't take a genius to work out that the Rugby League would hardly be rolling in it. Even so, it came as a real bolt from the blue when we discovered that our already depleted party was being whittled down by a further twelve, as a cost-cutting measure. Chief executive Maurice Lindsay blamed it on New Zealand's lack of publicity for the matches, and their overestimation of attendances. Whatever the reasons, he hardly left us in the best frame of mind for the remainder of the trip. Maurice has made some hugely innovative decisions for the sport over his lifetime but I have to say that wasn't one of them.

So I suppose we should have been pleased to get within three points of the Kiwis in that game, again losing to a late try, but once you've lost there is no real consolation in how you may have performed. I think that left us all hoping for the best but fearing the worst when we got to Christchurch for what amounted to a dead rubber – and crashed to a record 32–12 defeat, to give New Zealand only their second ever series white-wash against Great Britain. That was the lowest point of my career at the time, and I couldn't wait to get back to England, see the family and friends, and blow away the memories with a great Super League season. But as I was to discover, you don't always get what you want.

We had reached the last eight of the Challenge Cup, before losing at home to Salford, and then the rot really set in. We lost our first three Super League games of the season, and Dorahy quit as coach. As much as John had been a breath of fresh air when he arrived, it didn't come as a great surprise to anyone when he left, especially when you looked at some of the players he was working with. Warrington had established a great reputation for signing overseas stars over the years – Les Boyd is still a legend in the town, while the likes of Steve Roach, Phil Blake, Duane Mann and Les Davidson had all performed with honours in their day. Unfortunately the same could not be said for some of the other overseas signings who arrived at the time, and at one stage it seemed as if they were coming and going with almost as much regularity as some of the fans.

Then there was the infamous Iestyn Harris row, when he asked for a move, the club refused it, and it led to a stand off between Iestyn and Dorahy which would have seemed petty had it been a couple of eight-year-olds going at it. Iestyn found himself being ordered to train at stupid times, like five in the morning, although quite what that was supposed to achieve Christ only knows. In the end he was transferred to Leeds, but I think it left a very bitter taste in his mouth, and hardly had spirits rocketing among the rest of the lads either.

The place was in disarray, and we had the little matter of Wigan at home coming up as well. In hindsight that was probably the best thing for us, because the fans needed no winding up when the Pie-Eaters were coming to town – even if we had no coach and apparently no chance of winning. As it was, Paul Cullen and Alex Murphy took command for that one game, and against all the odds we beat Wigan. I had to laugh after the game, though, as the Fletcher Street End gave us a standing ovation.

Murph had spent all week saying that it was Cul's team, and he was very much in the shade. Clearly he felt we were going to get battered as well, and was getting his excuses in first. But once we'd won, you couldn't get him back down the tunnel. All of a sudden he had played a massive part in it and didn't he want us all to know it. Mind you, I don't really think any of us expected anything different from someone who has courted publicity so effectively all his life. So there we were, back up and running again, especially as we followed it up with victories over Oldham and Castleford, and had a new coach in position, in the shape of Darryl Van De Velde.

5

Time to Move On

As good as Warrington were to me, and as much as I loved my time there, I knew that if I was to live the dream of playing in big matches and picking up trophies, I would have to pack the bags and move on.

Mixing with the biggest names in the game in the Great Britain squad had really whetted my appetite and I was getting increasingly frustrated at watching finals on the telly, rather than being involved in them myself.

Don't get me wrong: I was perfectly happy at Wilderspool. I got on pretty much with all the lads, and the board were always great to me – and, contrary to what some people were trying to insist, it was never about money either. Bloody hell, I was still in my teens and picking up better wages than blokes who had worked all their lives in the same job. And I was doing something I loved as well.

But the fact remained that I was never going to achieve what I wanted as long as I stayed at Warrington, for all the big promises at the start of each season. I'd say I am a pretty easy-going bloke, but if there was one thing guaranteed to get my back up it was sitting at home watching lads I knew well playing in finals. The closest I got was a bloody ticket to watch from the stand – and the time had come for that to change.

The nearest I got to one was the Challenge Cup quarter-finals with Warrington – I wasn't even close to walking out at Wembley or Old Trafford. To be honest, I was getting more and more pissed off each season. Yes, it was great when we beat Wigan, Leeds or whoever. But doing it consistently was always a massive problem, and invariably we would follow a great win by losing against Salford, Sheffield or some club we felt we should have been whacking.

I still had a few years left on my contract – in fact I was only one season into a four-year deal, after signing a new one twelve months earlier. But things were really beginning to take their toll, in terms of that lack of success. It wasn't down to one man's lack of ambition, one player's falling out with the rest – it just seemed that no one there was going to be able to help me live up to my own expectations.

I think the deciding factor came when I went on the tour of Papua New Guinea, Fiji and New Zealand in 1996. I seemed to spend all my waking hours listening to the other lads telling these tales of the great games and big finals they were involved in. Iestyn Harris, who I'd come through the ranks at Warrington with, had moved on by then as well, and that really put the seal on it for me.

I wanted to be playing for a club which was buying the best players, not bloody selling them. I thought, 'How much am I going to win here if things stay the same?' The answer was pretty bloody obvious – not a great deal.

At least I didn't find myself in the same situation as Iestyn had, when he told Warrington he wanted to leave. I've never seen anything like it before and I don't suppose I will again. Paul Cullen, later to become Warrington coach, was part of the backroom team and he had to go training with him at times. I don't suppose that went down particularly well with Cul, either. To be honest, the rest of us players got on with our own jobs, as tends to be the case in situations like that, however crazy we all thought it was.

I was determined not to fall out with people if it could be avoided, but by the end of 1997 it was the worst kept secret in the game that I was off – and by the time I eventually joined Saints the whole world seemed to know about it.

There was still one final little twist before I could put pen to paper, though. By the start of the next season the deal had still not been completed, and when Warrington went off to their pre-season training camp in Wales I went along with them. It was absolutely crazy. How on earth could I possibly go through a pre-season with a club that everyone knew I'd be playing against when the competition kicked off again?

That was the strangest week for me, even though the lads were all great about it. They understood what I was going through and made it a lot easier than it could have been. In fact I am still really close mates with a lot of them, even though it doesn't stop them wanting to knock my head off when we play each other!

The weirdest thing was listening to them all talking about their ambitions for the season and what they were going to do, when I knew I wouldn't be a part of it. And at least the coaching staff had the good sense not to start working on new moves when I was around. It was more a team-bonding exercise, but I did begin to feel more like a gatecrasher than a member of the squad.

It was a world away from the pre-season training camps you get these days, when clubs head off to Lanzarote, La Manga or wherever. None of that for us. We were stuck in a hostel in the back of beyond, spending the days canoeing, raft building, charging over assault courses and stuff. I decided to make the most of it and just have a laugh, even though it was hardly my idea of the perfect break.

But I was determined not to rock the boat and wreck the chances of getting a move. I knew the powers that be could be stubborn if they felt someone was taking the piss, so I just kept my head down, went through the week with them – and when I came back I was pretty much a St Helens player straight away.

I've said how good my relationship was with chairman Peter Higham, and I didn't want that coming to a bitter end, either. In fact when I asked to go in the first place, I don't think I even put it in writing. That's how close we were and I still have all the time in the world for him. Obviously he didn't want me to go, but was honest enough to say that he fully understood my reasons and he was really, really good about it.

As we had done a couple of years earlier with my new contract, myself and my dad drove over to Peter's house in Warrington – only for far different discussions this time. In the end there was no official request in writing, no slamming my fist on the boardroom table and demanding out. Just a simple conversation over a cup of tea in his kitchen. If only every chairman was as good to deal with, eh!

Peter knew there was no point saying I had to see out my contract. He realised that forcing someone to stay was hardly going to help team morale, so he agreed to let me go as long as the price was right. I knew they weren't going to give me away, but when he said in the press that it wouldn't be for less than £1 million, I must admit it stopped me in my tracks. Fortunately it quickly became clear he had his tongue firmly in his cheek when he said that, even though there were a couple of weeks when I thought I was going to be priced out of a move.

By now Darryl Van De Velde had replaced John Dorahy as coach, and he, too, told me he fully understood why I wanted to move. He said he would support me as much as he could, but then seemed to change very quickly and hardly spoke to me again. In fact when I went back to Wilderspool as a Saints player, Darryl was a bit funny with me, which annoyed me a bit, but I was more than happy to put up with that if I was picking up winners' medals all over the place.

My agent at the time of the move was a bloke called David McKnight, who was hardly Higham's favourite fellow after a couple of incidents in the build-up to my transfer. He'd had various approaches over the previous months from clubs seeing if I was happy and would consider a move – basically McKnight was touting for business and you can imagine how well that went down with Warrington.

There seemed to be stuff about me leaving in the newspapers every day, but as far as I was concerned there was nothing from me personally, so it was a case of any publicity being good publicity. Naturally Warrington saw it a little differently and their reaction was to ban McKnight from the club. In fact they had refused to deal with him when it came to discussing my previous – and last – contract at Wilderspool. And thank Christ they did!

Even though McKnight was not allowed in on the talks, I had spoken to him about what I should ask for. If I'd gone in and demanded what he suggested, I would actually have ended up out of pocket. He told me I should go for a four-year deal on something like £40,000 rising ten grand a year, so that was my plan when I arrived at Peter's house with my dad.

Fortunately I hadn't had a chance to open my mouth before Peter said he wanted to get down to business at once – and promptly blew us both away with what he offered. Warrington came up with seventy-five grand a year for the first two seasons, rising to a hundred a year for the last two. Me and Dad just looked at each other and I couldn't put pen to paper quickly enough. I was only eighteen and was on the sort of money I could only have dreamed about. So you see that when I insist Warrington really looked after me it couldn't have been truer. They had always said that if a player makes the grade they'd see him right – they were as good as their word as far as I was concerned.

It was all a far cry from my first contract, of twelve grand, even though my wages had almost quadrupled by then anyway. What my last contract at Wilderspool did prove to me, though, was that I'd outgrown McKnight and our relationship had run its course – and that was something I only found out to my cost.

I must admit I did have a bit of a chuckle when I was driving home from Peter's because if McKnight hadn't been banned from the club Warrington would have ended up getting me for about half the price. Most of the time Higham wanted to rip McKnight's head off – on this occasion he would have settled for tearing his hand off instead, I'm sure. In the end McKnight actually did the deal for me to go to Saints, but by the time we parted company it was on anything but the best of terms. In fact I'd go so far as to say if I ever bump into him again I'd have no worries about sticking one on him.

When I went to Saints they offered me the choice of a sponsored car or a £7,000 allowance for the running costs of mine. I'd just bought a new one at the time, so took the money – or at least that was the plan. McKnight, for whatever reason, said it was best to pay it to him and then he would pass it on to me. We discovered later it was apparently to bump up the price of the company before he sold it. It was all above board, and everything was declared, but he convinced me that was the best way to do it, and because personally I'd never had cause to doubt him I went along with it.

But all of a sudden the payments to me dried up, even though the club had paid the money to McKnight, and I just couldn't get hold of him. He had some trouble with his company at the time, and was selling up, but something wasn't right. To this day I don't know exactly what happened, but all I do know is that the bastard never paid me my cash and I haven't seen him since. To be honest, as much as I am easy-going, it's probably best that way, too, because I'd break his neck if he turned up again!

That was all to come, though, and for now he was sorting out my transfer – there was another twist to be played out before St Helens sealed the deal – in the shape of London Broncos, as Harlequins were still known at the time. Money wasn't exactly a big problem for the Broncos back then, with Richard Branson's millions behind them, so when they moved in I was duty-bound to listen. And if first impressions were all you went on, I'd probably have ended up in the Smoke.

Peter had obviously given me permission to talk to other clubs by then, and I got a call from Brad Rosser, who was running the rugby operation for Branson. I told him I was interested in what he had to offer, and would wait for him to get back to me to arrange a date to meet up. Quick as a flash he asked me what I was doing the following day. When I told him I didn't have anything planned, he said: 'We'll send a helicopter up for you tomorrow.' Talk about a fast mover! Next morning the car was round at the house, I was driven to Barton airfield, and there was this absolutely mint Virgin chopper, all leather interior, like something out of a James Bond film.

They flew me and Lindsay down to Kempton Park racecourse, where I was met by coach Tony Currie, who took me straight to The Stoop, where they played. From there it was on to Richmond and a look around the house they had for me, which I have to say was absolutely beautiful. A few of the other lads lived in the area, and I was taken to Peter Gill's house, an Aussie who played for London then, and we all had a chat and a brew at his place.

Then it was on to meet the man himself, Branson, for dinner at his gaff in Holland Park. He struck me as a really genuine, nice bloke and it was an amazing place. I must say it was a world away from what you would usually associate with St Helens, Wigan or Warrington! In fact I was so blown away that I actually agreed personal terms with him, they'd impressed me that much.

They were offering a four-year deal and obviously more money than I was on at Warrington, while they also said they'd sort out a job in cosmetics within the Virgin organisation for Lindsay, which was obviously crucial to us as well. If I was going to be living in London, away from friends and family, at least I'd be off with the lads at training all day, but Lindsay could have been stuck at home, miles from anyone she knew, so they seemed to have taken care of everything.

Then came the stumbling block. The Broncos said they'd discuss the price with Warrington, but were not prepared to go above £200,000, which effectively saved me from having to make the decision anyway. I could see London's point, though.

The Bosman ruling was having an impact in every sport, and transfer fees were soon to become a thing of the past in Super League – certainly as far as massive deals were concerned, because there was a problem with the sell-on value if a player ran his contract down. In a nutshell, they weren't prepared to risk losing me for nothing at a later date – I guess you don't have Branson's sort of wealth without being fairly bloody shrewd!

If they'd agreed to pay what Warrington were holding out for, I suppose there's every chance I would have been packing my bags for London. Not that I was left to worry about being stuck at Wilderspool for another season or so – Saints made sure of that. As soon as word got out that I had been talking to the Broncos, St Helens showed their hand and things really scooted on.

I'd heard a whisper that Wigan were keen as well, but as soon as Saints came up with their offer that was that, and I was off down to Knowsley Road to meet coach Shaun McRae, chief executive David Howes, plus Tom Ellard and Mal Kay, who were the board, back then along with Howard Morris. It was clear that Peter's initial demand of a million was never going to be met, but when St Helens said they'd give £300,000 plus forward Chris Morley – who was valued at £75,000 – it was all systems go.

I must admit that, whereas I wouldn't have known too many of the Broncos because of all their Aussies, I was pretty good mates with loads of the Saints lads. I had already spent quite a bit of time with the likes of Chris Joynt and Bobbie Goulding through the international squad, so it was never going to take ages to settle in.

The main thing for me, though – on top of the fact that they were a bloody good team, obviously – was the way Saints played the game. They had always been known as the great entertainers, and the fact that they were always there or thereabouts when it came to the finals was a massive plus as well. They'd won the last two Challenge Cups, and also picked up the Super League, so I had every reason to think I would soon have a pretty decent stack of winners' medals.

Money-wise, I wasn't exactly on the breadline either. Don't forget that new deal at Warrington had taken my wages up to seventy-five grand, so I was hardly struggling, especially for a lad of my age. But Saints blew me away with another good increase, so things could hardly have looked brighter. I had joined a top club, bloody good money, and a load of sponsorship deals starting to come in as well. I was in dreamland – and just turned nineteen.

As I said, I'd always been pretty shrewd with my cash, so it wasn't a case of suddenly having enough to get my own house – I'd done that a year earlier, buying a place in Springhead, just around the corner from my parents. I'd paid a lot for it, and put a lot of time in too, but it was always going to be a good investment. I knew the folks were on hand if I needed them, and I still saw them every day, but for a teenager it was fantastic – you could put your feet on the coffee table and no one could shout at you for it!

To be honest I'd had a pretty good grounding in looking after myself by the time I was a house owner in any case. Mum and Dad had given me, Danny and Lee that from a very early age, so the washing machine and the oven weren't exactly alien to me. In fact one of my great loves is cooking and I think I'm pretty decent at it as well. Yes, we were spoiled a bit as kids at times, and never wanted for anything, but we always had to earn it too. I may not have liked it at the time, but it paid dividends for when I was living in my own place.

And while I would obviously have had to consider selling up if I'd gone to London, there was no need to move house with me joining Saints. All that was left was to pick up my stuff from Warrington – and one final chance for Okker to make a few quid from me!

Okker, or Roy Aspinall to give him his proper name – though I never heard anyone call him by it – was kitman, groundsman, odd-job man at Warrington. When it came to a scam and earning a quick buck, he was in a league of his own. As I found out. I knocked on the door of his little cubbyhole and asked if I could take my kit. Quick as a flash he said it would cost me £25 or my Great Britain tracksuit. In the end I swapped the tracky for my own kit – I don't think I ever saw Okker give anything away for nothing during all my time at Wilderspool!

Unlike football, where you can find yourself in a totally different environment at the other end of the country or indeed anywhere in Europe, rugby league is a pretty tight community and you come across the same faces all over the game. So there was no emotional goodbye to the lads at Warrington, no lingering look around the stadium knowing it could be years before I would be playing there again. Players come and go but a lot more relationships stay close in rugby just because of the geography involved, and I have caught up with them all regularly over the years since.

Obviously I was a bit sad at leaving, and would occasionally wake up and wonder if I had done the right thing. It was my first professional club, one I would always be grateful to for bringing me through and giving me a big break, but I knew deep down it was a move that had to be made. You can't spend all day, every day with the same bunch of people and not be pretty close. But things change, and it doesn't take long to settle into your new surroundings, and pretty soon I was part of the furniture at Saints.

In fact the first day I walked into Knowsley Road I remember bumping straight into my Great Britain team-mate Anthony Sullivan, who made me feel at home at once. In fact everyone was so easy-going that bedding in was simple. I also loved the fact that everyone was treated the same, be it an international star or a youngster still finding his feet.

The only downside was that Saints were playing Wigan at Central Park in the last of the traditional Boxing Day fixtures in December 1997, but I had to watch from the stands because my registration didn't come through until the January. Mind you, watching the way they knocked seven bells out of each other made me think it wasn't such a bad one to miss out on, if truth be told!

Anyway, there would be plenty of time for me to get out there on the pitch in the future. The more immediate thing was the pre-season – and probably the toughest one I ever went through. Shaun McRae and his assistant Mike Gregory had us on the running track at Sutton for virtually the whole of the build-up to the new season, to the point that a lot of the lads suffered from shin splints. It was the first time we went through such a preparation and, thank God, the last. We didn't seem to do much ballwork at all: it was just running, running and more running.

Fortunately I had always kept myself in decent shape, and had even improved my fitness when Darryl took over at Warrington, because he arrived full of new ideas and had never allowed any slacking. His big passion seemed to be the dreaded bleep tests – running between two lines a certain number of times within a given time – and, boy, did he put us through it. He was such a stickler that if anyone fell short he'd have them doing it again – and you could be certain that if they didn't manage it first time, they didn't have a hope in hell of doing so the second. I have to say that I never had to do a repeat. But if it was my forte, it wasn't one I was keen on proving again and again!

The funny thing at Saints was that they had the 'F Troop' as well, for all the fat lads, as we called them. You know, the ones lagging behind at the back – a label I was determined to avoid and, touch wood, have managed to do so far.

But while things were going great guns off the field, on it they didn't exactly explode into life and I made a steady but unspectacular start as a Saint. It's always pretty tough in your first season at a new club, and I was finding it was doubly so because of the expectations after they'd paid so much for me.

At Warrington I had probably had more responsibility, but as I had grown up at the club it never bothered me. It didn't exactly start affecting my game at Saints, but I knew that the eyes of the entire game were on me because of that big-money fee. And while I could really get in there and dictate the play, call a move or whatever in the past, I was never going to walk into St Helens and start doing the same.

In all honesty I found that first season at Knowsley Road a bit tougher than I would have liked, especially because Shaun played me at second row quite a lot as well. He would switch Karle Hammond between loose forward – my usual position – and stand off, so I found myself in an alien role to boot.

There was never really a time when I thought I was going to be a flop, though, and by the end of that first season I was flying – even though the club ended up without a trophy for the first time in a while. I knew there had been occasions in my debut season when some fans were questioning whether I was worth the money, but the size of the fee never played on my mind. I put enough pressure on myself with my own expectations and demands, and just wanted to get into a rhythm of playing like I had at Warrington.

At Wilderspool, whenever I thought a move was on, I'd be on the scene and demanding the ball or calling a play. Although I have never considered myself above anyone else, I've never allowed myself to be pushed around either, and I'm more than willing – and capable – of looking after myself if the need arises.

But by and large the fans at Knowsley Road have always been great to me, even though I was struck by how much they wanted to beat Wigan. We all know Saints' rivalry with their neighbours is probably the fiercest in the game, but it's only when you are directly involved that you realise quite how strong it is.

I'd only been there five minutes when one fan came over and said, 'I don't care what you do for the rest of the season, just make sure you beat those bastards from Central Park.' I still get that to this day; in fact only recently someone said exactly the same thing. It really is mad how much they hate each other, and it really surprised me at first. They proper love belting hell out of each other on the pitch, although thank God rugby doesn't tend to suffer the same problems with fans doing likewise.

The atmosphere in those games was like nothing I'd ever experienced, either. Warrington used to love it when they came up against Wigan in particular, and I know Wilderspool was known as 'the Zoo' by opposing teams because of the intimidating air. Saints and Wigan, though, was something beyond that, not just because they were the deadliest of rivals, but also because they were usually both going for trophies as well.

The fixture planners must have had a twisted sense of humour in ensuring Wigan's last ever home game at Central Park, before they moved to the JJB Stadium, was against Saints. Talk about going out with a bang! We knew we were in for a pretty brutal afternoon, because there was no way they wanted to say farewell to their home on the back of a defeat to their biggest rivals.

That's how it seemed to be going at first, as we went in front, and I didn't improve the home fans' mood when I actually managed to score as well. Unfortunately for us we couldn't see it through and Wigan managed to win, but you can't have everything.

Having said that, at the end of my first season I didn't have anything! Sheffield surprised everyone by winning the Challenge Cup, and Wigan – it bloody had to be, didn't it? – won the first Grand Final against Leeds.

We'd managed to get to the semi-finals, despite a pretty stop–start season, only to get hammered at Leeds. That's the way the whole campaign went really, with two great wins over Bradford but defeats in every other game against Leeds and Wigan. In fact we lost to Wigan *four* times that season, so it wasn't exactly a year to look back on with particularly pleasing memories.

I'd arrived at St Helens fully expecting to be in at least one of the finals, after all they'd done in the previous couple of seasons, but we finished potless, while our biggest rivals were triumphing at Old Trafford. At least things could only get better – thank Christ they did as well.

In hindsight I suppose I can say that finishing the season empty-handed only steeled everyone's resolve to make sure we put the record straight next time around. Not that we were exactly consoling ourselves with that fact at the time! It was horrible watching Wigan prance around Old Trafford with the trophy after beating Leeds, and I personally vowed that I would definitely be enjoying the same feeling at some stage.

I didn't have too long to wait, either . . . but, as ever, there was a hell of a storm brewing before I got my hands on a first winners' medal as a professional. Life was certainly never dull around Knowsley Road.

6

To Ell and Back

From day one at Saints I knew the pressure was on to deliver some silverware every season. That was just a sign of what the speccies had grown to expect, after the club topping the Super League and picking up a couple of Challenge Cups in the years immediately before I joined.

But as much as we felt it as players, coach Shaun McRae had it even worse, and when we finished my first season empty-handed the Australian paid the price. We all had a suspicion things were going on behind the scenes, and there had been the usual whispering campaign, so when Shaun left before the 1999 season kicked off it probably didn't come as that much of a surprise to be honest.

Of course rumours were rife about who was going to take over. But one day during the pre-season we were all called in and our new coach was unveiled . . . a certain Ellery Hanley. I can still remember the day he arrived and the players went to the club to meet the new boss. Personally I was delighted – Ellery had been my hero since I first picked up a rugby ball. He had been Great Britain skipper, won everything going at Wigan and played in my position at loose forward as well. He was the one guy I had tried to model myself on in certain ways from the very early days.

I know people say you should never meet your heroes for fear of being disappointed, but that definitely was not the case with Ellery. He was absolutely blob on, a top man and a top coach. Maybe there was a bit of a closer bond as well, with us both playing the same position, but even now I've got nothing but good words to say about him.

He'd been Great Britain coach a few years earlier and had done pretty well at that, and I couldn't wait to meet him. We hit it off straight away and I was very impressed with his views on just about everything. Ellery had been a winner for years and was not prepared to settle for anything less – and that suited me down to the ground. After all, I had gone to St Helens for that very reason, and here was a man as determined as me to get it. He just had a certain aura about him, and despite what others may tell you, his man management was exceptional.

One of the first things he did during that pre-season was make me vice-captain to Chris Joynt, which was a huge honour. I had always been a talker on the field anyway, whether in training or games, and he had obviously noticed that during his first few sessions. As far as his tactics went, Ellery tended to keep things simple, but certainly got the best out of us by allowing us to play what we saw. He was very big on discipline and fitness, but, then again, no one was going to argue that his ideas in that department were going to be of anything but a huge benefit to us.

He kept his personal life very much to himself, but that was good too. There was a very definite line between the boss and the players, but I think that's something you've got to have if you want to command total respect – and Ellery certainly had that. None of us really saw him away from the game, although we've spoken many times on the phone, I see him on occasions, and he was the first to congratulate me and Lindsay when Jake was born.

By now I was beginning to establish myself in the game, but that didn't stop me being in awe of the man at times. He'd been there, done it and printed the bloody T-shirt, never mind bought it. He'd not been retired for too long, and all the lads could remember his exploits on the field, so that just added to the respect he earned. We knew that everything he told us was from his own experiences, and I think that played a massive part in how we viewed him.

It was easy to listen to someone who had done as much in the game as Ellery and his mere presence gave us a lift every day. I suppose it was a sign of the respect we had for him that he never had to raise his voice to us from the day he arrived to when he left. He never shouted or bawled, never lost his temper; he simply had to open his mouth and everyone else shut up.

He used to make us laugh because he just couldn't help being super cool. He'd be on the training ground in his tracky pants and boots, with a black leather jacket and a black leather beanie hat – he just looks the dog's bollocks all the time. Ellery was still a top player as well, and would join in with the sessions. That helped because you knew he was never asking you to do anything, either with the ball or fitness-wise, that he couldn't do himself.

At that time we also had Nigel Ashley-Jones working as the conditioner. Nigel is an Aussie who arrived under Shaun and remains one of the best I have ever worked with. Ellery also had John Myler working alongside him, but there was never any doubt about who was in charge.

I found my game improving simply because of the attitude he instilled in you. That and his rigid discipline – I think we were all too scared to risk stepping out of line. His training sessions were legendary as well. If things were going wrong, he wouldn't put the balls away and flog you with a run or fitness work. He'd just tell us to go home, forget about it and come in the next day with our heads right. That's what we did and it certainly seemed to work.

I wasn't so stupid as to think I had learned all I could. It's no secret that you never stop picking things up, and if you relax on your skills and basics it is very easy to get into bad habits – and that was something I wasn't about to do. But the players were also allowed to play a bit more, despite him being very big on defence, and I don't think we ever had the basics so fine-tuned as when Ellery was in charge.

We always did pretty short sessions, but they were quality ones too. He was absolutely spot on with his timing of them as well. If he said we were going to have a 28 minute session, it would never be more than a couple of seconds out either way. Nigel would have his clock on the job, and bang on the button Ellery would call a halt. The lads all used to laugh about how precise he was, but that was just his way – absolutely spot on with everything he did.

And it certainly worked. Yes, Ellery had grand ideas, but he got grand results as well, and no one can ever take that away from him. No one ever crossed him either, not among the players – we knew there would only be one winner if we tried it on. There was a time when Tommy Martyn wasn't too happy because it looked as though he might struggle to get a new contract. But despite a little bit of friction, Ellery left before it came to a head, so nothing ever blew up. I remember Ellery getting stuck into me once, because I had been giving away too many penalties. It wasn't a case of bawling me out. As I said, he didn't work like that. He just sat me down for a quiet word and it was more like he was disappointed in me than angry. You don't want to let down your hero, do you, so needless to say it worked.

One thing that didn't, however, was his signing of Darrell Trindall from Australia before his second season as coach. Tricky, as he was known, had a big reputation Down Under and it was clear he was a very gifted player. But he also had a bit of a reputation as something of a lunatic, and he did more to live up to that one than to his playing abilities. Actually I got on pretty well with him, but Tricky was clearly a wild card and you could tell he had that crazy streak in him. It wasn't long before he showed it, either.

He had been out one night, which in itself you couldn't slate him for; we've all done it at one stage or another. Where Tricky really slipped up was crashing his car. He was over on his own as his missus was still back in Australia, and he took a few of the younger guys under his wing as well. As you can imagine, that wasn't really appreciated by the club.

I don't know if Ellery was unaware just how much of a loose cannon he was, or simply felt he could harness it. But when someone is that much of a nutter, I don't think you can change them. It was the way Tricky was, and it didn't exactly augur well for a long and fruitful career with Saints.

Ellery also signed an Aussie forward called Phil Adamson, and pretty soon the rumours were going around that Eric Hughes, the football manager, had bought the wrong one. Around the same time Matt Adamson was in the Australian Test team, and there were all sorts of whispers that he was the one we should really have got. There was a falling out between Ellery and Phil before too long because the coach didn't really rate him and consequently didn't play him that much. We never did find out if we'd blundered in getting the wrong fellow, but as players we weren't about to get involved in the politics of transfer business, were we?

Needless to say, Phil's St Helens career wasn't the longest on record. But Trindall was the one getting the headlines, not really for the right reasons, and eventually Saints let him go. He'd also arrived, unknown to us, with a long-term shoulder problem and you didn't need more than one hand to count the number of games he played for us. Pretty soon the combination of his injury and his wild side meant he left St Helens. No one knew it was coming, but when it did I don't think too many of us were surprised, either.

But all that was for the future. For now we were concentrating on impressing our new coach, and I think we did a fair job of it too. Of course there were setbacks, none worse than losing 30–0 to Wigan of all teams, in Swansea, when Super League took the games on the road to try and help development in Wales. Yet even when things really went tits up, Ellery would never come in and start slamming the dressing room walls. He treated victory and defeat pretty much the same – outwardly at least – and would immediately be looking towards the next game, planning his video sessions and stuff.

Yet if that Wigan defeat was a stunner, it was nothing compared to the storm which blew up halfway through Ellery's first season in charge. In fact make that midway through his *only* full season in charge. It came early in July, when Ellery lost his temper with the Saints board, and they weren't about to take that lying down and almost immediately he was suspended as

coach. Us players hadn't got a clue what had happened, because
we were all in Southport, where we'd gone for a day's wind-
surfing, as an alternative team bonding exercise.

When the bus brought us all back to Knowsley Road it was
swamped with press, and we quickly discovered what had gone
on with Ellery. We were all gobsmacked, absolutely amazed,
especially when the board banned Ellery from having any
contact with the players. We weren't about to have that, and felt
we had a right to talk to him, so when Ellery got word to us that
he wanted a meeting, we were all there.

We all met up at full-back Paul Atcheson's house and it was
pretty emotional. Ellery wanted to see us as a group because he
had no idea if he was going to get his job back. He told us it
wasn't about money, but we all knew that – he was hardly
struggling for a few quid after a successful playing career and
shrewd investments. Ellery, as I said, wanted to win everything
and didn't feel he was getting as much help from the board as he
should. He wanted to do things his way, and we were all behind
him – that showed from the fact that we all showed up at Patch's
house to see him.

Fortunately for us, Ellery made his peace with the board –
albeit an uneasy truce – and was back in work within a
fortnight, and it was full steam ahead. Even so, the seeds had
been sown, and, boy, was that eventually to blow up again big
style. But more of that in time – for now we were all sailing one
happy ship again.

One of Ellery's strongest points was his ability to make you
feel you could take on the world, and before each game he
would get us in a circle in the dressing room. We had one game
at Leeds when we got stuck in traffic and ended up having to
change on the coach before we got there about twenty-five

minutes before kickoff. Ellery was as cool as you like, keeping everyone relaxed, then he suddenly turned off the lights. He gave us his pep talk, everyone in a circle while he said something positive about each player, in the pitch black. It certainly did the trick, because we played superbly and hammered them.

Everything was looking rosy and we ended up going into the play-offs having finished second in the table, one place behind Bradford Bulls, earning ourselves a trip to their ground for the qualifying play-off semi-final. Mind you, I don't think too many who witnessed our performance at Odsal that day would have been rushing to back us to win the Grand Final.

Their place has never been a particularly happy hunting ground for Saints and on this occasion it was an absolute bloody nightmare, because they whacked us 40–4. At least the play-off system allowed the loser of the game between first and second another chance the following week, against the one other remaining side from the top five, as it was.

Just about everyone expected that to be Wigan, but in the first ever game at the Warriors' new JJB Stadium, Castleford stunned the game by pulling off a memorable victory, and in doing so booked themselves a trip to Knowsley Road. We knew we'd have to pick ourselves up from the thumping at Odsal, and no one more than winger Chris Smith, who'd had a nightmare in that semi.

Ellery, typically, had given him nothing but support, just as he always defended his players. You could never accuse him of being anything but 100 per cent behind us, and I know Smiggy really appreciated that. He was in the team again the following week, and we booked our ticket to face the Bulls at Old Trafford with a great performance against Cas.

Scrum half Sean Long started the game on the bench because of a wrist injury, but when he came on he took them apart, and had a stormer as we went through to the Grand Final, only the second one staged since Wigan had beaten Leeds the year before. So there we were, preparing for the biggest game of our lives, against the team which had thrashed us only a fortnight earlier.

But funnily enough, I can't really remember that semi-final being mentioned by anyone in the build-up to the final. Of course we knew we had to raise our game, but we were just delighted to get a second chance – and this time we didn't intend to let ourselves, the fans or the club down. Personally I thrived on all the preparations, the suit fitting, media open day, the lot. This was what I'd signed for, and it was a brilliant week.

Fortunately I have never really suffered from nerves. I look forward to the big games rather than dreading them. And I've never been one for superstitions like some people. The only routine I tend to follow is having a rub before the game, but none of that putting your right boot on first stuff or anything like that, although I do insist on taking care of my own boots, rather than leaving them with the kitman; it puts my mind at rest. And I only ever wear the same pair of moulded or studs, depending on the surface. I couldn't be doing with having some for training and some for playing – I hate breaking new ones in at the best of times, so keep what you're comfortable in is my thinking.

But none of that was going through my mind in that dressing room at Old Trafford. I just wanted to get into the tunnel, walk on to the pitch and get my first taste of a big final. It's funny but I can still recall Russell Watson, the opera singer, singing 'Nessun dorma' as part of the pre-match entertainment just before we came on to the pitch. If that doesn't get the hairs on the back of your neck standing up, nothing will. I was ready to go and couldn't wait to get started. We also came out wearing the old-style Saints tracksuit top of white, with a red V, which seemed to lift our fans even more. Surely we couldn't blow it now.

Having said that, the way things went in the first half at Old Trafford you'd have struggled to find a neutral in the ground who would have backed anything but a comprehensive Bradford win. We were on the back foot throughout the first half, and it really did look as if I'd have to wait at least another year for my first taste of winners' champagne. They were in front 6–2, after Henry Paul went scooting in for a try from a scrum. Forward Sonny Nickle had chased him all the way and Henry probably only scored because he slid the last few yards on the wet surface.

There was no doubt we were really chasing the game and we were under a hell of a lot of pressure. I'd say that was the most sustained defensive effort we had to put in all season and it was very intense. But for all that, Paul's try was the only time they managed to get over our line before half-time, and at just four points adrift we knew we were still bang in it. The older heads in the side wasted no time in trying to relax the youngsters at the break, and I remember Kevin Iro, a vastly experienced Kiwi international, playing a particularly big role. He was a very quiet bloke off the pitch, but had played with Ellery at Wigan and was a big influence on the others in the dressing room – and especially in that game.

Even so, within two minutes of the second half starting we were further behind – then we were thrown a controversial lifeline that helped turn the game. Leon Pryce was convinced he'd scored when Michael Withers sent him down the left and clear – in fact at the time I think everyone thought it was a pretty routine try. But referee Stuart Cummins wasn't certain, and went to the video ref – and thank God he did! As we watched the replay on the big screen, it seemed that Withers' fingertips had just brushed the ball in the build-up to the try, and the ruling went in our favour, deciding there had been a knock on.

If that had been given I honestly think the game could have been just that bit beyond us, because it was so tight. Of course we'd have kept going to the end, but it was obviously not going to be a high-scoring match, and who knows if we'd have managed it. Fortunately we never had to find out, and we'd also had one disallowed ourselves when the video ref ruled that Freddie Tuilagi had knocked it forwards before going over as well.

It was still nip and tuck, and time was running out. But then Apollo Perelini made a great burst for the line, and, with Bradford still on the rack Iro, the Beast, went over for the try that brought us level. Sean Long kicked a brilliant goal from out wide, and we hung on as Bradford suddenly found themselves having to try and save a game they must have thought they'd got won. Those last few minutes seemed to drag on for hours, but then it was all over, we were the champions and everything I had left Warrington for was mine. It was a fantastic moment, the greatest of my career at the time, and I wanted to savour every second.

The dressing room was just like one big party, and we ended up going back to the club for a proper one as soon as we could. The only drawback, if you could call it that, was the fact that several of us had to report to the Radisson hotel in Manchester the next day, because on Monday we were off to New Zealand with Great Britain for the Tri-Nations tournament. Lindsay was pregnant with Jake at the time, so wasn't drinking, but I bloody was and had sunk quite a few by the end of the night. But there was still one final little twist to the evening which leaves me sweating when I think about it even now.

Lindsay had not long passed her test and had just got a new car, but was still pretty nervous about driving. When I'd gone for the coach I'd driven hers, so it was there to come back from the club afterwards. But when my dad left the party, with my kitbag in his boot, we realised that it also had Lindsay's car keys in it, so we were stuffed. I was due to report with Great Britain the next day, but was stuck in St Helens, with no way of getting back to Oldham. It was a total nightmare. Then winger Anthony Sullivan, who was also going on the tour, said we could borrow his car because he obviously wouldn't be needing it. The only problem was that it was a Golf VR6 and there was no way Lindsay would drive it. I ended up breaking one of my cardinal rules and drove us home at 4.30 a.m. I was an absolute mess and thank Christ I wasn't pulled over. That would have been it: no Great Britain tour, and God knows what else. It's the only time I have driven in a state and it leaves me cold when I look back now. The weird thing was that as I was driving one way down the M62, Smiggy phoned. He had been out in Manchester before going back to the club and we passed each other on the motorway.

Fortunately we managed to make it home and the next day I reported for Great Britain duty with my head banging. And looking at most of the other Bradford and Saints lads in the squad I wasn't the only one. If the Aussies had seen us then they wouldn't have fancied us to give them much of a game. Mind you, as it turned out we didn't, but more of that later.

As far as Saints was concerned, things couldn't be going

better. The season had finished on the ultimate high and we couldn't have been in better spirits as we reported back for pre-season training. Little did we know all that was swiftly about to change, and in the most dramatic fashion. We traditionally held a pre-season dinner and players' awards, with all the board and sponsors there. The coach always made a speech, and Ellery stood up to make his. The players knew that he felt the board at the time hadn't helped him as much as they could on certain things, but couldn't believe it when he finished his speech by calling them all a bunch of dinosaurs. You can imagine how that went down with them all, in front of people who were pumping money into the club. But then again, Ellery always did say what he thought, whether it was good or bad, so it was no surprise that he was doing the same here.

If that wasn't bad enough, he made things worse for himself at the annual Super League launch, which was being held in Bradford. Every club turned up with their coach – except Saints. He copped a load of stick in the media for that, and I know the bigwigs who ran the game were thoroughly embarrassed and not at all pleased with him.

There was loads of speculation that he could be sacked, but when the 2000 season started he was still in charge, and we knew a few good results could take the pressure off him. Unfortunately we got off to the worst possible start, kicking off with a real drubbing by Melbourne Storm in the World Club Challenge. Then we went out of the Challenge Cup at Leeds – when I went over for a try courtesy of a pass from Tricky, who was making a very rare appearance – so it was the Super League or nothing when we kicked off at home to Bradford.

They were clearly still smarting from that Grand Final defeat, because they came at us with all guns blazing, while we were way off our best and ended up losing. For a board of directors who had probably been waiting for their moment ever since they had suspended Ellery the previous season, enough was enough and he was dismissed on 11 March. Everybody knew that Ellery would never back down, so maybe it had been on the cards for months, I don't know. What I did know was the fact that we were losing a bloody good coach just a couple of weeks into the new season – hardly the perfect way for champions to be setting off on the defence of their crown.

I don't know if something was in place before Ellery left, but Ian Millward was quickly brought in as his replacement. Ian had worked miracles with Leigh, albeit at the level below Super League. He had taken them from the foot of that table to one of the emerging sides in the game, with pretensions of eventually challenging the Super League big guns themselves. That had been enough to earn Basil, as everyone called him, a crack with one of the top teams and we settled down for a new era under a new boss, with everyone suddenly finding themselves in the position where they had to prove they were worthy of a place.

I was hardly in the ideal frame of mind for rugby at the time, either, because Lindsay was due to give birth very shortly, although I don't think I actually told Basil that. In fact when we went to Hull for his first game in charge, just a week after Ellery had gone, it came after I'd spent two days dashing to and from the Royal Oldham Hospital, Lindsay having been taken in on the Wednesday. The funny thing was that Basil was shocking with names, and didn't really know anyone when he arrived either. In fact he spent the first three weeks calling me Paul Schofield. He eventually got it right, but was a bloody shocker when it came to remembering things like that,

Anyway, we really turned on the style for him at Hull and

ended up giving them a real beating. It had gone particularly well for me, scoring a try and having a good game, so I was buzzing when I came off, if not in the mood to hang around and celebrate. As soon as the hooter went, I went racing to my mum and dad on the sidelines to ask if they'd heard anything, because they were keeping in regular touch with Lindsay's mum, Eileen. Nothing had, so I had a quick shower, jumped in the car with them rather than the team bus and we raced back home.

As soon as I got in I was on the phone to the hospital, but they told me to get some rest because it was unlikely anything would happen that night. I must admit I was pretty shattered, what with the game and then the mad dash home, and got my head down at just gone midnight. But I'd not been asleep for more than five minutes when the hospital rang to say Lindsay's waters had broken, so me and her mum – who was staying at ours – raced there. I spent the night alternating between trying to give Lindsay the support she needed and trying to fight sleep when I sat in the rocking chair in her room. But at 10.18 a.m. she gave birth to Jake and it was just the most incredible feeling in the world, far better than anything you could experience on a rugby pitch.

I must admit the timing could have been a bit better, though! I was due to be an usher for my mate Mick Slicker, the Huddersfield player who was getting married that day. Needless to say that was out, so my brother Lee did the business instead. He was just thankful that I hadn't been down as the best man. It was also the same day, 18 March, that a very close family friend, Phil McLean, died. Phil had been a good mate to all of us, and had coached my younger brother Danny since he was six or seven right through the juniors. I remember the *Oldham Chronicle* had a picture of a rugby ball and the announcement of Jake's birth on the same page as the one about Phil's death. It was a tremendously emotional time, but for two reasons as far removed as you could ever imagine.

ON YER BIKE…Shooting around the ATC track in Royton, on my 50cc Yamaha.

TAKING STOCK…Me and Danny enjoying our day out watching the stock car racing.

LITTLE ANGELS…Me (left), Danny (centre) and Lee.

BAD HAIR DAY…
I cut my own hair before this
school photo. Clearly not
one of my strong points!

SUNSHINE GANG… Lee (left), next to Danny, Mum, me and Sam the dog at the beach.
Dad was taking the photo.

MAY DAY…
Mayfield line up
before our Cup
final against Orrell.
Howard Leach,
such an influence
on my career,
is on the right.

SECRET
DRINKER…
Having a sly sip of
a pint, with Danny
and Lee. I must have
had a few, actually,
as I'm wearing a
Castleford shirt!

DOG'S LIFE...
Me and Boss,
and my close
mate Wes Rogers
with Otis.

WATER WAY TO GO...Waterhead Under 14s celebrate winning the Barrow Sevens.
I'm fourth left on the back row.

FULL STEAM AHEAD...Making a break in my early days with Warrington.

WIG WHAM!...
Causing problems for the Wigan defence in my Warrington days.

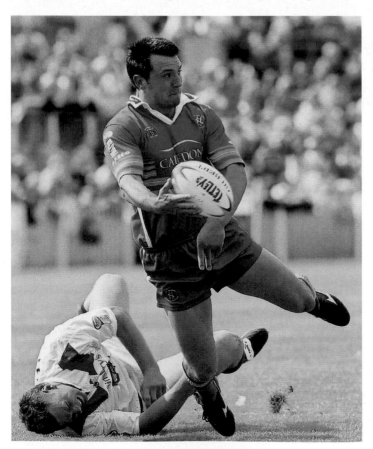

PASS MASTER...
Slipping the ball out
against Wakefield.

SUPER STARS…The party starts following Saints' 2000 Grand Final win.

GAME FOR A TAFF…Touching down for England against Wales.

CHEER WE GO… Celebrating a memorable win over the Aussies.

OH BROTHER…No prizes for guessing who came out on top in Saints' game against our Danny's Wigan.

7

Basil's Brush – A New Broom

I must admit that it was a strange experience when Ian Millward first arrived. Nothing against him, but when you've won the Grand Final four games – albeit five months – earlier, you don't expect a new coach to be on the agenda. Yet that was exactly the case, and suddenly we were all trying to impress the boss who, at the same time, was trying to prove he was worthy of the big reputation he had earned at Leigh.

It must have been strange for Basil as well, to be fair, because most of the playing staff were probably better known than the coach, which certainly hadn't been the case when Ellery breezed in. But he struck me as an amiable sort of bloke, very approachable, if a world apart from the previous guy.

Ian was keen to stamp his own authority and ideas on the club, but was very confident in his ability and, considering all he ended up winning, you can't dispute his success. It was odd having a coach who wasn't averse to raising his voice when he felt it was needed – quite unlike Ellery.

As far as the training was concerned, that couldn't have been more removed from what we had grown used to either. Ellery, as I said, kept things very simple and worked on the basics. Ian, on the other hand, was off the wall with some of his ideas – they were crazy at times. He was always looking to do something out of the ordinary and during his reign the club must have bought every single piece of training equipment on the market.

One day all these vests arrived, with Velcro straps on the shoulder and wrists. Ian was keen to introduce boxing into the training sessions because some techniques are similar to the tackling in rugby league, and apparently these things were designed to help you keep your hands up – although quite how it worked none of us could quite fathom out. Whatever, it was all very technical, as most of his sessions seemed to be.

He was absolutely blob on when it came to technique and some of the players were probably really working on it for the first time, but some of his ideas were over the top. He had us hitting the tackle bags with tennis balls in our hands. What on earth that was supposed to achieve was beyond us. Apparently it was something to do with keeping your hands ready to react and tackle, but I don't know where the balls came in. As far as we could see, it was just a load of 'em!

I'm not saying his suggestions didn't work but we seemed to spend a hell of a lot of time scratching our heads. One thing that did go down particularly well was his love of team bonding – there weren't too many arguments among the lads about that one. Ian wasn't averse to having a beer with the lads himself, and he also made sure the girlfriends and wives were involved a lot as well. He certainly made it a fun place to be at times.

We had gone from a coach who we only really saw at work to one we socialised with as well. Under Ellery we had a lot of alcohol bans, too. If we had a big game coming up there was a total ban in the week. Sometimes if, for example, we were playing Wigan on the Good Friday, Ellery would say he wanted three good wins going into it, so no alcohol whatsoever beforehand. I assume people stuck to it!

But with Basil there was none of that. Of course he expected us to look after ourselves and not go daft, but we weren't stupid and realised that if we had a beer, it had to be in moderation as well. And never at any stage getting close to the match, either. It led to him developing a really good relationship with the lads, even if some of his video sessions were done with such detail that it was almost like being back at school on occasions.

You couldn't deny his methods seemed to work, though, because we basically carried on where we left off under Ellery, and were pretty much right up there all season. In the end who topped the Super League table came down to the final game of the season, when were faced Wigan at Knowsley Road. Unfortunately the wheels came off big time and they battered us.

That left us having to negotiate a tricky qualifying play-off, albeit at home, against Bradford Bulls, who had beaten us twice in the league that season already. Even so, home advantage meant we were chock-full of confidence, and getting a sniff of Old Trafford once again.

And in hindsight maybe it wasn't too bad having to do it the hard way, because that match against the Bulls is probably the most famous in Super League history – and there will certainly never be a game decided in quite such dramatic circumstances.

It had been a real arm wrestle of a game, but with just seconds left on the clock they looked to have won it, and held an 11–10 advantage. I actually had the ball and the crowd were all counting down the last ten seconds, when I was fighting to get to my feet, with Henry Paul trying to hold me down until time was officially up.

When I actually played the ball there were just four seconds left, and what happened next was absolutely unreal. We were pinging it around like the Harlem Globetrotters, desperately looking for a chink in their defence and the chance of a break to set up a drop goal, if nothing else. The crowd couldn't believe it when Sean Long launched a big kick right across the pitch, and Kevin Iro swapped passes with Steve Hall on the right wing.

Back to the left it came, and Dwayne West spotted his chance and made a break into space, racing past a couple of despairing defenders. He passed the ball inside and second rower Chris Joynt, of all people, had kept pace with him and took the pass. Anthony Sullivan, one of the fastest men in the sport, was on his shoulder and screaming for him to hand the ball on, but Joynty backed himself and raced away from James Lowes to score the match winner.

People have asked me since if Longy's kick across the field was something we'd planned, but when you get to that stage of a game plans go out of the window – you're just desperately looking to do anything that will stretch the opposition's defensive line and open them up a little. When Joynty raced over, Sky TV brilliantly captured the emotion of it all as they filmed Bradford coach Matt Elliott sliding from his seat to the floor, totally gutted.

We were going absolutely berserk, even though we had the conversion attempt to come. It was pretty much from in front of the posts, but to be honest it didn't matter, as we were already in front. Longy wasn't going to miss the chance of a laugh, though, and actually tried to take the kick wearing a huge St Bernard head, which our mascot had lost as he jumped in with the celebrations in front of the fans. Unfortunately referee Russell Smith was having none of it, so Longy – minus his false dog's head – slotted it over and we could really start celebrating.

Even so, the job was far from done and we had a trip to Wigan to earn our place at Old Trafford – and this time we were determined to avoid a repeat of twelve months earlier, when Bradford had stuffed us at Odsal and sent us into that sudden-death, last-chance game with Castleford. It must have been the best performance by any team to visit the JJB Stadium, because we really got our revenge – and a real psychological advantage – by thrashing them to book our place at Old Trafford once again.

We were well aware that the previous games counted for nothing in a one-off final, so there was never any danger of complacency. But we'd also experienced how good it felt to win the Grand Final, and we all wanted more of it. For a long time it seemed as though we were going to walk it, as we shot into a 13–0 lead, with me grabbing a drop goal. But Wigan, to their credit, fought back and got to within touching distance thanks to a couple of tries, and it looked as though my one-pointer could be the difference.

But then we cut loose again and Chris Joynt, Freddie Tuilagi and Tim Jonkers all grabbed further tries, and in the end we saw it out with something to spare. I remember saying to Kez Cunningham a few minutes before the end 'we've done it again, lad', and he just had a massive smile on his face. It's fantastic when you're nearing the end of the game and they need three tries to win, which you know is way beyond them, and you can start your celebrations early. We all knew what to expect at the hooter – the lap of honour, the celebrations, the party – and we were determined to enjoy it just as much.

To be honest, I still think that every final just gets better each year. It's because you know exactly what it entails, everything that comes with it, and you want it every single season because it's that good. And it doesn't come any better for the fans – beating your deadliest rivals convincingly, in the end at least, to become champions. That's a case of bragging rights of the highest order.

In all we played them five times that season and won four of them, and the fans actually had some T-shirts printed after Tommy Martyn got two tries to beat them at the JJB in the fourth meeting. You still see the odd one knocking about, with the words Tommy's Double Does The Treble.

And after the final there was, of course, the party back at the club again. Only this time without a set of car keys in sight for me, until well into the following day. This year it went off without any scares or needing to avoid police patrol cars, and the thing I really remember is Freddie Tuilagi's fantastic version of 'Mambo No. 5' on stage at Knowsley Road. There was more than a hint of sadness about things, too, because Freddie was leaving for Leicester rugby union, Apollo Perelini was joining Sale and other lads like Vila Matautia, Julian O'Neill, Steve Hall and Scott Barrow were packing their bags too. It was a truly memorable end to a season that had started with such a storm of controversy.

As luck would have it, a load of us were supposed to be linking up at the Radisson hotel again for international duty the next day. England had a World Cup to prepare for, and we were going to America for warm weather training as part of the build-up.

But this time Ian had insisted to the international bosses that we get a day's grace so that we could actually enjoy the celebrations; we didn't have to join up until Monday tea time. Of course once they had allowed us an extra twenty-four hours, they had to do the same for the Wigan lads, and by the look of them when we all linked up at the airport they'd enjoyed just as big a drink as us.

There was myself, Paul Wellens, Sean Long, Andy Farrell, Gary Connolly, Kris Radlinski and Tony Smith all with banging heads and still feeling pretty rough two days after the final. The only difference this time was that we weren't going over to face a New Zealand or Australia, but to put the finishing touches to our preparations – and what an eventful trip it turned out to be.

We were staying in Florida, and personally I thought it was fantastic. We trained at the Wide World of Sports Complex, and then they opened the fun park itself for us an hour early, so Sky Sports could get some shots. That was brilliant, getting to go on all the rides – without queuing! – and we went on the lot. They couldn't get us off the rock and roll rollercoaster until we'd done four on the bounce, and the whole thing was unbelievable. We had the place to ourselves and went back to being kids again for a few hours. Then we were off to the Epcot Center for a feed and a massive fireworks display. David Howes, the England manager, did a brilliant job in sorting us out.

John Kear was the coach at the time and he brought David Waite, another future Great Britain boss, over for a couple of days.

At first he just ripped into the lads, probably because he thought we were just out to enjoy ourselves rather than concentrating on the real reason for being in the States, and at first he struck me as a schoolteacher type – not surprising seeing that's what he was trained to do as well. But once we got to know him, he ended up having a great sense of humour.

One of the days over there we went for a game of golf, me and Wello against Waitey and Sean Long, and it was an absolute riot. Every time David hit a decent shot, Longy would be yelling: 'Nice one Terry, good hit Tez.' I'm not sure he knew what to make of it, but in the end, as I say, he turned out to be a top bloke and all in all the Americans really looked after us.

The final part of the build-up was a match against the USA, and we already knew it was hardly going to be a close call. Rugby league is very much a minority sport compared to things like baseball, basketball and American football. It was very much a minority sport compared to most things the Yanks play, in fact. So it was always going to be more of a fitness workout than a serious competitive game and we ended up winning 110–0. If only they were all that easy. Even so, that doesn't mean you are going to avoid injuries – as I swiftly found out.

I started the game on the bench, but got the nod to go on, made one break and immediately did my hamstring. It was the worst kind, a tear, a proper job, and I couldn't tell you how gutted I was. A bloody nothing match and it had put my whole World Cup in jeopardy. Needless to say, my mood changed somewhat from that moment.

I spent the whole of the remainder of the stay in Disney's Wide World of Sports Complex over there, which fortunately has brilliant rehab facilities. I was in the ice bath, the hot bath, the ice bath and so on for hours, desperately trying to recover in time for England's opening game against Australia at Twickenham little more than a week or so later.

Even so, it didn't look optimistic. But then Howesy suggested I saw Tommy Smales, a former Great Britain scrum half who ran a pub in Featherstone, but who also had a great reputation for curing muscle problems, hamstrings and the like. We stayed the night in Staines after coming home from the States, but Howesy arranged for me to fly straight back up the next day, and by five o'clock the following afternoon I was in Oldham again.

Tommy knew I was ringing him the minute I was home, and he told me to get over to his place, the Travellers' Rest, for seven. I thought he meant the next morning – in fact he meant there and then, which gave me two hours to get my stuff together and across the M62. I didn't know much about him at all, but the likes of Ellery swore by him; they said he was an absolute magician when it came to hamstrings, so that was good enough for me. And let's be honest, my prospects weren't exactly glowing unless he could work a miracle, so anything was worth a go.

There was none of this fancy Dan stuff with Tom; he was full-on, hands-on treatment, and then he got me in his car and took me up to the cricket pitch nearby. By now it was about 10 p.m., and there I was, on the field behind the boozer, with the car lights on so we could see what we were doing. It was certainly the most bizarre treatment I'd ever had. He actually had me running pretty much straight away, only at about ten per cent, nothing more than a slow jog, but gradually building up.

Then it was back down to the pub again for more treatment, more massages and stuff, and then up to the cricket pitch for some running. He had me slowly increasing the level of the runs, just to stretch the hamstring. It was really throbbing, but I got through it and knew he was doing me a lot of good, even though I was absolutely knackered by the end of it. I suppose it wasn't surprising; I'd got back from London, gone straight over to Tommy's and didn't get home till gone 1 a.m. – knowing I had to be back there again in seven hours for another full dose of treatment.

All in all I went to see him every day for a week, and he had me back in the England camp in Leeds at the end of it, so fair play to him. My leg seemed almost 100 per cent: I was virtually sprinting again, less than two weeks after I could barely walk with a torn hamstring. Everyone had said how good he was, and I'd not heard a bad word about his treatment – now I could vouch for it myself.

Nowadays, of course, everyone knows that the best thing for injuries is actually to work the muscle, so he proved to be way ahead of his time. Back then most people would have ordered me to rest it and put ice on the problem area, but everything shortens up and it makes your rehab a lot longer. That's why, at the time, some were quick to query his methods and I know the Saints physio, asked a few questions.

But I had been under the care of England physio Allan Tomlinson, and he was quite happy for me to give it a go, and it certainly seemed to pay off. Tommy may not have been the traditional type of medical expert, but he proved to be way ahead of the rest and I was delighted. Mind you, that wasn't a feeling that lasted too long.

John Kear kept me back for the opening games, against Australia in the opener, and I also missed wins over Russia and Ireland. But come the semi-final against New Zealand I was raring to go, and John threw me straight back into the side for that. Pretty soon I was wishing he hadn't. We got absolutely tonked and I had a real shocker; I was crap. I was totally off the pace, my timing was off, everything was off.

In hindsight maybe I shouldn't have played, because I hadn't seen any serious action since the Grand Final about six weeks or so earlier, not to mention my injury, and bloody hell it showed. I may have been fit in general terms, but my match fitness wasn't sharp enough and whether I was 100 per cent ready to play I don't know. But it was the semis of the World Cup and you're always going to convince yourself that you are ready with a place in the final of any sport's most prestigious competition at stake. I know Tommy pulled a rabbit out of the hat in getting me back, but returning against the Kiwis probably wasn't the wisest decision I've ever made.

Not that I have anything but total appreciation for the way John Kear put his neck on the block in selecting me, despite me not having played a game in the tournament up to the last four. But it was a massively disappointing end to a year which had seen us winning a second Grand Final, only to end on a huge low just a couple of months later.

Even so, there was no time for wallowing in self-pity. My close season lasted just over a month before I was back in full training; we had a World Club Challenge against Brisbane Broncos to prepare for. Having been walloped by Melbourne in the same competition twelve months earlier, it was the ideal incentive for all of us. And personally I wanted to show the Aussies that I wasn't the player they had last seen performing well below standard in the semi-final. Fortunately revenge was just around the corner – and I was to play a hefty part in it, as well.

8

Bronco Busting

We knew from bitter experience against Melbourne a couple of years earlier that there is no such thing as an easy game when you are facing the Aussies, be it in a Great Britain shirt or in the World Club Challenge. So we were under no illusions that it would be anything but a real dogfight against Brisbane Broncos, when we faced them at the Reebok Stadium for the right to call ourselves world champions.

The Aussies had proved themselves top dogs in another aspect too, over the years – having a file of ready-made excuses to hand. It's funny, but whenever a team from Down Under lost the World Challenge it never seemed to be simply that they'd lost to a better side. It was always a case of 'we had a load of injuries, we were jet-lagged, we weren't match fit'. You name it, they suffered from it.

This time, however, the Broncos brought over a full squad, fielded ten of the side which had won the Aussie Grand Final, and were at pains to insist how seriously they were taking the game. That was pretty bloody obvious from the kickoff, as they established an 18–6 lead and were good value for it as well. Not that we were playing badly, in fact we were going pretty well – they were just taking their chances better than us.

Stand off Shaun Berrigan proved that when he burrowed his way over the line from dummy half on their first serious attack. Phillip Lee added another for them, and Brad Meyers scored their third try pretty soon after half-time. Our only reply had been a try from yours truly, and a kick from Sean Long. Even so, at 18–6, I suppose a few people were expecting a demolition job – but this time we were made of sterner stuff. We also had the added motivation of a few comments from Brisbane beforehand, basically saying that their game was a lot better than the English one.

The other thing that seemed to work for us was a big change in the weather, because in the second half the heavens opened and hailstones came lashing down. I know those aren't the best conditions for playing open, flowing rugby, but we were a little more used to the dodgy climate than Brisbane were, and we really got into our stride.

A lot is made about how momentum plays such a big part in rugby league, and we certainly had it with us that day as Longy inspired a fantastic comeback with an angled run to score a try. Then, little more than two minutes later, he sent Paul Newlove racing clear and Chris Joynt was there in support to go over; Longy added a goal to tie up the scores. Fair play to Brisbane, they showed exactly why they were Australia's top side by pounding our line, and I remember making one tackle to stop Wendell Sailor, their giant winger, which ultimately proved pretty crucial.

Even so, it was a real arm wrestle in the closing minutes and you couldn't have picked a winner with any confidence. But with only six to go, Keiron Cunningham set me up for a drop goal from fifteen metres, and suddenly we were in front. Once again they came steaming back at us, but we held firm and with just over a minute left Longy booted a second drop goal for us and we were champions. I don't think any other domestic game had given me quite as much satisfaction, especially after my last visit to the Reebok had ended in such dismal failure against the Kiwis in the World Cup semi-finals.

We had proved that the British game was not dying on its feet after all, and Brisbane could have no complaints about missing star men. They brought over the likes of Sailor, Berrigan, Lote Tuqiri, Gorden Tallis, Darren Lockyer – all world-class players who would walk into pretty much any side in the game. It was the full army and it had needed a truly great display from Saints to win it. The only downside, if there could be one after that, was that the celebrations were very short and sweet, because for all our delight at winning the crown we had a full season just around the corner.

Our pre-season preparations had been fantastic, and we had gone for a week's warm-weather training in Lanzarote. Given the climate at the Reebok against Brisbane, though, we would probably have been better served going to Greenland. It was all a far cry from my early days at Warrington, when we'd been sleeping in a hostel on an outdoor pursuits week in Wales. Mind you, the game as a whole had progressed since then and these days every club flies off somewhere for a week or so to complete their build-up for the new campaign.

We knew we had to hit the ground running straight away, too, because, of all the ties to get in the Challenge Cup, we were paired with Wigan, although at least we were at home. Plus, of course, we had already proved our quality in the World Club, so we knew we were pretty sharp. Unfortunately for me, not as sharp as Paul Johnson's knee, as I discovered fairly soon into the fourth-round game.

I was just running the ball in, tried a little step but slipped, and my jaw caught PJ bang on the knee as I went over. It was a complete accident on his behalf, but I knew straight away what I had done because I couldn't put my teeth together. I'd been pretty lucky with injuries up to that point, and my only real problem had been against Leeds the previous season, when I had cracked my eye socket.

That came when Andy Hay caught me, although I managed to finish the game and only realised what I'd done in the showers afterwards. I blew my nose and my eye popped, and came up like a bubble. The doc knew what I'd done straight away and he told me: 'It's obvious you've cracked it because the air is getting through your sinuses', so off I went for a scan, which showed a hairline fracture.

Even so, I had been back in action the following week because the main problem there is the risk of infection, and that was sorted out with a dose of antibiotics. I didn't even miss a game, but this time it was a different story. I was rushed to hospital as soon as I came off, and I remember pestering them to let me phone the ground to see how we were doing. The good news was that we had won, so at least I still had the prospect of coming back for the latter stages of the cup, touch wood.

Even so, I was facing six weeks on the sidelines, the longest I had been out since I first picked up a ball in anger. It was six weeks of absolute hell, as well. Obviously the main thing was the fact that, for whatever training I could do in the week, there was no game to look forward to at the end of it. But the extra torture came in the shape of Mick McGurn, our conditioning coach from Ireland, who seemed to take a real sadistic pleasure in making us suffer during his various fitness regimes. He was into running marathons, a real fitness freak, and with him in charge of my recovery I knew there was no danger of me returning in anything but peak condition.

All the injured players trained the day before the game – fitness permitting, obviously – but I also did quite a few one-on-one sessions with Mick. One of them was an absolute killer, total pain, and it still brings me out in a sweat just thinking about it. Mick took me over to Sherdley Park, where we did an hour and a half's running up and down the hills there. Then it was straight back to Knowsley Road, where we did fifteen consecutive 320-metre rows on the machine, with just thirty seconds recovery between each one. Then, just to cap it, we went straight into a two-hour weights session. But if it was hell at the time, I certainly reaped the reward later in the season, and I still put a lot of my success that year down to the fact that Mick had me in such great condition when I returned. I'd never been pushed so hard in anything, but I don't think I'd ever been as fit either.

I hadn't had the longest of pre-seasons – none of the lads who had been in action for Great Britain at the end of the previous year had – so that six-week break probably did me a lot more good than I was prepared to admit at the time, too. So I was raring to go when I came back for our Super League game at London, even though I was a bit wary for the first time about how well my cheek would hold up; it's not something you can really protect with padding or anything.

I didn't have long to wait before I found out, as London forward Jim Dymock gave it a pretty severe testing very early on. I'd been tackled, and as I lay on the floor he gave me the old facial, rubbing my face into the ground. To be honest, it was probably the best thing that could have happened, because although it was still a bit tender there was no reaction and I could get on with the game knowing it was almost as good as new. I got a few more bangs on it throughout the eighty minutes and it was a bit sore at the end, but no worse than usual, and when I went for X-rays just to check nothing had been dislodged it was all clear.

I could also get back to eating proper food as well, which was a blessing. When I was out, I was on mash, stews, soup, anything that didn't require a great deal of chewing. I'd had a titanium plate inserted into my cheek and four screws under my teeth to keep everything in place. But, as you might expect, I didn't get much sympathy off the rest of the Saints lads, either, who took great delight in calling me the Elephant Man and a few other things besides. All in all, I lost over a stone and a half. So you can imagine how pleased I was to be back in action. And, to cap it all, we beat London as well, when two tries from Keiron Cunningham won us the match.

For me it was a massive psychological boost to get a game under my belt, because the following week we had the Challenge Cup semi-final against Leeds, and there was no way I wanted to miss that one. What a cracker it proved to be as well, as I put us in front with a try that was all down to a bit of local knowledge. I knew that Barrie McDermott, the Rhinos' prop forward, loved to offload in the tackle, so when he tried it near the halfway line I sneaked round the back, intercepted the pass and raced over.

I probably shouted for the ball as well, which some might see as illegal but I rate as smart play. Maybe there's a bit of gamesmanship in there, but everyone does it, and at the end of the day it's all about winning. That's all semi-finals are about –

sod it: whether you win by one point and play crap, or thirty and have the game of your life. Reaching the final is all that matters in games like that.

The Rhinos equalised with a try from Mark Calderwood, and that was really the story of the game. Neither of us could kill off the other, and it was all level with a couple of minutes left, when Tommy Martyn banged over what we thought would surely be a match-winning drop goal. But when we looked at the official clock, rather than the one on the stand which only showed sixty seconds left, there were still five minutes to go and we were anything but safe.

But then I got another chance and managed to romp over, and this time it was certain – we were heading to the Challenge Cup final at Twickenham. There was no time for celebrating, though, because after whitewashing Wakefield we were back at the JJB again for a derby against our deadly rivals. And if the semi-final at their ground had been close, this was tighter still, and there was still nothing between us at the final hooter.

Wigan had a 100 per cent Super League record at the time, and, with a ten-point lead going into the final ten minutes, looked odds on to extend it. But then Dwayne West went over for one try and I grabbed another after a pass from Vila Matautia. His ball was actually too low to pick up, but I shinned it over the line, dived on it and screamed at referee Stuart Cummings to go to the video screen, because I knew his first reaction would have been to disallow it, as it must have looked like a knock on.

Fortunately he did so and the try was awarded; we just had to survive two missed drop-goal efforts from Andy Farrell and we had sneaked a point. If that was supposed to lift spirits before we faced Bradford Bulls in the final, it didn't work, because the week before we were due at Twickenham, Warrington put fifty-six points on us at their place.

We had a decent side out and most of the lads due to play the following week were in the line-up. But they were red hot that day and absolutely blitzed us. Maybe a few of us did have half an eye on the following week's game, but that was no excuse. St Helens simply do not get beaten like that, not with a full-strength side anyway, and it was a real eye-opener.

We knew that any repeat of that kind of form would see the Bulls dish out similar punishment, and we were bloody determined that wasn't going to happen. Fortunately it didn't. It won't go down as one of the prettiest finals rugby league has ever seen, but when the hooter went we were 13–6 to the good and Challenge Cup winners once again.

Personally I rate that day as one of the outstanding performances by Saints, and a few of the Bulls lads told me afterwards that they felt they could have played all week and still not scored. Our defence, not something Saints were particularly known for, was tremendous and we were really clinical in the manner we kept them out. The weather was so atrocious that it was never going to be pretty and the condition of the field was crap as well. To be honest, I haven't really got a good word to say about Twickenham. Well, I have – shite – but I don't suppose that's exactly what the Rugby Union would want to hear.

And as far as the standard of the game was concerned, basically who cares? It's all about winning them, and we had done it. We scored two fantastic tries, thanks to a couple of fantastic kicks from Longy and a drop goal from Tommy Martyn that eventually gave us breathing space at the end. It also meant that we were the holders of the Super League, World

Club Championship and Challenge Cup – the first time it had ever been done.

Two of the guys who played a major part in that success very rarely seemed to get the headlines, but as far as we were concerned David Fairleigh and Peter Shiels were both heroes. They had only arrived from Australia that season but I feel the pair of them – especially Dave – were two of the best overseas signings this country had ever seen.

Fairleigh had been the forward of the year at Newcastle Knights the previous season, while Shiels was constantly under-rated. I don't think anyone, including the Saints fans, really accepted how good they were until they'd gone, and we all realised what we were missing. Personally I thought they were brilliant; I used to run so many plays off those two.

But if that Twickenham win over the Bulls was the sublime, there was no doubting the ridiculous that season – at Headingley the following week, when Leeds Rhinos put seventy points on us. Now you can always accept a defeat, even though none of us likes losing, and Leeds is always one of the toughest places to go. But losing by that score was very, very tough to accept, and really took some getting over. Toni Carroll helped himself to four tries that day, and we were shocking.

Of course we had done a fair bit of celebrating after winning the final, but not so much that it had affected our preparations and there was no excuse for such a performance. They were a lot better than us on the day – the scoreline says it all – but it was a hell of a rude awakening for all of us and you don't come down to earth much quicker than that.

But really that seemed to sum up the season for us. One week we would be celebrating a fantastic win, the next we'd be crashing to a defeat against a side we would expect to stroll past.

We spent two weeks of that 2001 campaign in second place, but, that aside, we were never higher than third and ended the regular season in fourth place.

The annoying thing was that we lost a lot of games by the narrowest of margins, such as getting beaten by a point by Wigan, drawing with them and Warrington, and going down by six at Hull. If we'd turned those into victories then it could have been so different, but harping on about it wasn't going to bring back the points. Then there was the other side of the coin, when we would look like absolute world beaters, and would have beaten whoever was up against us.

We put seventy points on my old mates from Warrington, when I got thirty of them myself, in our best attacking display of the year. I remember actually being a bit pissed off that I missed one of my twelve kicks at goal, because I wanted to finish with a 100 per cent record. Then we'd lose by a couple against Castleford, and ended the Super League fixtures when Wigan put forty on us at the JJB, so all in all it was not a particularly memorable season given what we had achieved.

Mind you, it didn't half end on a high for myself and Ian Millward, who scooped the prizes at the end-of-season Man of Steel awards dinner. Ian was rightly named coach of the year, for leading us to that quadruple, and I won the biggie – as the outstanding Super League player of that season.

I looked anything but set for the most memorable personal campaign of my life back in June, however, when I copped a really bad one in the Lancashire against Yorkshire game at Headingley.

The Rugby League were trying to get the fixture established along the lines of the traditional State of Origin games in Australia, where New South Wales and Queensland constantly produce some of the most bruising games you will ever see. There was the usual outcry from some quarters, with people saying it was hardly going to help players who had too many games as it was, but if we were ever going to beat the Aussies they had to be taken seriously, with the best players on show, and the chance for fringe internationals to step up a level.

Well, there was no problem with the intensity level, as I discovered to my cost fairly early on when Tony Smith caught me with his elbow. I shot up to try and smash him, and he ended up doing the same to me. It was in no way deliberate, and I am actually a good mate of Casper, but he raised his arm to protect himself as he saw me coming, and caught me an absolute pearler. I ran straight into the point of his elbow and cleaned me out, knocked me right off my feet.

I can't remember too much about it, even though apparently I walked off with a bit of help off the doc, Chris Brooks, and someone else. Then I just recall coming round on the table in the dressing room, getting up to have a look at the damage in the mirror, and being totally shocked at what I saw.

My teeth had gone through my lip, and it had split almost all the way up to my nose. It was a real mess. Luckily Brooksy is an expert at that kind of stuff, and did a real good job on me, to the point that you can hardly even see the scar these days, even though I ended up with fifty-odd stitches in it. The funny thing was that Longy had come into the dressing room to see if he could help, because he wasn't playing, and ended up having to hold my lip while Brooksy did the stitching. Longy's never been too clever around blood and stuff, and he probably felt as bad as I did. He told me later that at one time he went all woozy and nearly collapsed. The next day I got a phone call from Casper full of apologies, but there was no need.

You wouldn't have put much money on me being back in action within a fortnight, but that's what happened; Brooksy did such a good job that I only actually missed the following week's game against London. And things could hardly have gone any better when I did return, at Wakefield, because I got my first hat-trick for Saints. Not that it did us a lot of good in the general scheme of things, because we ended up fourth, missing out on the Grand Final, and after the euphoria of what had gone before that was a massive downer.

We hadn't been helped by a load of injuries throughout the season, though. Longy hadn't played since May after a late tackle from Huddersfield's Brandon Costin left him with a badly injured knee. Tommy missed eight weeks after a hernia operation, and Paul Newlove was also sidelined for a lot of the campaign with a badly damaged Achilles tendon. Take those three out of any side and it will suffer; we were no different.

So I suppose we actually did well in getting to within a step of returning to Old Trafford for the final – although at the time there was no cause for celebration. We beat Leeds in the elimination play-off, then went to Hull and won by four points in the elimination semi-final, to set up a sudden-death shoot-out at the JJB against our neighbours.

When it came to the game at Hull we were really down to the bare bones and relying on a lot of kids who, for all their potential, clearly weren't ready for it just yet. John Kirkpatrick came in and actually scored a crucial try at Hull, while the likes of John Stankevitch and Mike Bennett all got first-team experience that was to prove invaluable in their development over the coming years.

When we went to Wigan for that semi-final in October, nobody was really giving us a prayer, but there was a growing sense that we could turn the whole thing around and pull off another shock, despite being huge underdogs. We were certainly well enough prepared, and we had never actually lost a knockout game in eleven attempts under Basil. We started off well enough, too, and at 6–6 were more than punching our weight. But then they cut loose to go fourteen points clear and ended up winning easily. I think it was just a case of one game too far for our battered squad, and we ended up getting a fair amount of credit for staying in contention for so long.

So there was to be no measuring up for Old Trafford suits, none of the build-up to a Grand Final which I enjoyed so much – although there was still the most memorable personal award of my life to come. The Man of Steel dinner is traditionally held during the week before the final, so I headed off to Manchester in my penguin outfit with the rest of the lads – and couldn't believe it when my name was read out by Sky's Eddie Hemmings. I'd already been announced as the winner of the Players' Player award, a real honour to be chosen by my peers, but this was something else.

I knew my form had probably been as good as in any season of my career, even though nights like this were the last thing on my mind when I was drinking soup because of my broken jaw at the start of the year. But I remember standing in the gym with David Fairleigh in the run-up to the Wakefield game in June, just after I'd bust my lip with Lancashire, and talking to him about the possibility of a quick return.

Basil was mulling over the idea of throwing me straight back into the side, and Dave told me: 'You're having a great season, these are the sort of matches you've got to be playing in, because if you carry on as you are, you're going to be in with a big shot for the Man of Steel.'

His advice convinced me to start putting a bit of pressure on Ian to pick me and I don't suppose you could argue when I ended up with that hat-trick and seven goals to boot. I remember casting my mind back to that conversation in the gym as I was making my way up to the stage to collect my trophy off Hemmings. Looking back at the illustrious list of players who had done so before me was amazing – men like Ellery, a hero to me when I was still making my way in the game. Adding 'Paul Sculthorpe' to that list as the outstanding achiever in rugby league was a brilliant feeling. I really was on cloud nine. Plus I also had the chance to make amends for Saints missing out on Old Trafford in the big one – an Ashes series against the Aussies once again.

There is no bigger contest in rugby league than Britain against Australia, even though they had the upper hand for far too long, and we were brimming with confidence that we could finally put the record straight. The first Test proved it as well as we ended up beating them 20–12 at Huddersfield. David Waite had made a big difference since he became our international coach, and the set-up had certainly become a lot more professional under him.

Waitey made it a lot more like a club unit and we all really enjoyed being in camp. He hadn't made wholesale changes, just tweaked a few things here and there, and the benefits were obvious when we ran out at the McAlpine Stadium in Huddersfield. He got the right people in and we stuck together for a few years, which fosters a great team spirit. There wasn't a thing he didn't seem to know about the game, either, and I don't think I've ever come across anyone who loves his rugby league quite as much as he does.

Anything you needed to know about the game, Waitey could tell you off the top of his head. We had gone to La Manga to prepare for the Ashes and within a couple of hours of arriving we were all broken up into little team meetings. He'd have the wingers and centres in one room, the back rowers in another, and so on. He spent about fifteen minutes on each player, and even though there is only so much information you can take in we had a full dossier on everyone we were up against – which foot he liked to step off, which way he preferred passing, which side he was uncomfortable tackling on, we knew everything by the time of the game. Sometimes you thought there was simply too much to remember, but generally speaking it was good and we knew the information was always there if we needed it.

Come the match itself, it turned into my best in an international shirt as we went one up and within sight of a famous series victory, and I got the two tries which ultimately proved the difference between us. The second, a few minutes from the end, was especially pleasing because it put us two scores in front and we knew it would take a real disaster for us to lose from there. The Aussies had fought back to level it at 12–12, with two tries in eight minutes, so we knew what they were capable of. But this time there was to be no late drama, no heartbreaking defeat at the death, and we were buzzing.

It wasn't a feeling that was to last too long: the second Test at the Reebok turned into a total reverse and we got battered. They ran riot, ultimately winning 40–12, and that was only after we clawed back some respectability when the game was already lost. We were forty down after fifty-five minutes, and there were a few sneaking doubts that it was going to be the same old story – raise hopes by winning one game, only to blow it over the next.

Waitey remained positive, however, and emphasised the good work we'd done in the first Test, instilling that feeling of self-belief back into us. Obviously we couldn't simply forget what had happened in the second, but we wanted to go into the decider on the back of positives, and by the time we ran out at the JJB Stadium spirits were high once again. We knew we needed the game of our lives, but we were all convinced we could produce it.

When Paul Johnson went over for us after only three minutes our confidence couldn't have been higher, and even though they fought back to lead 12–6 at half-time there was still really nothing between us. Unfortunately it wasn't to be, and by the final hooter they were 28–8 in front, after tries from Matt Gidley, Brad Meyers and Darren Lockyer. We'd blown it again. All the neutrals – not that there were too many of them – felt the scoreline was very unjust, but so what. We'd lost, end of story, and it was a massive, massive disappointment given how we'd started. Having said that, things were put in perspective somewhat by events in the stands, when Aussie coach Chris Anderson was rushed to Wigan Hospital after suffering a heart attack in the first half. Fortunately he recovered well enough, but it showed you the pressure of top-flight rugby league.

I looked back on that series a lot over the following months, wondering just what we could have done to win, and I still think there was one crucial factor that went against us. The first Test had been refereed by an Englishman, Bob Connolly, and the Aussies had, predictably, made a big fuss about that. When we won, they didn't exactly calm down and take it, either.

So perhaps it was no surprise that for the next two we had an Australian official in charge, in the shape of Bill Harrigan, as Anderson's men got their own way again. It's not sour grapes, because they probably did deserve to win the series in the end, but there's no doubt that we didn't get a fair crack of the whip with the fifty-fifty decisions after the first Test.

But I have to admit that we always seem to bow down to everything the Aussies want, and over the years that has bloody annoyed me. It's the same in Test matches, World Club Championships, the lot. Take the World Championship this season as a prime example. For ages there was a lot of talk about us playing the match Down Under, but then the Aussies started spouting off about how hardly anyone would turn up because they're simply not interested in the British game or the British players, so it was played over here. Then we have to listen to the same old excuses about jet lag, not being prepared and everything. They don't just seem to want to have their cake and eat it; they clearly begrudge anyone else having a bite as well.

And as far as the change in referees was concerned, that caused us massive problems. The Aussie and English games have a totally different interpretation of things, and there have been times in the past when, even with one of 'our' officials, it seems to be controlled their way. We spend the whole season in Super League jumping off tackles quickly, but then when Harrigan was in charge we were being mugged on the floor and nothing was happening about it. And as for that one-off Test we'd played in Australia, there wouldn't be a hope in hell of them returning the favour, and I still wonder what on earth that game was supposed to achieve.

Losing the Ashes series just proved another kick in the guts for the English game, although I had the personal honour of finishing runner-up to Aussie Andrew Johns in the Golden Boot award, given to the world's best player, and making the world dream team. In fact I was chosen as the top loose forward and joint best stand off, with Brad Fittle.

Even so, that still could not mask the disappointment of the season in general. Saints had missed out on the Grand Final and the Ashes heartbreak just compounded the disappointment. True, we had won the Challenge Cup, but by the time Old Trafford comes around that's all forgotten and there was a definite sense of emptiness when I eventually got to put my feet up for a few weeks, despite those personal highs.

9

Grabbing the Bulls by the Horns

When the 2002 season started I suddenly found myself under the brightest personal spotlight of my career. Over the years I had grown used to finding myself in the headlines, fortunately for the right reasons. This had followed me from the early days at Warrington, through my record transfer to Saints, and beyond. But if the expectations were great when I first came to Knowsley Road, they were nothing compared to the ones this time.

Not that I was complaining too much about it – after all, I had won the Man of Steel award in the previous season, presented to the player whom a selected panel of experts believe has made the greatest contribution to the game over the previous campaign. But if the pressures beforehand had been great, this time they were enormous – including, I should add, those that I placed on myself. There was no way I wanted my great season to be followed by a dramatic dip in form, which so often happens in many other sports.

I have to admit it was pressure I welcomed, though. After all, you don't get high expectations if you're crap, and I knew I was not too bad! Things started quite promisingly as well, and while Halifax pushed us close in the quarter-finals of the Challenge Cup we never looked like losing en route to a semi-final against Leeds Rhinos, a match that still sends a tingle down my spine when I think of it.

As usual with games between us two the tipsters could hardly split us and the only thing everyone agreed on was that it'd be close. You wouldn't have got too many in either camp disagreeing with that prediction, either. But it turned out to be one of those days when every little thing went right for us and we absolutely monstered them, 42–16. I managed a try myself, but this wasn't a day so much for personal performances as for the team display, which still rates as one of the best I have ever been involved in at any level.

It set us up nicely for the final against our old rivals from Wigan – and sparked the first of what seemed eventually to become almost regular controversies under Ian Millward. The week before the Challenge Cup final at the end of April we were due to travel to Odsal – never the easiest of venues – for a Super League game against Bradford. Everyone knew Basil wouldn't field his full-strength line-up with a trip to Murrayfield around the corner, but he effectively put out a reserve side and the Bulls ran in fifty points. The RFL were up in arms about it, and Saints ended up getting fined £25,000 – although, having said that, it was nothing compared to the stink it caused when he did it again a couple of years later.

Obviously the players knew it wasn't exactly going to be our strongest team, and we did have a few knocks as well. Basil brought in Heath Cruickshank, Dave Whittle and Paul Southern from Leigh, all on loan, although Heath ended up staying for quite a while afterwards. Another one of Basil's crazy ideas, and, given that we ended up losing the final the following week, it couldn't really be viewed as an unqualified success.

I think there are pros and cons to having a break during the season. Obviously this time there were more cons, given that Wigan beat us. If you play there is always the risk of injuries, and a week off can freshen players up. But on the other side of the coin, if you're struggling for form it can help to keep playing, because you don't recapture it on the sidelines, and you always want to go into finals in the best possible form, preferably with a decent victory under your belt.

Fortunately, losing to the old enemy at Murrayfield did not affect our season too much, and we quickly got back on the winning trail with eleven wins out of the next twelve games. Sandwiched in between a couple of them was a bizarre trip to Australia, for a one-off Centenary Test that, to be honest, we could have all done without. Personally I couldn't see why it should happen in the middle of our Super League season, and I'm sure the Aussies wouldn't have been so quick to jump on a plane had it been the other way around.

Obviously everyone jumps at the chance of playing for their country, but this time the whole bloody trip seemed to be one mad rush from start to finish. Saints played Hull away the night before we left, and it was a typically tough game which we edged 32–30. Straight after the game everyone involved in the international piled into a mini-bus and we headed from The Boulevard to the Radisson hotel at Manchester Airport to meet up with the rest of the British squad. The next morning we were off to Sydney, arrived on the Tuesday, played the Aussies on Friday and flew back on the Sunday – to face a game against London seventy-two hours after returning. It was absolutely crazy.

That trip to Australia is the one and only time I have ever

suffered from jet lag, but, given the speed of it all, I suppose it isn't surprising. We were in a restaurant on the actual day of the Test, for our pre-match meal, and the room started spinning. I remember thinking 'this is crazy, putting players through all this for a one-off game with nothing resting on it'.

It's always tough to play them at the best of times, so to go there in the middle of the season, with a one-week turnaround, was totally ludicrous. The spirit in the squad was good enough, I must point out, probably because most of us had played together for such a long time. So there was never a problem with the lads themselves, and, fair dos to the Rugby League, we were staying in a fantastic spot in Manly. You can never knock playing for your country, but you want to do yourself justice on the field and we were on a hiding to nothing, because that was never going to happen really.

Even so, none of us were prepared for what happened as we slumped to a record 64–10 defeat. You can imagine the stick we got, both in Australia and back home. It's at times like that when you just wish people would actually look at things with a bit of common sense, and realise what we'd all gone through. None of us would ever have admitted it beforehand, but I think we sensed we were going to struggle because of the schedule if nothing else. The preparation went okay as well, but we took to the field with players busted from the previous week even before kickoff.

I was hardly in the greatest shape myself, either, and had been on a drip throughout the week running up to the Test because of an infection in my arm. It had happened the week before we left, when we'd beaten Bradford in a real toughie at Knowsley Road. Lesley Vainikolo and Mike Bennett were scrapping in the corner and I went in to help sort it out. But Lee Gilmour, later to become a team-mate at Saints, grabbed me as I arrived and shoved me into the wall around the side of the pitch. We have a laugh about it now, with me winding him up about his cheap shot, hitting me from behind! It wasn't funny at the time, though, as I cut it pretty badly, which became infected and basically left me with a hole in my arm.

As soon as I arrived at the Radisson, the team doctor put me on a drip to get the antibiotics into my system as quickly as possible, so it was not exactly the best way to prepare for facing the best team in the world. The game itself got off to a bad start for us as well, and we seemed to be losing players left, right and centre. Kris Radlinski was injured, Paul Johnson popped a shoulder, Ryan Sheridan got knocked out and Keiron Cunningham had a knock as well.

But none of that shows up in the record books, merely the fact that we got hammered, on Lindsay's birthday as well, and no one wanted a place in rugby league history for that reason. The worst thing was that we were sitting in the dressing room afterwards absolutely devastated, because we knew it was a one-off game, with no chance to put things right in the next Test. At least you are usually talking of a three-match series, so if it's all gone wrong in one it can be swiftly forgotten if you win the next. And although the Aussies seemed to exclude me from much of their criticism, and actually thought I'd played okay, that was no consolation. We always win together and lose together, and this was no exception. But unfortunately people didn't see the background, or the problems we had faced, and that didn't stop them giving us loads of shit about it.

That was one of the occasions when it was actually a benefit to have a game pretty quickly after returning, which in our case was a home game against London on the 19th. At 22–14, it wasn't exactly a resounding victory but at least it was good to get back to winning ways and I was delighted with my own performance. I think the fact that we hadn't had time to draw breath between fixtures meant that it didn't really catch up with me until after the match – but, take it from me, I slept bloody well that night! Australia and back in a week is a tough enough ask if you're doing it on holiday. Throw in a couple of high-intensity games as well and you can see that it's not something your average bloke in the street would cope with very easily.

At least there were no real dramas for the remaining couple of months of the season, and I even managed to grab twenty-four points myself in one match, when we stuffed Warrington 72–2. That match actually went a long way to ensuring we finished the regular twenty-eight-game Super League ahead of Bradford, after we ended up level on points. It came down to points difference, and the fact that ours was better by fourteen was due in no small part to that stroll against my old team. But just to prove how close the Super League was becoming, we were pushed all the way by London – who ended up back in eighth – in that last match, before edging home 18–16. Before the kickoff there was a real drama, when Chris Joynt collapsed in the dressing room. It transpired that he was suffering from a virus of some sort, but it was really worrying when he went down.

Our finishing position gave us a week's break, and while the arguments rage about whether that is really beneficial or not I can't see the harm in getting the chance to rest for a few days. After the season a lot of the Saints lads had gone through, that was a real blessing in disguise. I don't go along with all those who say it is better to keep playing every week to the Grand Final because you'll go to Old Trafford in winning form. After nearly thirty league games, plus the Challenge Cup run and the trip Down Under, the last thing most of us needed was another match. Although I suppose anyone who saw our qualifying semi-final against Bradford would argue that we had got it wrong, because we lost it 28–26.

That was particularly disappointing for me because I had the chance to level it in the dying seconds. Tony Stewart brought us back to within two points with a try in the left hand corner in the last minute, which gave me a conversion to take it into extra time. If we'd done that, we would have really fancied our chances, but unfortunately I fluffed it. I hit the ball true enough, but it faded past the post and that was that. I'm certain we would have won had it gone to extra time, because we'd have been on such a high at dragging it out of the fire, but it wasn't to be.

As it was, the set-up gave us the safety net of a final eliminator against Wigan, who had thrashed Leeds in their play-off game the week before. This time we made no mistake and beat them 24–8, with me scoring a try as well. It was a really horrible, wet day and when Sean Long put a kick up I went sliding in to touch the ball down. But victory came at a price because I pulled my quad muscle kicking off in the second half. I'd felt it in the last training session twenty-four hours earlier, and was playing in cycling shorts, but it was clearly a problem and not the best preparation with which to go into the final.

It didn't affect my actual game that much, but there was no way I could get involved in the kicking. Fortunately I was still able to run okay, and remember charging at our Dan on one occasion and getting a real whack off him. I'm sure he hits me harder than he hits anyone else, and he doesn't seem to miss that much, either. But I suppose I had the last laugh because we were the ones going to the Grand Final, and although I had plenty of sympathy for him not so much that I'd have changed places.

I knew exactly what it meant to walk out at Old Trafford for the biggest game in the rugby league calendar, and couldn't wait to get another taste. But first there was the little matter of the Man of Steel awards night, and I knew I was in the frame once again.

Obviously it was the topic of much conversation in the dressing room, and we all had our ideas about who would win. From what I could gather it seemed to be a straight fight between myself and Wigan scrum half Adrian Lam, who had had a fantastic season. My dad seemed even keener to find out, and was desperately trying to discover who'd won, but with no success. As you'd expect with the biggest personal prize in the game, it was the last award to be presented, and Eddie Hemmings, the Sky Sports commentator who was MC-ing the evening, did a bloody good job of building up the tension.

There are no nominees for the Man of Steel trophy, unlike the Players' Player – won by Lammy, by the way – and the rest. He started off by saying that the winner had just come off the back of a play-off semi-final. But as both me and Adrian had played in it, that was hardly the greatest clue in the world. It was only when he said: 'This year's winner is setting a new record for winning it twice in succession', that I realised it was me – and what a fantastic feeling it was. To be honest, that was probably a greater shock than when I'd won it the year before, because I knew I'd had a real good year then, and although I'd not been disappointed with my form this time Lammy had played out of his skin all season. It meant more to me, as well, because everyone can have one good season. Backing it up with another is the hard part.

A place in the history books as the first man to win it two years running was a superb feeling, just the thing to put me in the mood to follow up with a Grand Final winners' ring. Obviously there was never any danger of any drink being taken so close to Old Trafford, but I don't think I needed any. I was floating around quite nicely just with the honour of having picked up the award. In fact those two Man of Steel trophies are the only ones I have on show in the games room in my house. As I have said, the rest are dotted around the place, and a few are in Jake's special drawer in his bedroom.

So on we went to Old Trafford, and what some rate as the greatest Grand Final ever. Looking back on what happened, you'd certainly be hard pushed to beat it for drama. It had been nip and tuck between us and Bradford throughout the regular season, and there had only been a two-point gap in our semi-final a fortnight earlier. There wouldn't have been a bloody gap at all if I'd managed that last-minute conversion, either.

The upside for us was that we had won a Grand Final before and knew how good that feeling was. It wasn't something we wanted to miss out on again. Everyone was predicting one of the tightest finals rugby league had ever seen, and they weren't disappointed. And as confident as we were, we knew it would be bloody tough – the one thing you could guarantee from every game against the Bulls was coming off with a few bruises.

There was just one problem as far as I was concerned – I was still struggling with the muscle I had aggravated against Wigan, and was well strapped up for the final. I wasn't exactly doubtful – I don't think the entire Saints pack could have kept me out of that one – and was always going to play, but I knew I was far from 100 per cent. Amazingly we managed to keep that out of the press throughout the build-up, and even more surprising was the fact that the Bulls camp seemed to be in the dark about it too.

The most frustrating thing was that I knew I wouldn't be able to do any kicking, not even for field position. Little did I know that that fact was to play a crucial part in the destination of the trophy. Unfortunately for us, we didn't get off to the best of starts and Bradford raced into a 6–0 lead and then seemed to have gone further ahead when they got another try under the posts. But the decision was passed on to the video referee and, after what seemed ages, it was disallowed for a knock on by Jamie Peacock. Even TV replays couldn't determine for certain whether it was the right decision or not, but bollocks to that – we weren't complaining.

Then I had to put my injured leg to the test when Michael Withers popped a pass out near the line, and I just managed to beat Robbie Paul to the loose ball. But another kick from Paul Deacon put them 8–0 up after twenty minutes, and we were most definitely under the cosh. The one thing you can never do with Saints, though, is write us off – and once again we proved it. Longy put a kick up, and Lesley Vainikolo and Brandon Costin hesitated. Martin Gleeson reached it first and somehow got the ball out of a pack of bodies, for Chris Joynt. He spread it wide to Sean Hoppe, and, despite being swamped by defenders, he managed to find Mike Bennett, who scored. Longy kicked a great conversion and suddenly, from looking out on our feet, we were only two points adrift.

If Glees had done superbly to get to Longy's kick for the first try, he excelled himself a few minutes later, with a great tackle on Costin that sent the ball spinning free. Keiron pounced on it, to send Longy over for a try down the right, and he picked himself up to add a fantastic conversion. Bradford, naturally enough, threw everything at us and they were up in arms when they claimed I'd obstructed Paul Deacon near our line, but the ref didn't give a penalty – just goes to prove what I've always said about Russell Smith being the best official in the game!

But if we thought that was a sign that things were going in our favour, the Bulls had other ideas and when Robbie Paul went over, and Deacon kicked the goal, they were back in front at 14–12. If that was bad, worse was to come when Michael Withers just managed to get over in the corner, and on this occasion the video referee's decision didn't go in our favour.

It was time for us to really show our bottle, and myself and Peter Shiels both went close, before Glees gave us a lifeline by scoring down the right. And with fifteen minutes left we tied it up at eighteen apiece when Longy kicked a penalty from in front of the posts.

Alex Ferguson famously called the run-in to the football season 'squeaky bum' time, and for those final few minutes at Old Trafford I knew exactly what he meant. It was pretty obvious that a drop goal could prove the difference, and we must have had about six goes between us, myself, Longy and Tommy Martyn all missing with our attempts. I was often the one who we set it up for, but obviously with my leg not being right I wasn't first choice.

Even so, when the opportunity arose I just thought 'bollocks, it's a Grand Final and I'm quite prepared to tear the muscle if it means a winners' ring'. So when they teed it up for me and I had a go, I nearly hit the bloody roof in agony. I didn't even have the satisfaction of seeing it go over, because it ended up closer to the sodding corner flag.

It looked certain that we were heading for extra time, but then, with no more than a minute on the clock, Keiron set it up for Longy and he popped the drop goal over from about twenty-five metres. I sometimes wonder what would have happened if my leg had been okay, because maybe the lads would have been trying to tee me up instead. Thank God for my dodgy leg. There was still no time for celebrating, though, because we knew Bradford would try a short kickoff and we had to be in position to combat that. When we regained possession, that appeared to be that. But with less than ten seconds to go and the crowd counting down, Chris Joynt went to ground from dummy half in front of Deacon and Lee Gilmour. Deacs jumped out of the way and they were screaming for a voluntary tackle – an offence that would have given them a kick at goal. Whether he'd have got it from near the halfway line, out wide, is open to question, but you have to say that Joynty bounced straight back up when he realised what was happening and the ref let it go.

This time there really was no way back for Bradford, and the hooter for full time went, sending us wild. The Bulls, though, were wild for a vastly different reason, and I know it still annoys them when they look back on it. But all those people who say that they lost the Grand Final because of it are just bloody crazy, absolute jokers, and all the whinging in the world wasn't about to put the mockers on our celebrations. A lot of folk have asked me if I find it frustrating that the incident still seems to be the major talking point of the game, but not at all. I actually found it one big laugh that everything else which went on in eighty minutes is apparently forgotten and if they think it cost them the game they're crazy. The way I see it is if they talked about it, it's because it clearly troubled them, so I'd just have a chuckle to myself. At the end of the day we were the ones with the winners' ring on our fingers, and rightly so, and in my view they can say what the bloody hell they like. Read it in the record books, as they say.

Once again we had a great night and it's safe to say there were a few banging heads the next day. But once again there was no time to put our feet up and reflect on a job well done, because we had the little matter of a Great Britain series against New Zealand over the coming weeks.

I knew I wouldn't be playing in the first Test at Blackburn's Ewood Park because of my leg, but it still hurt to be watching from the sidelines as we lost 30–16. But the doc did a great job and I was back in the side for the second game, at Huddersfield, and we got a fourteen all draw. I was delighted with my own performance, and the icing on the cake came when I was named man of the match.

So it was all on the third match at the JJB Stadium, home of our bitter rivals Wigan. The RFL had decided that, should the series be drawn, whoever won the last game would win the Baskerville Trophy on offer, and that gave us that little extra incentive. We created a hatful of chances and fortunately I scored the try fourteen minutes from time which eventually – with Andy Farrell's conversion – proved the difference as we held out in a desperate finish for a 16–10 win. That was almost as good a feeling as winning the Grand Final, because I'd never been involved in an international series victory before and the Kiwis were no pushovers. They'd proved that by stuffing us 49–6 in that World Cup semi-final a couple of years earlier.

I know that international rugby league doesn't have half the profile of union, but that doesn't mean the pride in playing for your country is any less. The funny thing is that however many times you play for Britain you only ever get one cap, which always used to be presented after your second game. I remember when I got mine – through the post! I wasn't expecting a parcel, but this envelope arrived and when I opened it there was a Great Britain cap.

But if rugby league and its players were still something of a mystery to plenty of people in the south, I knew that rugby union knew all about me. That was proved when Leicester started making noises about being keen to try and get me to switch codes.

There had been talk of it throughout the season, but I just ignored them as the usual rumours that go around. Then I discovered that Leicester coach Dean Richards had spoken to Andy Clarke, who was acting as my agent at the time, on a few occasions and wanted to know if I was interested. Playing union for a living wasn't something I had ever considered, because in my opinion there is simply no contest when it comes to which code is best. But I had to consider the wider options, and the fact that I'd be set up for life should I sign because of all the sponsorship that would obviously follow was probably the most crucial. I did realise I'd be making a hell of a lot of money – not that I was exactly on the breadline as it was – and I discussed it at length with Lindsay and Mum and Dad. Everything had to be right, because I'd be taking Linds away from her friends and family too, and there were the kids to consider.

Naturally I spoke to Saints chairman Eamonn McManus about it, and he was as good as gold. He came up with a new five-year contract, and I had no hesitation in putting pen to paper, because I'd enjoyed my time at the club so much. I'd been successful since leaving Warrington, but there was still plenty I wanted to achieve in the game. There had also been talk of me becoming Great Britain skipper at some stage, and for me you cannot get a higher honour than captaining your country. It came down to the fact that, although money is important, you've got to enjoy what you do, and I know I'd never enjoy playing union as much as league. And you can have all the money in the world but it doesn't guarantee happiness, which was paramount to me.

I knew my family would back whatever decision I made, but Dad made a very telling comment when he said: 'Don't forget, you've got to realise that you'll be doing this every single day, do you think you will be happy with that?' Fortunately Saints had made sure it was a decision I never really had to make, although I think that had I been put in that position I'd still have made the same one. There were plenty of things for me to prove. So once the prospect of union had gone away, I could finally put my feet up and look back on the best season of my life – Grand Final winner, another Man of Steel trophy and a first series win with Great Britain. Plus I finished runner-up in the Golden Boot again, this time to New Zealand scrum half Stacey Jones. I couldn't have been in greater spirits as I prepared for the new season. Unfortunately Sydney Roosters made sure I came crashing down to earth with a pretty painful bump once it got underway . . .

10

Down to Earth

Our Grand Final win had sent us into another World Club Challenge against Aussie champions Sydney Roosters, who had won their own Grand Final by trouncing New Zealand Warriors – who were coached, ironically, by Daniel Anderson, the man who was eventually to take over at Saints.

We warmed up well enough, with a seventy-point drubbing of UTC, one of the French sides in the Challenge Cup – although before that we had a bizarre cross-code game with Sale Sharks at Knowsley Road. We played the first half under union rules and lost 41–0, and won the second under league 39-0.

But the one we were all licking our lips over was the chance to take on the Aussie champions and perhaps restore a little pride after Britain's hiding in Sydney the summer before. The Roosters were a pretty formidable unit, with my old international team-mate Adrian Morley leading the pack, so it was never going to be easy. Even so, we had no idea quite how tough a day at the office it would turn out to be.

After losing one World Challenge against Melbourne, our determination to put the record straight couldn't have been greater as we walked out at the Reebok Stadium. Unfortunately we didn't get off to the best of starts when Jason Hooper had an early try disallowed for a marginal forward pass by Tommy Martyn to Paul Newlove. Once again, just as in the Grand Final, television evidence hardly gave a conclusive verdict – although this time the decision went against us.

That was a sign of things to come, as nothing really seemed to go for us on the night, although I have to say that the Roosters were as good as we were poor. Had that try from Hoops been given then who's to say that things wouldn't have been different, but we're all masters of hindsight I suppose. I'm not saying we would have won, but it could certainly have put a different slant on things – and at least we'd have got on the scoreboard and maybe stopped them getting on such a roll.

As it was, we didn't manage it all night, while the Roosters ran in thirty-eight unanswered points to make it a pretty shoddy game all round for us. The major talking point centred on a new rule change, which left pretty much everyone in the dark really. At least, it did that night, in any case. They were already 18–0 up when Brett Finch seemed to knock on as he came in to tackle Sean Long. Finch was quick to pick up the loose ball and send Todd Byrne away for the try which effectively killed any slight chance we had of getting back into it.

Of course we all appealed for a knock on, but the video ref gave it, because of a new instruction which said the game continued if you didn't strike for the ball in the tackle. Fair enough, at eighteen down it would be tough to say that was the game-breaking decision, but it left a pretty sour taste in our mouths. I remember being interviewed by Sky after the game, and saying that the video ref must have been the only person in the ground who thought it was a good try. But then Eddie and

Stevo, the two commentators, insisted it should have stood so it must have been the correct ruling: we all know those two are never wrong.

I suppose there was always going to be some controversy over it, as there always is when any new ruling comes in, but it was just unfortunate that it came in such a high-profile game. And when things are going against you, everything seems to go wrong. Yes, they were outstanding on the night, but by the same token we weren't too clever. The Roosters had won their own NRL competition on the back of an awesome defence, and every time we had the ball they seemed to be in our faces, with no room to play. That showed with the big fat 'nil' next to our names on the scoreboard at the end.

Sydney skipper Brad Fittler absolutely ran the show from stand off; he had an outstanding game. At the time he was my hero, the complete player who had a bit of everything in his locker. It was an education being on the same pitch as him and I believe he was the greatest in the world at that time. It certainly made a big difference to the Roosters' fortunes when he left. The thing that really rubbed salt in our wounds was the fact that we didn't manage a single point, although as it went on we realised that the game itself had gone from us. I'm not saying we threw the towel in – no Saints team would ever do that – but it's hard to take when there is still loads of time left and you know you've no chance of winning.

Still, at least we had an entire British Super League season to put it right. That was what we were consoling ourselves with in any case – unfortunately things didn't go exactly to plan.

The cynics didn't need much encouragement to come out of the woodwork, and after that Roosters game a few of them were already writing our obituaries. There was a certain satisfaction in proving them wrong by rattling up forty-six points against Bradford, of all people, in our first game. Sadly there weren't too many other high spots throughout the coming months.

We were still unbeaten in our first five league and Challenge Cup games, and had cruised into the semi-finals, when we went to Huddersfield for a Super League fixture. Sadly it turned into another bad day at work, as we lost 36–22, a defeat that sparked a run of four more on the bounce, including one of the most heartbreaking of my career. It was a shocking day, one of the worst I can remember. Following the Huddersfield match we slipped up again at home to Leeds, albeit by only eight points, but we had the chance to right that one pretty much straight away as they were our opponents in the last four.

We seemed to be well in command as we controlled things early on, but we knew better than anyone – having pulled off numerous great escapes over the years – that things can turn on their head pretty quickly in this game. I remember scoring a try under the posts, and booting five goals – if only it had been six, I'd be able to look back at the game in a totally different light.

That chance of a sixth came in the final few minutes, when Darren Smith went over for a try which put us six points ahead with the kick to come. With only three minutes on the clock it would certainly have won us the game, and even though it was right on the touchline, I was pretty confident because I'd been absolutely smoking them all day. Unfortunately it wasn't to be, and I still beat myself up about it even now. I just wish I could have my time again, because I feel that I rushed it. The number of times I've looked back at what I could have done differently. Maybe I'm being a bit hard on myself, but that's how I see it, and if we'd hung on then I would never have given it a second thought.

Obviously they tried the short kickoff to try and regain possession, and we did the job for them when we knocked on. They pressed forward and got a penalty near the line when Tim Jonkers picked up the ball in an offside position, and Danny McGuire managed to squeeze over in the corner. I remember standing under the sticks while Kevin Sinfield lined up the conversion, thinking: 'It's not all lost yet, he could easily miss this.' Sadly it wasn't to be, as Sinny booted the goal from right on the touchline – a kick Leeds chief executive Gary Hetherington later called the most important one in the history of the club. That may have been stretching the point a little, but it was certainly one of the most painful of my career.

So into extra time we went, and when you've been pegged back in such devastating fashion it's always hard to lift your-selves. The balance seemed to have swung their way and you'd have to say that when a team's come back from the dead like that, they are always favourites in the extra period. But there were still a couple of twists in the tail, and within a minute we thought we'd scored when Mike Bennett won the race to reach a Longy kick – only for the video referee to decide after several looks that he was just offside. It was a real arm wrestle, but they edged in front by a point when Sinny dropped a goal at the end of the first half.

That's the way it stayed until two minutes from time when Mick Higham went within inches of a try for us, before he was submerged by a massed defence, and Sinny almost immediately went sixty metres and sent Danny McGuire into the corner for a try. Just to make it worse, Sinfield kicked another bloody goal from the touchline as well. I'd been beaten in Challenge Cup finals before, when Wigan did us up at Murrayfield, but this one hurt even more.

It was the first time in my life that I'd lost a semi-final and it wasn't an experience I wanted to become a habit. It still probably rates as the most painful loss I'd ever experienced. I guess I was pretty tough to live with for the next few days.

There was no time for wallowing in self-pity, though, because our next game was against our old rivals from Wigan, who had just been beaten in the semi-finals themselves by Bradford. What better way to regain the winning habit than against your neighbours, and we were long odds-on favourites when they named a side with nine regulars missing, and four of the team making their debuts. When we raced into a 22–12 half-time lead those odds looked well justified, but somehow they dragged themselves off the canvas and the most incredible of fightbacks saw them win by two points. The pain of that defeat wasn't nearly as bad as the loss to Leeds, but that's not to say it wasn't acute.

That was our fourth loss in a row – the first time that had happened since my time at Warrington – and we were all pretty low for a while. As far as the fans are concerned, you can lose to most teams but not to Wigan. When it comes on the back of a semi-final defeat as well, it doesn't come much worse. At least one member of the family was happy enough, though, because our Dan was in the Wigan side that day. As for us, we had to get back on track quickly or the season could have totally slipped away – and fortunately we were up against my old Warrington mates the following week.

I don't know what it is, because they are a top side, but we always seemed to have a bit of an Indian sign over them, and so it proved once more as we reached a half-century of points and I ended up with twenty of them. I know it was my old team-mates who were on the receiving end, but you certainly don't have any sympathy in situations like that. Obviously I've still got a lot of mates there, and have all the time in the world for the club – after all, they gave me such a good grounding in the professional game – but I was a Saints player now and you've got to have a ruthless streak if you're going to be successful in anything, and that win had got us back on track. At least that's what we thought, until we went to Hull and promptly got a good stuffing.

The fixture list had given us a home game against Wigan again just a couple of matches later, and once more they had the last laugh – and once again after we had gone into a comfortable early lead. We were 14–0 up and on our own patch, but young Luke Robinson came off the bench for them and scored a hat-trick as they ended up winning 38–34. Funnily enough I was talking to our Dan about that recently, and, needless to say, he looks back on it with somewhat different memories from me. He hasn't got the better of me in too many matches, but that was one of them – as he is very quick to remind me.

That defeat actually saw us slip out of the top six, and for a team with the expectations of Saints that was disastrous – especially when we lost again to Leeds next game. But just to prove what a crazy season we were having, we promptly went to Bradford, who were to finish as league leaders, and won 35–0.

It was pouring down at Odsal and we absolutely kicked them to death. We were putting their wingers under huge pressure with some big kicks and ran riot – even though it was a win that only lifted us back to seventh, still out of a play-off position. It was the perfect example of how to play the conditions, and was the second game in a run of nine straight wins which took us up to fourth.

Sadly that was as high as we were to go, and just to make matters worse we also had two points deducted for breaking the salary cap, a rule designed to keep clubs in some sort of financial check. We really needed a flying finish to the season if we were to have a chance of retaining our Grand Final crown, because finishing in fourth place means away fixtures in the play-offs, and the tallest of orders for any side. But any hopes of that were blown apart as we lost four of our last five games.

We got past London easily enough in the first of what were now sudden-death play-offs to set up an elimination semi-final at Wigan – who ended our season by putting forty on us. We had a great second half, which we won 18–6, but unfortunately the damage had already been done, and we pretty much knew we were a beaten side by the break. Winning one half of rugby meant absolutely nothing to us when we lost the match itself and, after the highs of twelve months earlier, it was a shocking way to finish – even though it wasn't entirely out of the blue, as we had struggled for consistency all season.

Personally it was something of a nightmare as well, because I was starting to have a few problems with my hamstring, which kept me out for quite a few games. I knew from past experience, when I'd worked with Tommy Smales on a similar injury with Great Britain, that you can't take any chances with hamstrings, and I sat out too many matches for comfort that year. It was also pretty obvious that I didn't have a prayer of landing a third Man of Steel award, and Jamie Peacock was a worthy winner. Even so, the biggest prize in rugby league lay just around the corner – an Ashes series against the touring Aussies.

Britain hadn't won a series against them for over thirty years, despite going bloody close on a few occasions, but spirits were soaring at our chances of making history. That would certainly have turned a pretty shocking season into the most memorable of ones – if only. It wasn't anything like some of the awesome touring squads they'd brought over in the past, and even their coach Chris Anderson said it was as weak a party as they'd come over with in years. Every game was in the balance throughout as well – but every game also went their way in the end.

In the first Test, Brian Carney went over for his second try and we were hanging on to a two-point lead with just five minutes left. But then Darren Lockyer broke our hearts by snatching it for them, leaving us with a mountain to climb if we were to save the series.

If that was bad, worse was to come at Hull in the next match – and after we had raced into a comfortable lead to boot. Unfortunately after scoring twenty points in the first quarter, we didn't manage another for the remaining hour, and they pipped us by three points once again and the series was lost with one game still to play. By the time of the third game, at Huddersfield, we were almost expecting them to come back and hit us in the dying stages – once again when we were six points to the good with less than five minutes to go.

But they raced in for two quick tries and that was that – whitewashed by a supposedly below-standard Aussie side. It really was soul-destroying because we'd been so close in every game, and, given a different bounce, a different decision, a different pass we could have been in the record books. As it was, they were the ones enjoying their place in history as the first Australian outfit to win a series three nil in almost twenty years. If it taught us one thing it was to keep your intensity levels as high as possible for the whole eighty minutes – even though we had talked about the importance of that beforehand – and it remains a thorn in my side that I have never managed to help Britain win the Ashes.

Obviously that's something I would have loved to do, but to be honest my first priority has to be Saints, and remaining injury free with them. They were superb over my knee injury, and were just as good when I ruptured my Archilles in June. But I must admit it does make life pretty tough when you're having a shortened close season every year, and it really takes it out of you for the following campaign. Financially it doesn't exactly change your life, not that anyone who pulls on an international shirt lets money come into the equation.

We got around two grand for a win, but unfortunately seemed to be collecting the £500 losing money with more regularity. Throw in the fact that you never really get the chance to take the family away, or simply put your feet up and prepare for the following season – and I had done that for ten years – and it was beginning to take its toll.

My pre-season seemed to be starting in January every year, while for a lot of the others who weren't involved it was beginning in November. Fortunately Daniel has changed things around since arriving at Saints, and he actually does a split close season now. Whereas in the past it used to be a straight six-week break – with a later return for those who were involved in a Great Britain series – now it was two lots of three, with training in between. It was three weeks off at the end of the season, then three weeks doing stuff like weights, and then another break after that, which seems to work a lot better.

Personally I always felt six weeks on the bounce was too long a break, and I always found myself getting bored after a bit and going down to the gym on my own. Even so, when you come in after such a break, the first week back in training absolutely kills you. It was murder, you'd get really flogged, so I think everyone benefits from how Ando does things. Hopefully we will see that with our results over the coming seasons, as well.

11

Gambling Fever

The 2004 Super League season will go down in the record books as one of the more unforgettable in St Helens' colourful history – and not entirely for the reasons we would have all hoped.

It could hardly have started in more scintillating fashion for us, as we rattled up seven straight wins in both league and Challenge Cup, to lay down the marker that we were going to be the team the rest had to worry about once again.

Cup wins over Bradford, Leeds and Hull meant that, whatever happened, no one could ever accuse us of having a soft route to the semi-finals, and, it was to be hoped, a trip to the Millennium Stadium. And personally I was on a high as well, after Ian Millward handed me the captain's armband at the club.

To be honest, retiring skipper Chris Joynt had always involved me in everything and I'd learned a hell of a lot from his style of captaincy. He was great to play under but had decided the time had come to stand down, and I was the obvious man to replace him. As vice-captain I knew that, all being well, it was a question of time before I took over but it was still a hugely proud moment when Ian made it official.

It was never going to make any real difference to my game because I've always been quite a talker during matches anyway. But I must admit it did cross my mind that, if and when Saints were winning the big finals again, I would be the one shaking hands and hoisting the trophies in front of our fans.

The way we started that season gave all of us every reason to believe I wouldn't have long to wait, either. The fourth-round Challenge Cup win at Bradford, in particular, was a fantastic display as we whacked them 30–10, when young Mark Edmondson got a great try. Then two tries from Paul Wellens helped see off Leeds in the next round, which was another boost, as they had started the season really well and were actually top of the Super League for the entire campaign.

So we were brimming with confidence after claiming such prized scalps, and not even dropping our first point of the season, in a thrilling draw with Wigan, could put the dampeners on things.

Sean Long's improvised drop goal a couple of minutes from time had earned us a point, but probably the major talking point was a mass brawl. I'd been in there, helping out the lads, and referee Karl Kirkpatrick had put the whole thing on report. Dom Feaunati was suspended for three games for his part, while on the Wigan side Andy Farrell was fined £500. Fortunately for me I was found not guilty, so I had no complaints with rugby league's justice system over that one.

But if that Good Friday showdown against Wigan had earned a few unsavoury headlines, for all it was a great game, that was nothing compared to the storm which was brewing. Two days later we travelled to Odsal for the second of our Easter fixtures and a few of us were feeling the heat a bit. So Basil decided he would give some of us – most of us, actually – a break, especially with the Challenge Cup semi-final against Huddersfield coming up in a fortnight.

Contrary to what some people appear to think, we *did* have quite a few injuries in the camp, but that didn't stop the shit hitting the fan when Ian fielded a weakened team. I think even a few of us were surprised at the way we started, though, as Martin Gleeson – one of the few regulars in the line-up that day – put us ahead with a try early on. But then Jon Wilkin got sent off after only nine minutes and that, plus the fact that we had five debutants in the side, saw us on the wrong end of a 56–8 scoreline.

The trade papers were full of letters from people moaning that they'd been short-changed, and Bradford coach Brian Noble didn't exactly douse the fire when he said: 'We came to fight George Foreman and ended up with George Formby.' Even so, the Saints board backed Ian's decision and the Rugby League, unlike two years earlier when they'd slapped a big fine on us for the same thing, took no action either. Unfortunately for us, and for two players in particular, that was not the end of things.

Four days later, on the day we were to play Salford in the Super League, the news broke that Glees and Longy had placed a grand on Bradford beating us. The RFL immediately announced they were launching an investigation, but then Huddersfield threw their two penn'orth into the debate as well, which I felt was bang out of order.

Chief executive Ralph Rimmer called for both our players to be banned from the semi-finals the following week, which didn't go down well with us. If the official body took a decision then we knew we'd have to live with that, but it was absolutely nothing to do with the Giants; they just saw it as a chance to have an easier passage to the final.

Talk about backfiring: all that effectively did was to do Basil's job for him because we certainly didn't need any motivational team talks when we walked out at the Halliwell Jones Stadium for the semi. Longy was outstanding, a clear winner of the man of the match award, having a hand in four of the five first-half tries we scored, and adding another himself after the break in our 46–6 win.

That sent us into another final showdown with our old Wigan mates, who now included our Dan in the side. And we had already been given another little boost beforehand when the RFL announced both Longy and Glees would be clear to play as their report into the alleged betting scandal would not be ready before the match.

No prizes for guessing what happened in that game, either – Longy was one of a host of outstanding performers for us on the day, and we ended up winning 32–16, despite having a real fight on our hands in the first half. A month later we got ample revenge on the Bulls as well, when we beat them 35–30 at home – but just three weeks after that we lost Glees and Longy effectively for the rest of the season.

In his defence Glees had put forward the fact that he scored the first try of that now infamous game, but the RFL were having none of it. They banned him for four months, Longy for three. In addition both players were fined £7,500 each and ordered to pay costs of over £2,000 – far outweighing anything they would ever have won on the game.

Whenever we'd discussed the incident in the club beforehand, we'd actually been having a bit of a laugh about it. The bet itself was never really relevant to any of us, and I'd like to emphasise that there was never any suggestion that it had affected anyone's performance on the day. We knew that game would be tough, even if we had been able to field a full-strength line-up, so it wasn't exactly rocket science that Bradford were hot favourites. I suppose the mistake Longy and Glees made was actually placing the bets in their own names – not, I hasten to add, that I know of any of the lads who do have a flutter on our games and do so in the guise of other account holders.

And another point worth making is the fact that, until this came to light, we'd never been given any official ruling that we weren't allowed to have a bet. That, obviously, was amended pretty quickly and players forbidden from betting on Super League fixtures. I think they were moaning about 'insider info', but the result was a foregone conclusion really as soon as everyone saw the team-sheets that day. And I do wonder what would have happened had we somehow pulled off a miracle result and actually won the game – meaning the bookies were a grand to the good and Glees and Longy had done their money.

The decision to ban them both sent shock waves through the club, because although we all expected them to get fined, and pretty heavily at that, we didn't really contemplate having to do without them for so long. Personally I thought the punishment was way over the top, and having to do without two Great Britain internationals certainly didn't make our job for the rest of the season any easier. There was massive disbelief throughout Saints, but there was sod all we could do about it even though it was such a big blow. And at least the RFL announced that they would both be available and considered for selection when it came to the Tri-Nations series at the end of the season.

Despite their ban, they were both still allowed to train at the club, and when the news of their betting first broke, Longy came up to me and said: 'Give us the keys to your folks' caravan, because we want to clear off for a bit.' The entire media were, obviously, trying everything they could to get in touch with the pair of them and they just wanted to escape the heat for a while.

My mum and dad had a caravan at Fleetwood, so the two of them headed off there for a bit. It was hardly a fortnight in the Caribbean, but it got them out of harm's way for a while. It was certainly a strange old time, and one of a variety of things that seemed to land Saints in the headlines for events off the field over the years. Basil didn't say a great deal to us about it, because his main concern was bringing the team together for the rest of the season. Fair enough: we had to do so without two hugely influential players, but we had a job to do regardless.

In fact in the very next game we put forty points on Widnes and were still picking up some handy results, until the wheels came off with a vengeance at Leeds in July, when they thrashed us 70–0. I was in the stand at Headingley that day, but it hardly softened the blow having to sit and suffer that particular eighty minutes. My hamstring had gone at Hull the week before, in a game which I should never really have played.

I'd felt it go in the warm-up, but it was too late to do anything by then and I took the field. I had the leg well strapped and thought that maybe I could muddle through. As it was, I lasted no more than fifteen minutes because it was clear straight away that I couldn't run properly. That was the start of the injury problems that were to dog me for a couple of seasons and stemmed from my lower back.

That was more of a physical pain – the mental one came from watching that Headingley hiding, which really was the lowest of the low. And the mood hardly improved a few days later, when the dramatic news came that Warrington Wolves had signed Glees, who still had over half his ban to serve, for supposedly around £200,000. Losing him was going to be a real body blow, and one that stunned us players, although we did actually end up getting a player who would make an even bigger impact, in the shape of Jamie Lyon from Australia.

It was something we had to shrug off, however, if we were to have any hope of reaching Old Trafford again – although from finishing fifth, it was going to take a superhuman effort. We finished the regular season by going to Odsal to play Bradford again, and by a quirk of fate that was the game in which Longy made his comeback from the ban. I don't think I've ever heard a player get booed so roundly and for so long throughout. But unfortunately, despite his kicking four goals, this time there was to be no fairytale return as they rattled up sixty points.

That left us facing a play-off trip to Wigan, and although we ran them to six points, we couldn't see it through and that was that – out of the play-offs at the first attempt, the earliest stage we had gone out in the seven years since play-offs were introduced. How different things would have been with Longy and Glees in the side for those months we had to do without, no one will ever know. What I will say is that Saints were a better side with them in it, and a tough task became a mountainous one when they were sidelined.

Once again, though, there was the chance of redemption and salvaging something from the dying embers of the season in the shape of the Tri-Nations tournament, with the Aussies and New Zealand. And on a personal level, I'd got a fantastic sponsorship deal with Gillette in June, becoming only the third British sports star associated with them. Considering the others were a certain David Beckham and Jason Robinson, I was in good company.

On the field, though, it wasn't exactly the stuff of dreams. And when Australia and New Zealand played out a draw in Auckland in the first game of the Tri-Nations, we knew we were in for a hell of a battle. The rest of the tournament was being played over here, and the Aussies gained their first win by beating the Kiwis at QPR's Loftus Road ground in London – but not before they got a hell of a fright first – so we were going to have to be at our best if we were to be in with a chance.

Our own tournament started at the City of Manchester Stadium, and was all going superbly as we led 8–4 at the break. Glees had stormed back into the British set-up by going in for the first, after I slipped an inside pass not far from our own line, and Brian Carney shot over for the second straight from dummy half. Sadly Faz missed both kicks, and that was ultimately to prove crucial.

A minute before half-time Willie Mason went storming through me to cut the gap to four points, and then Luke Rooney, who was turning into a real try machine, scored brilliantly in the corner. Just before that I'd tried a drop goal which agonisingly came back off the crossbar, after Nathan Hindmarsh got a hand to it and took a lot of the pace off the ball. Brett Kimmorley, Longy and Faz all missed with further attempts, but then in the last minute Rooney got another try and we were beaten.

That turned the second game, against New Zealand, into a real do-or-die occasion, and we showed great character in picking ourselves up for a 22–12 win. What made it even more pleasing was the fact that we came back from 12–2 down at half-time. We really blitzed them straight after the break, Stuart Reardon scoring two of our three tries in that period.

When we went to the JJB Stadium and beat Australia 24–12, we couldn't have been more confident. Plus we had the satisfaction of giving them a bit of a battering as well. Just two minutes from time, with the game in the bag, Aussie second rower Craig Fitzgibbon dropped the elbow on me, which left me absolutely raging. Funnily enough, we had always got on pretty well, and he tried to apologise to me pretty much straight away. I was having none of that and flew at him. He was saying: 'What are you doing, I've said sorry', but I just answered: 'Fuck that, it doesn't take away what you've done', and it was all on.

We were all in there, when Mark O'Meley blind-sided me, coming in from behind, and swinging punches. It doesn't say much for his aim that he failed to connect, and I must admit I got a great deal of pleasure from getting a couple of good ones off on him, right on the button. I probably shouldn't say it, but it was very pleasing because it also showed the Aussies that we were all in it together, and no one was prepared to take a backward step if they tried the rough stuff. We won the game and then we won the fight – it's not often the Aussies get a hiding twice in the same match!

When the whole team joins forces and stands firm like that, I think it sends out a real message to the opposition that it's one for all, and maybe it made them realise we weren't the pushovers they always considered us to be. The only problem we'd had was that for all we knew how to beat them once, knowing how to do it consistently was another matter.

Whatever, it set us up nicely for the final against Australia, and most of the bookies actually had us as favourites for once – and it was hard for anyone to argue with the fact. We still had another game to go against New Zealand because of how the tournament was formatted, and Brian Noble took advantage to rest several of us. It was actually a replica of our earlier game against them, because we trailed 12–4 at the break, but a couple of tries from Carney eventually saw us home by two points, and meant we finished top of the table, a point ahead of Australia and five clear of the Kiwis.

So we couldn't have been more confident as we walked out in front of forty thousand Elland Road fans, all desperate to see Great Britain finally win a trophy against their old rivals. Sadly all hope evaporated pretty sharpish and all glory went to the Aussies as we suffered the same old story. By half-time we were on our backsides – in fact after twenty minutes we were pretty much dead and buried – as they went 18–0 up. Losing would have been bad enough on its own, but to end up getting stuffed 44–4 was shocking. The fact that we'd kept them pointless for the last thirty-five minutes was absolutely irrelevant – they already had enough on the bloody board by then.

To be honest, that was another match I shouldn't really have appeared in, and if it had been a run-of-the-mill Super League game maybe I wouldn't have. I'd been having problems with the lower back since that defeat at Hull near the end of the regular season, but there was no way I was going to miss the Tri-Nations final. I'd not been able to extend my knee properly for ages, which was putting my back out, but within five minutes of the kickoff I had nothing really in the tank.

I'd actually made the problem worse a couple of days before the final when we were doing a bit of wrestling in training. I still remember it was in the in-goal area at Salford's Willows ground, when I just twisted and my back went into a spasm. But I decided to go with the injections in my back, obviously not something you want in an ideal world, but I hoped that when the adrenalin was flowing it would help me through.

Playing with jabs wasn't something I had made a habit of doing, but sometimes needs must. I remember a few years earlier I was elbowed in the sternum by Kelvin Skerrett against Halifax, which was still one of the most painful injuries I'd ever had. It didn't actually keep me out of any games, because I had five injections straight into my rib cage, but recalling the pain still makes me wince.

So there was no way I was going to sit out a Great Britain and Australia final – every player in the world would do everything in his power to play and I was no different. If we'd got off to a decent start and looked like winning, maybe it wouldn't have been quite the problem, either, because when you're on top the pain never seems quite as bad. The fact that I was really feeling it after only ten minutes tells you all you need to know about the game, and all in all it was a pretty shocking day. Unfortunately, worse, far worse, was to come in the injury stakes . . .

12
Dan and Dusted

Around 4.30 p.m. on 15 May 2004 I should have been celebrating the happiest moment of my career, the fulfilment of a lifetime's ambition, first dreamt on the windswept playing fields round the back of my mum and dad's house in Royton.

Instead all I could think of was my brother Danny slumped on his backside, tears pouring down his face – and all because of what my team had done to him.

Don't get me wrong, I wouldn't have swapped winning the Challenge Cup for anything. Well, nothing in sport, anyway. How many great players have never even reached the final, let alone led their side on to the stage to receive the trophy? And I wasn't just picking up a winners' medal, I was the man collecting the most famous cup in rugby league.

But there were other things to attend to before I could think about raising the most famous trophy in rugby league to the thousands of St Helens fans who had no idea of the inner torment I was going through at that moment.

It's funny how many things race through your mind when the

hooter goes for full time. Delight, obviously, is the first, quickly followed by relief at mission accomplished. But then so many other things flood into your head – in my case my wife, Lindsay, and son Jake (we've since had a little girl, Lucy-Jo).

And if I was going through hell at what I'd done to our Danny, it was even worse for Mum and Dad, Linda and Doug, sitting in the stands at Cardiff while everyone around them was going mad.

It's funny when I look back on that match now, because the first thing that still comes to mind is the sight of how upset Danny was. I remember trying to pick him up off the turf and cheer him up a little – but having been in that position myself, when Wigan beat us at Murrayfield, I know there's not really much anyone can say when you've lost a final.

We'd been together from the first time either of us first picked up a rugby ball – in fact he got me a bollocking off my dad because I wanted to play football at the time! – and had just become the first brothers to play on opposing sides in the Challenge Cup final.

But fair play to him, he texted me as soon as he got his head together and basically ordered me to have a good night. That took some doing because he was going through hell himself. To be honest, though, I wouldn't expect anything else from him because we're very close, even though he tries to knock my bloody head off every time we play each other!

Mum and Dad had actually told the pair of us that they planned to have a quiet night out in Cardiff – if that's possible after a rugby final – because they were in an awful position when it came to what to do.

They knew one of us would be throwing the drinks down and celebrating the best moment of his life, while the other would be doing the same, only trying to forget a game that would go down as one of his worst memories.

So in the end they decided it would be unfair on one of us if they went to the winners' party, because they'd be feeling as much sympathy and sadness for one of their sons as delight for another. After the game, though, Dan was having none of it. He grabbed them and said: 'Your son's just picked up the Challenge Cup, now go to the party and celebrate it properly with him.' I have to take my hat off to him for that. It can't have been easy, and I know he was as gutted as I've ever seen him, but he was determined that our parents would enjoy the moment as much as possible.

Obviously Mum and Dad weren't bothered which side actually picked up the cup. In a way they couldn't win and they couldn't lose. But all they wanted was for the pair of us to play well and to come through without injury.

As for the game itself, we knew all too well how dangerous Wigan could be when they got a sniff of a trophy. After all, we had experienced it ourselves in the Challenge Cup final of two years earlier, when we had gone to Murrayfield as over-whelming favourites, only for the Warriors to emerge as victors.

This time, though, we got off to a flying start when Willie Talau swooped on to a loose ball and sent Lee Gilmour over for the opening try after only three minutes. There was a hairy moment soon after, when Terry Newton dived through a pile of bodies to go for the line and the ball came free. They claimed I had dislodged the ball in a two-man tackle – illegal in rugby league – which would have meant a penalty to them or even a penalty try. Fortunately for us video referee David Asquith decided otherwise, and we escaped.

It was only a brief stay of execution, however, as Newton did eventually tie it up, and Wigan were only denied the lead when the video ref ruled that Craig Smith had knocked on in a move that saw Kevin Brown go in under the posts. It was a crucial turning point, because within a couple of minutes Longy kicked a penalty to put us back in front, and then Willie grabbed the first of his two tries.

I felt awesome that day – like I could run and run all afternoon, and had a pretty good game as well. In fact we all just ripped into them. Apparently I was in the running for the Lance Todd Trophy as man of the match, along with Willie and Paul Wellens, but no one could argue when it was given to Sean Long. At least a Saints player getting the nod meant that Saints had won the game.

The day was capped for me when I got over for a try as well. I remember making a run for the right-hand corner at Adrian Lam, and from a quick play-the-ball Longy dummied to go left, gave it back to me and I went through a gap. That was the moment I really knew we were going to win, and I must admit I didn't really give Danny a thought at that instant!

Everyone was screaming that we couldn't relax, how Wigan had loads of players who could do you a lot of damage – but, sod that, we'd won it and it felt bloody great! It certainly helps you enjoy those last few minutes a hell of a lot more – and the night wasn't too bad either, even though the sight of Danny so upset did keep haunting me.

So there it was, the first cup I collected as skipper – but, as I said, that nagging feeling of disappointment on our Dan's behalf as well. Mind you, for all that the celebrations were a little tainted for me because of it, I wouldn't have swapped places and let Wigan win it instead, you understand.

People have asked me thousands of times what it's like to play against my brother, and if I am ever tempted to go easier on him because of family ties. Well, I can say here and now, not a bit of it – from either side. In fact we probably go out to smash each other more than anyone else because of that, to be honest, and there are certainly no favours asked or given.

I remember one game against Wigan, when I had a bit of a do with David Vaealiki, one of their overseas players. He had dropped on me and I banged my arms upwards and caught him back. But then Dan came in and lay all over me, holding me down, while Vaealiki smashed me, and all the time our kid was just laughing.

The great thing about rugby league is that, for all we try to knock hell out of each other on the pitch and however much things may boil over in the game itself, as soon as it's over we will have a drink and a laugh together in the players' bar afterwards. And of course I am closer to our Dan than anyone else, so it goes way, way beyond that with him.

We both look out for each other off the pitch – me, Dan and our Lee are all very close and that will never change. We're not just three brothers, we're three best mates as well. Dan only lives around the corner from my house and I see him just about every day. Lee is still in Oldham and works away a lot, but that doesn't mean we aren't just as close.

Despite the age gaps – Dan's a couple of years younger than me and Lee's a couple older – we have never had to act as each other's minder or anything. I've certainly never had to save Dan from any trouble, probably because he's always been so bloody big and daft that he can manage it pretty well himself. Mind you, we all know that if ever the need arose we'd all be there for one another.

Of course we had our ding-dongs when we were growing up,

just like any set of brothers, but nothing out of the ordinary. But when the first whistle goes, me and our Dan always end up looking for each other on the pitch. Over the years I have come to realise that whenever I try to get a big one in on him, he always seems to sneak a pass out and put us in the shit.

There was another time we were playing Wigan when, right from the kickoff, myself and Jason Hooper said that we'd put it straight into Dan's arms and hammer him with a real biggie. Stage one went to plan, and the ball dropped straight to him.

But when we went to smash him, he just went through us and ended up putting Brett Dallas over for a try. That taught me a lesson and I stuck to regulation, run-of-the-mill tackles on him after that.

So that day of the final in Cardiff I wasn't going to blow it for Saints by concentrating solely on one player. And after the way things had gone in the lead-up to the game, we honestly couldn't see anything stopping us.

One of the greatest things about getting to big finals is the week running up to the game. From the moment you walk off the pitch in the last league game before the final, everything is geared towards coming out of the tunnel with a full house screaming for you.

That year preparations had gone particularly well, too. Certainly a million times better than when we'd been at Murrayfield. On that occasion our build-up had been crap, to be honest. We were training on a pitch in Scotland you'd have had second thoughts about letting your dog run on, and the whole thing was really negative.

None of that this time. Everything went really smoothly, we were in the best hotel in Wales, and we felt we could have taken on the bloody Aussies and beaten them, we were in such form.

In fact that was the season when a lot of people were saying that Saints were going to win the lot. I think Ian Millward would have entered us for the Grand National if he could, and still been convinced that we'd win it in a record time! As you can gather, confidence was never really that much of a problem for our old gaffer!

No one could argue that we won the trophy on the back of an easy draw, either. By the time I got my hands on the cup, we'd beaten Leeds, Bradford, Hull and Huddersfield. Wigan meant that we'd come up against the other five sides which – along with us – led the way in Super League. Talk about doing it the hard way!

It's funny in the dressing room before a final, because everyone is still trying to keep their preparation exactly the same, but you know deep down there's not a hope in hell because of what's at stake. Personally I've always been one for having a quiet word with individuals, rather than punching the walls or screaming and shouting.

And when you come out of that tunnel at the head of the team, the feeling is like nothing on earth. Goose pimples don't come into it, although I guess I've been pretty lucky in that I've never suffered that much from nerves. I just tend to have a look around, try and find the folks in the crowd, and keep my mind focused.

A lot of players get so psyched up that they can leave a bit of their game in the dressing room, but I have to confess that I love it all – the bigger the game, the better as far as I'm concerned. Maybe I'm a bit of a poseur deep down!

That night we all went up to the Angel Hotel in the middle of Cardiff – wives, girlfriends, kids, parents – and had a good old drink. I can't actually recall too much of it, but people have told me I enjoyed it – and the banging in my head the next morning seemed to suggest the same.

To be honest, you don't really savour a big victory in a final until the next couple of days after the match – I think it took us that long to stop drinking! The following morning it was down to breakfast – cornflakes with lager on aren't too clever, believe me – and then the hard labour of lugging all those crates of beer on to the team coach.

Eamonn McManus took us to a little boozer in Knutsford on the way back, and God knows what they thought. There was this sleepy little pub in a quaint Cheshire village, and suddenly twenty-four steaming blokes burst in with no shirts on, all singing – and not one of them in tune.

Longy, as ever, was the ringleader, but it was all pretty well behaved. Well, as much as it was going to be with us in that state, and from there it was on to Knowsley Road. I expected a fair turnout, but the fans packed the stadium and we all got interviewed in the middle of the pitch by Alan Rooney.

Funnily enough, I've got the DVD of that day and my interview is the only one missing. I didn't think I was slurring that much. In fact I thought I was talking pretty good sense – but then again, it wouldn't have been the first time!

Needless to say that one went on into the night as well, and it was a while before we all sobered up. It was certainly memorable, for good and bad reasons. At the time I remember thinking we could take on the world, and injuries were the last thing on my mind. I couldn't have been more wrong on that score . . .

13

Bye, Bye Basil

After the controversy that followed us throughout the 2004 campaign, largely because of that infamous gambling incident and the subsequent fall-out, we all went into the following year just hoping that the headlines would all be rugby related – and all for the right reasons. Some hope of that, as it turned out to be a total nightmare for me, and one Ian Millward will want to forget as well.

On the field it could not have started much better, as we won twelve of our first fourteen in cup and league, and by early May our only defeats had come at Leeds and by two points to Wigan at the JJB. But I was having increasing injury problems and the fact that I had made only sixteen appearances come the time to up stumps at the end of the campaign tells its own story.

I had gone okay in the earlier games, but my knee was continually sore; it was just throbbing all the time, around the joint. Funnily enough, playing itself was not a problem, but I wasn't sleeping properly and struggling a hell of a lot. It was all day, every day and I seemed to be living off painkillers. The best way I can really describe it was like having a headache in my knee.

I remember there was one time in mid-season when our Dan and Natalie, my mate Jonathan and his wife, and me and our Linds went to the Superbikes at Brands Hatch. Maybe it wasn't the best idea, because it was a long day and there was lots of standing around. That was actually the day I decided enough was enough, and to get the knee sorted once and for all.

We were stopping in a hotel in London and I didn't get a minute's sleep all night. I just spent hours and hours sitting on the edge of the bed, in absolute agony. That was in the August, and we were getting close to the business end of the season. Saints had been in pole position throughout, so there was every confidence we were going to go all the way to Old Trafford once again, too.

It was the week before St Helens played Warrington away, and that match at the Halliwell Jones Stadium ultimately turned out to be my last of the season. After that I just couldn't carry on. I went for a scan, which showed I had damaged the joint surface of the knee. The bottom line was that if I tried to go on, in the long term the damage could have been even worse. Obviously I wanted to get things right, and in my mind I had all but written off the rest of the year in any case, so that was me on the sidelines.

The ironic thing was that it came just a month or so after I had been given the ultimate honour of being named the new Great Britain skipper. Obviously, as someone who'd been around the international scene a while, I was involved in the senior players' meetings with coach Brian Noble, so he knew me as well as any of the lads in his squad.

There was a committee of senior internationals, usually made up of captain Andy Farrell, me, Jamie Peacock, Keith Senior and, latterly, Brian Carney. After one meeting Nobby asked me to stay behind for a minute and told me: 'I want you to be my captain.' Talk about buzzing! I was absolutely elated, the realisation of a thousand schoolboy dreams. My name had been mentioned for ages as a Great Britain skipper of the future, even though Faz never seemed to miss any games. So I suppose it was no real shock that I was the man chosen to replace him – although it doesn't matter how strong a favourite you are for something, you've still actually got to achieve it.

One of the first things Nobby asked me was who I thought should be vice-captain, and I had no hesitation in suggesting Jamie. We'd played together for a while with Britain, I knew all about his game and what he was like, and he was the obvious candidate. I was really looking forward to working with him.

Back then, things were going great on the field as well, such as running in sixty-six points at Bradford with Saints, and beating Wigan 75–0 in the Cup – in a game that will live long in the memory for a host of reasons. And most of them involved Ian Millward.

Basil was enjoying an increasingly stormy reign at St Helens, and things began to come to a head when he was found guilty of breaching the regularities concerning the technical areas in front of the dugouts, during our Challenge Cup win over Huddersfield in early April.

He had also been referred to the RFL's disciplinary commissioner for what they called an 'off-field' incident during our Easter Monday home win over Bradford. It was clearly getting a bit much for the St Helens' board, and on 4 May – the day after I got the Great Britain captaincy – he was suspended by the club. Eamonn McManus came in and spoke to the players, saying that assistant Dave Rotherham would be taking charge until the situation was sorted one way or another.

It didn't look too clever for Basil, who had been in the news for a run-in he'd had with the Warrington press officer, when there were tales that he had used some choice language. But it all came to a head one day at the training ground, as we were going through our usual sessions ahead of the weekend's game.

Brian Carney, the Wigan winger, was fronting a DVD on Super League's top tries and Joynty's memorable 'wide to West' try in the play-offs against Bradford had been named the winner. Brian was to interview him for the tape, nothing else, no sinister reasons or trying to spot our training-ground moves. But when Alex Turner, our press officer, turned up Basil went absolutely ballistic. He was giving it to him for inviting a player from our big rivals over when we were training. He really tore into him and was going way over the top. Amusingly Brian told me that he hadn't even watched any of our training session. He said later: 'I honestly didn't see a thing. And even if I had, I'm not clever enough to remember anything relevant and take it back to tell our lads.'

It had reached a point where Basil was doing a lot of press for himself as much as for Saints, but it proved there was certainly never a dull moment at our place. If it wasn't coaches being suspended, it was players in gambling controversies, or Ellery having a run-in with the board.

But things really kicked off when it was revealed that Basil wouldn't be coming back at all: he had been sacked. To be honest, there was a bit of a mixed reaction among the players, because for all those who backed him there seemed to be as many against him. Personally I'd not really had any bad experiences with Millward, and it came as a shock when they chose to get rid of him.

I must admit I didn't like the way he treated some of the

younger, inexperienced players. Basil knew that because they were still kids there was no chance of any of them speaking back to him. He didn't really have a pop at any of us senior ones, but in my view the younger lads may have felt bullied.

Mind you, I wasn't telling him anything I hadn't mentioned already. At the end of the year Ian used to give us all forms to fill in, wanting us to do our review of the season, what we liked, what we didn't and what we thought should be changed. You didn't need to put your name on, but I did in the two years when Ian kept the idea going. So he knew exactly what I thought of how he treated the kids, but I never got the chance to do the third year's form because he was on his bike before then.

When Basil got the bullet, I felt it was my job as captain of Saints to do my bit and try and lift the lads. It's a cruel side of sport, but life goes on, even if the coach doesn't, and we were playing Hull away in a few days. There was a lot of talk between the lads, and I remember telling them: 'He's not on the field with us, we've still got a bloody good team, let's do what we are best at and go out there and play.' Clearly Churchillian speeches weren't my forte, because we got hammered.

I rang Ian soon after he got the flick because, as I said, I didn't have any problems with him. I just wanted to do it out of courtesy and to wish him all the best; it was something that was only right as captain.

I was also fairly close to the Saints board, and had realised that some of the things Ian had been doing weren't going down too well. He was always in the paper with Everton manager David Moyes or whoever, rather than doing what he was being paid to do. The split between the players over Ian was very broad, and there were not many above half who were disappointed when he did go. When it gets to that stage, it's tough for the coach to carry on in any case, if you've only got 50 per cent of your players onside.

It was so ironic when Wigan – who snapped him up as their new coach – were drawn to play us at Knowsley Road in the Challenge Cup quarter-finals, just over a month after he had left us. I only saw him briefly, in the tunnel before kickoff, and we exchanged pleasantries. After the final whistle I don't think he was particularly in the mood to talk to anyone.

We got thirteen tries, including a hat-trick for Mark Edmondson, while I got nineteen points with the boot. That 75–0 drubbing was Wigan's record defeat for the second week in a row, having gone down 70–0 at Leeds the week before. But if I had sympathy for anyone it was our Dan, a Wigan player, rather than Basil. This is a ruthless game and no one would feel sorry for us if the boot was on the other foot.

It was just great to be a part of such a monumental win, in what I rate as the biggest derby in rugby league as well. It also set us up, almost incidentally given all the headlines about the size of the score, with a semi-final against Hull – and a game which I still remember with a shiver. We were red-hot favourites once more, but we got absolutely smashed on an awful day for the club. They played well, we were shite, and we got blitzed. They kicked us to death and bashed us in the forwards. And just to make it worse, it was only a week before my season came to an early end at Warrington.

As I said, things weren't too bad with my knee when I was on the go. But when I was at home after training, or whatever, it was excruciating. It was okay if I kept it loose, but you can't be moving around all the time, and when I wasn't I had bigger and bigger problems.

So off I went to see the specialist, who told me that although he felt I could possibly play on and get through the season, the pounding we get every week in this game would only lead to even more damage. He discovered a big fragment where the cartilage should have been, and there was just bone clashing with bone in the knee. That had splintered other bits off and I was heading for major problems if I continued. I had no plans to announce my retirement just yet; I felt I had years left in me, so any lingering doubts were quickly put to bed by his diagnosis.

I discovered it was going to be a six-month recovery period, whether I could get through that campaign or not. Of course my decision wasn't made any easier because I was so desperate to captain my country, but there was just nothing I could do. Even if I did get through that year, I would have missed God knows how much of the next one. So I took it on the chin and sat out the remainder of the season, plus the Tri-Nations tournament at the end of it, and channelled all my thoughts into getting back for the 2006 season.

Within a week of making the decision to call it a day for the year I was having surgery. I had a micro-fracture, and they put me in a leg brace for three weeks, in order to keep it straight and let the blood clot in between the surfaces of the bone. It was just for protection, but in all I couldn't even put my foot down for a total of twelve weeks. Have you ever tried going that long without plonking your foot on the floor? It was absolute torture and I am sure you can imagine what a barrel of laughs I was to live with.

Simply going upstairs was a total ballache, and even heading off to the toilet was a drawn-out operation. Obviously I couldn't drive, either; the whole thing was just horrendous. At least I consoled myself with the thought that this was finally going to be the answer to all the problems – some hope. I was swiftly told that there was more wear and tear on the lateral side of the knee, because I had been unable to extend it properly, and other parts had been compensating. This was merely a case of fixing some of the damage that the main problem was causing – although I did not know it at the time.

When it came to the crunch and things should have been showing a marked improvement, they were still bad a year later, when I headed down to London to see yet more medical experts. They told me that the fact I had been unable fully to extend my knee was causing more wear and tear, and had also thrown the alignment of my hips out. I was basically playing on a bent leg, and that was causing hamstring problems as well. It was always my left hamstring, left calf, left everything – but because of how the body overcompensates it was all stemming from my right knee.

I took some comfort from the fact that when I had been playing I was constantly in pain, but at least after the surgery I could rip into my rehab work, and have something to aim for. Not that it was easy to accept at the end of the week, when I should have been looking forward to getting out there on the pitch, but instead knew I'd be sitting and sulking in the stands because I couldn't help the lads. The Great Britain situation didn't improve my mood, either, knowing that I had been given the chance to lead out the lads, but it wasn't going to happen – not this season, at least.

I went to all the Tri-Nations games at the end of the season and spent a few days in the camp with the rest of the squad, but obviously it was never going to be the same. I was as frustrated as anyone when Britain lost their first two games to New Zealand and Australia, only to raise their hopes again by stuffing the Kiwis – and then promptly having them dashed when the Aussies did us again.

At least I had been keeping myself busy with my work for Gillette, the sponsors of the Tri-Nations. They had signed me up as one of their three sporting faces, and I was certainly in good company – their other two were Jason Robinson and David Beckham. I did a couple of photo-shoots with Jase, but Beckham stayed in Spain to do his, so I never actually came across him. The deal had come courtesy of Tony Colquit, one of the bigwigs at Gillette, who later worked for Saints as well. They wanted me as rugby league's ambassador, and it was the biggest deal of its kind in the history of our sport.

None of which, of course, was actually making my knee any better, even though it was helping to make me feel part of things. What didn't help was the fact that Jake always seemed to be catching my knee at that time. It was such a relief when, after those twelve weeks, I eventually got permission to put weight on it again just three days before the first Tri-Nations game at Loftus Road.

I went down to watch that one with Apollo Perelini, our conditioner at Saints, Willie Talau, who was catching up with his old New Zealand playing pals, and my mate Jonathan. I remember the British team shot back up north straight after the game, but the Kiwis went out and we went along with them. We ended up at their post-match function at the Walkabout bar and had a great time. Although in my case I suppose it would have been more fitting to find one called the Hobble-about. At least I knew that, barring disaster, I would be back and 100 per cent for the start of the season. Unfortunately for me, disasters of the injury variety were becoming all too familiar.

14
Final Misery

Come the start of 2006 I was really champing at the bit to get out there again. I'd trained right through the winter, although obviously my match fitness was a bit down because I'd had all that time when I couldn't do any running. Fortunately I have always been naturally fit and even though that can't prepare you for the contact and bashing, it still left me in good stead.

Daniel Anderson decided I still needed an extra week when it came to the big kickoff at Harlequins, which was a bit frustrating, but I was raring to go in the next game against Castleford. It was my first competitive action for six months, and I felt really good. Obviously winning 44–8 helped, but the pleasing thing was the fact that I played the full eighty minutes. I got a fantastic reception off the Saints fans and I felt ten feet tall.

Ando was still determined to take things steady with me, and told me he was going to play me in a couple of games, give me a little break, put me back in again, and play it like that. And as much as I wanted to play as often as possible, I could see his logic, so that was how it went. To be honest, looking back I still probably wasn't 100 per cent at any stage, as good as I felt in comparison to before, but that didn't stop Saints rattling up thirteen straight wins at the start of the season.

When our first defeat came, as it was inevitably going to at some stage, it was at Huddersfield – probably not the side most people would have tipped to send us crashing – when we went down 19–16. Even so, we quickly regained our winning ways and included Bradford among our victims as we reached the last four of the Challenge Cup.

But the week after stuffing Catalans in the quarter-finals came one of the defining games of the season for me, when we lost by a point to Hull at Knowsley Road. That was bad enough in itself, but I was starting to have real problems with my leg once again. I had struggled with my lateral movement throughout, and just couldn't push off my right leg. Ando, as I said, was picking my games carefully and had rested me for the odd one here and there. But things were far from right when I was on the field, even though I had the extra incentive of a Challenge Cup final to look forward to again, after we stuffed surprise package Hull KR by fifty points in the semis.

Huddersfield had shocked everyone, probably even a few of their own fans, by beating Leeds to reach Twickenham, the venue, once again, for the final. But while I have some great memories of the Challenge Cup over the years, this one was totally different – even though we won. We beat them easily, 42–12, but I just didn't feel as if I had contributed a great deal. To be honest, I thought it was rubbish! Even when you win the game, the feeling is never quite the same when you've given a poor performance, and that was hard to take despite the fact I had another winners' medal.

The lack of lateral movement with my leg meant that I was

being forced to play a different style of game from my usual, simply because I couldn't step sideways. I was stuck in the second row, basically running straight lines, and it really wasn't enjoyable. I knew that I couldn't make half the impact or difference that I should have if I'd been totally right. I'm not blowing my own trumpet, but knew I was better than I was showing at the time, and when you've been lucky enough to play at a very high standard it's hard just to put in a run-of-the-mill performance.

I spoke to Ando about it several times, but his answer was the obvious one. He just kept telling me that he couldn't play me in the middle because I couldn't run properly. In an all-action, constantly moving sport like rugby league, naturally that has a massive impact on how you and the team go. He didn't need to tell me, because you can't play around the rucks if you can't move. I've always set my own goals, and don't need anyone to tell me when I'm falling short of them, and this was no different.

The really bloody annoying thing was the fact that the press and some neutrals clearly didn't realise the reason I wasn't playing too well. They just put it down to the fact that I was off my game, but had no idea of the true situation. Basically, I was being asked to play a different style as that was all I could do because of my fitness. It was bugger all to do with anything else. At least the people who really mattered knew the score. My family, team-mates, the club, close pals . . . they were well aware of the situation and they were really the only ones who counted. Not that it made my mood any lighter. When you're used to being able to make a difference suddenly failing to do so is very frustrating. That was probably as low as I felt, and things didn't exactly pick up to any great extent either as time passed.

Ironically, despite having such a stop–start season that

eventually ground to a halt entirely, I did actually manage to lead Great Britain out for the first time. It came after we had beaten Salford at home in Super League, which probably went down as my best game of the season. I had built my knee up to a certain strength, and felt really good. So good, in fact, that I was man of the match in our 28–6 win, capped by the fact that I scored a try as well. I made a few breaks, saw a lot of ball because I largely played in the middle that day, and I was convinced I was back on track and could play out the season.

It was the first really positive thing to happen that year, and I was in the best possible spirits when New Zealand came over for a one-off Test in June, and the fact that it was at Saints' Knowsley Road ground put the icing on the cake for me. I worked hard on the knee all week after the Salford win, and was as pleased as punch when I walked out as skipper of my country, in front of the fans who watched St Helens week in, week out.

Unfortunately every silver lining seemed to have a cloud for me, and this was to prove no different. I started really well and felt strong, but after only eighteen minutes Kiwi second-rower David Solomona tackled me bang on the side of the knee and tore the medial ligament. It was totally unconnected to the injury I'd just come back from on the other leg, but I knew it was serious straight away. With a medial problem, the knee just goes all wobbly and physio Rob Harris diagnosed it immediately when he came on to treat me.

I went for a scan at once and that showed a 90 per cent tear. On top of everything else I'd gone through it was terrible news and left me totally gutted. The most frustrating thing was listening and hearing everyone say that I was injury prone. In twelve years of playing the hardest sport of all at the top level, I had suffered only two major problems, which both happened to be in the knee, and I just struggled to get it right. If I'd been getting knock after knock, and a variety of them, then, fair enough, I'd probably say I was jinxed myself. But when you're coming back from the same problem each time, then sod that – that's not being injury prone, that's just bad luck.

I have to be honest and say it did raise a few doubts in my mind as to what the future held for me as a player, and – as with every operation – the surgeon told me there could never be a 100 per cent guarantee that everything would be fine. He could only do his best, and me do mine, and hopefully things would recover perfectly – but they were worrying times, no doubt about it. There was even the slender chance that I might have played my last competitive game, although I was determined it wouldn't be the case, and fortunately never came close to reaching that stage. I want to play on for as long as possible and see no reason why I shouldn't do so. But there was no denying the fact that it had been an horrendous couple of years.

I know there seemed to be something of a whispering campaign that I was finished, although no one had the sense – or perhaps that should be the bottle – to put it to me face to face. And for all those who thought the worst, there were plenty out there offering me support. My family and friends, plus everyone at the club, were 100 per cent behind me and for that I thank them. Everyone who mattered was telling me that I'd be back to my best. It was just a case of knuckling down when the time came, and working bloody hard – and hard work is something I'd never shied away from.

Lindsay in particular was hugely supportive, especially when I was off my leg. She was doing everything for me, and it must have been like having another kid in the house. She probably thinks it still is, to be honest. It can't have been easy for her, and

I know there were times when I probably snapped when I shouldn't have. The worst thing for a professional sportsman is not being able to play. You desperately want to take out your frustrations on something out there on the pitch, but even when I was training there was no chance of that.

Over the past eighteen months or so I don't think I've ever done as much work with sponsors and stuff. I suppose they all knew that I was available, so just thought, 'Scully's not doing anything, let's get hold of him.' That was good news in terms of keeping me in the spotlight and involved to some extent, because we've all seen over the years how quickly players can slip away and get forgotten when they're sidelined, retired or whatever.

But it's bloody hard when you're working in the gym by yourself, and not enjoying the craic with the lads on the training ground. Obviously I still saw them around the club, but missed the involvement of playing kick tennis, or simply being in the thick of all the mickey-taking. It was especially tough when all I could do was upper-body work on the weights. I had my own rehab programme, but naturally that did not involve being out there with the rest of them.

Thank God Jason Hooper was having problems with his knee at the same time! We basically kept each other's spirits up as we did a hell of a lot of training together, while fellow Saints team-mate Vinnie Anderson kept us company for a while, too, with extra training. We'd all head down to the David Lloyd Centre out of hours to do as much extra work as we could, because we were so desperate to get back as quickly as possible. Me and Hoops are really close, but perhaps that's no surprise given how many months we were in rehab together.

I was also doing a hell of a lot of training on the bike, and it makes so much difference when you've got someone alongside you going through the same. Apollo Perelini was really good too, be it in training or a supportive phone call. Obviously I couldn't drive for a time when I first had my knee done, and Apollo was great, coming round to pick me up and run me around. He joined me for a lot of the upper-body work, and there's no doubt that when you're big and strong you feel a lot better – even if you can't get around as you should. Apollo supported me all the way, from training to just cheering me up with a quick call.

I've already said how, despite my coming back later in the season, the knee was so bad that I ended up walking off the training field before our play-off semi-final against Hull. But although the season had been written off before we played them again at Old Trafford in the Grand Final, that week was a personal nightmare for me. I'd been involved in enough already to know exactly what I'd be missing out on, and it was a shocking time. If I'd been selfish, I suppose I could still have been involved, because Ando had told me he was prepared to select me for the semi. It was tough, knowing I could have risked taking someone's place and only lasting ten minutes, and that was something I'd never do.

If another player had done that, I'd have been furious, so I wasn't about to act the hypocrite and do it myself. But on the Tuesday of the week of the Hull semi-final that September, it was obvious I was finished for the year anyway, because I couldn't even get through the session. The day I called time on the season certainly wasn't a day for the kids stepping out of line at home!

Yet gutted though I was at missing out, in some ways it was also a relief eventually to go for surgery, because at least then there was a definite decision and I knew where I stood. Or at least where I hobbled. On the day of the final I was actually working at Old Trafford, doing some television, but at the end of the day I am a player and the only thing I wanted to do was play – especially in such a big game. It goes without saying that I was delighted when Saints won, and at 26–4 it was hardly the closest of our Grand Final victories, even though it still took a lot of winning, but being at the celebration party back at the club was a weird feeling.

You never feel quite as involved when you haven't played, so things were a bit subdued to say the least – or that's how they started anyway. A few of the lads were preparing to head off for Tri-Nations duty with Great Britain the following day as well, which kept them in check to some extent. I was just throwing down a few drinks, but was struggling to get about regardless of that, because I had a leg brace on to help keep it extended.

It was the first time I'd worn it while dressed in the club suit and, needless to say, the trousers weren't the best fitting ones on show that night. The brace ended up ripping a bit out of them, and by the time I was blind drunk at the end of the evening the trousers had been split right up the leg until they were eventually cut off completely. Everyone seemed to be coming up and making the rip that bit worse, so – with alcohol-induced common sense – it seemed like a good idea to cut them off that leg altogether.

I forgot all about them for six months, while I was concentrating on rehab, because clearly there wasn't great call for me to don the official St Helens suit for anything. But come the day of the World Club Championship against Brisbane, and my long-awaited return to action, I found myself facing a real dilemma.

We were all required to go in our official club get-up, but try as I might I just couldn't find the trousers to the suit. Obviously I did what all blokes do in that situation – blamed the wife! I was convinced Lindsay must have put them somewhere, or left them at the dry cleaners or something. She actually went round all the shops with my club blazer, desperately trying to find a pair of trousers to match, but came home empty-handed. Then she suddenly realised and said: 'Don't you remember getting them all ripped and cutting them off at the club?' As soon as she mentioned that, it dawned on me, even though it didn't solve the problem.

But then I remembered that Vinnie Anderson, who had left for Warrington at the end of the previous season, would probably still have a pair, so I gave him a bell. On the day I was playing my first game in six months, I had a mad dash to Vinnie's, wearing a bog-standard pair of navy trousers, picked up his old club pair and I hurriedly got changed at Knowsley Road before heading off to face Brisbane. It was a distraction I could have done without after the six months I'd just endured. But at least it ended all smiles – especially when we became world champions just a few hours later.

15

Tour de Farce

The highlight of any professional's career is being selected to play for his country, and when I got the call to represent England in the World Nines in Fiji back in 1996 I was walking on air. Okay, it might not have been the headline sporting event of the year, but in my eyes it couldn't get much bigger.

I was only eighteen years old, still wet behind the ears compared to all the seasoned pros out there, so, as much as I was establishing myself at Warrington, playing for England was something way and above that. I realised it was only a nine-a-side competition and a world away from a Great Britain Ashes series, but so what.

We flew out via Los Angeles and had a stopover there. It was funny, because as soon as we got to LA we bumped into a load of lads from the other countries, who'd had the same idea, so we linked up and had a great time. We had hardly landed in America before we were all packed off training to this grassy area right near the airport. It was like something out of Boyz 'N The Hood!

It was that close to our hotel that we just walked there, went through the session and walked back – which was when we were told something which left us all rooted to the spot. One of the locals was chatting to us and asked where we'd been training. When we told him, he said: 'I honestly don't know how you haven't been shot, because it's rife with that around here. When these guys see someone else on "their turf", especially a bunch who they don't know, they don't mess about.'

We'd gone out with a squad of thirteen or so, and could easily have ended up losing a couple straight away! It was a real shock and put things in perspective a bit. But we came through unscathed, and flew on to Fiji for the tournament itself. In all we were there for about ten days, even though the competition was supposed to take place over two, and it turned into one of the best holidays I've ever had.

But we were in for another eye-opener when we went to visit the stadium, because the surface was a real shocker, absolutely rock solid. Even so, we put in a couple of great displays on the first day and beat Tonga 18–4, before following up with a 34–0 win over Morocco and a slender 4–0 victory over Italy.

We were all geared up for another day on a ludicrously hard surface, but it absolutely bucketed down overnight and it got so bad that the second day was actually postponed. When the tournament resumed twenty-four hours later conditions could not have been more different: we found ourselves playing in knee-deep mud. In the end we made the semi-finals, before losing to Papua New Guinea, which left us facing Australia in a play-off for third place.

Now it might not have been a full-blooded Test match, but you always want to beat the Aussies, and we gave them a hell of a game before they eventually sneaked over for the winning try in extra time. I even had the satisfaction of scoring a try when I intercepted a pass from Ricky Stuart, one of the all-time great half backs, so all in all things had gone pretty well for me on my international debut.

The next step was being selected for England's European Championship squad, and I made my full international debut against France in Gateshead, when we absolutely monstered them and I scored a try to make it even more memorable. That proved to be the only time I actually played in the same side as the great Shaun Edwards, and when you look back now it was certainly some line-up. The likes of Martin Offiah and Jason Robinson were in there, and it was an honour to be able to call them team-mates.

Then it was on to Cardiff Arms Park, and victory over the Welsh, which saw us finish on top of the table and crowned European champions. I knew it wasn't the most important tournament in the world, but if nothing else it also proved you were in the frame for Great Britain – and with a tour coming up at the end of that 1996 season put you right in the shop window for selection.

You're supposed to be informed of your selection by post or phone, but from my experience you tend to find out off Teletext – not the best way if you're one of those who miss out – and the letter usually comes the next day. Even so, until that official confirmation arrives you are still on pins. Fortunately I had no need to worry, because when Phil Larder announced his squad for Papua New Guinea, Fiji and New Zealand, I was in – my first tour.

I was absolutely buzzing when we boarded the plane at Manchester. I wasn't quite so full of beans forty-seven hours later when we eventually touched down in Lae airport after a truly horrendous journey. It seemed to go on forever, and one of

177

the trade papers had a picture of us all stretched out on the floor at Port Moresby airport, waiting for the connecting flight. There was no chance of relaxing when we got to the hotel either – not with Neil Harmon around. He was a vastly experienced forward, who played for Leeds, Warrington and Huddersfield among others, and it soon became obvious to me that he was one of the real jokers in the squad.

The film *Scream* had just come out, which all the lads were on about, and Neil wasn't about to miss the chance for a wind-up. I was rooming with Chris Joynt and heard all this laughing outside my room. I stuck my head out the door to see what was going on, and Harmon had the bloody mask on from the film – I nearly shat myself!

He has to be one of the funniest men I've ever met, and for the rest of the time in Papua I borrowed his mask and caught out loads of the lads around the hotel. But if that was a laugh, the matches over there were anything but. Rugby league is an absolute religion over there, but it isn't the safest of countries and there were guards all over the hotel, stopping us from going out and wandering off.

We were supposed to go and watch their National Cup final, which was basically between teams from two of the biggest tribes in the country, but because the flight took so long we ended up missing it. Thank God we did as well: there was a mass riot and four people were shot. When we went to the ground to train, before our Test match against PNG, the pitch was just covered in rocks and stuff – anything spectators been able to get their hands on to throw at each other.

Come the match, I was on the bench but came on after three minutes when Joynty split his head open. It went quite well and we edged it by two points, but there was as much drama getting to and from the ground. We'd had to change at the hotel, drive the bus on to the side of the pitch and run straight on, because of the threat of being mobbed by the thousands of fans. I don't think they had anything nasty in mind, but we weren't about to wait and see. It was the same story after the game – drive the bus to the edge of the pitch, jump straight on without a shower and get changed back at the hotel again.

The press lads were on the same bus, and when the officials were asking if everyone was on board we all shouted to go as there were no more to come. I'll never forget the sight of Dave Hadfield, one of the larger members of the press corps, running to try and catch the bus with about eight million locals chasing him. He's not the fastest in the world – I think I'd still have beaten him with my leg in a brace – but he shifted that day. We all thought it was hilarious; strangely, Hadfield didn't have quite the same opinion.

Fiji, the next leg of the tour, had its rough bits as well, but we were in a pretty decent hotel – even though it was the same story about getting bussed straight on and off the pitch for the match. In terms of the scoreline, it couldn't have been further removed from the PNG Test, as we won 72–4, and this time I was in the side from the off. But just fifteen minutes in there was an almighty brawl involving all twenty-six players.

They had a prop forward called Mal Yasa, who played for Sheffield Eagles, who'd had a bust-up with our scrum half, Bobbie Goulding, during a Super League game the previous season. When it all kicked off in the Test, Yasa went racing thirty metres towards Bobbie, and we all expected him to step out of the way.

But Bobbie wasn't one for taking a backward step, and he simply moved to one side and caught Yasa with the best punch

I think I've ever seen, and absolutely flattened him. Bob actually escaped any punishment off New Zealand ref Jim Stokes, as he sent off Yasa, and sin-binned Denis Betts from our side and Livai Nalagilagi from theirs.

That win set us up nicely for the real business of taking on the Kiwis. As we were flying into Auckland airport, the captain was giving us the spiel about New Zealand, and how proud they were of it being such a trouble-free country. Just our luck, then, that we arrived at the Sheraton hotel to find all this police-incident tape around the area because there had been a murder in the cemetery opposite. There was actually another killing during our stay, and some of the lads were even interviewed by the police, obviously not as suspects but just in case they'd seen anything that could help when they were out.

I played in the first game, a twenty-two-all draw with a Lion Red XIII, missed the defeat by a New Zealand XIII as Larder rested his Test match line-up, and was in from the start for the first Test at Auckland. I went pretty well, too, and we were 12–4 ahead with less than ten minutes to go. But then Adrian Morley – together with me the other young lad of the squad – came off the bench and was ludicrously penalised and sin-binned for holding down Sean Hoppe in the tackle. It had gone on all game but referee Bill Harrigan only decided to take action then, and with Moz off the field they ran in two tries and edged it by five points.

Moz, naturally, was distraught, even though no one in our camp was blaming him, and even some of the Kiwis told us it was a pretty harsh decision. We knew we should have won, so were still pretty confident of squaring the series in the second Test at Palmerston North – only for events back home to leave everyone reeling.

The day after the midweek team played the Maoris the shattering news came from RL in England that twelve players were to be flown home. They felt that because there were no games left in between the two remaining Tests there would be plenty surplus to requirements, and manager Phil Lowe had the unenviable task of drawing up a list of those who had to go.

It was a real shattering blow to morale, and with just twenty-one players left – and a lot of those carrying knocks – we were down to the bare bones. News of the decision quickly spread throughout the squad, and it was the only topic of discussion. Jon Roper, a close team-mate of mine from Warrington, bumped into me and just said: 'I'm going home – they're sending a load of us back.' We were gobsmacked; it was a ridiculous decision, and I think Larder and Lowe were as pissed off as the rest of us, and it left them with a massive job on their hands to prepare for the next Test.

The injury situation was so bad that Tulsen Tollett, who spent most of his life in Australia despite being qualified for Britain, was actually recalled – having initially been dumped with the rest of them. Tulsen had flown to see family and friends in Brisbane, but came back when he got the call. Quite a few of the lads insisted they'd have told Britain where to stick it, had it been them, but it was another example of how things could have been handled so much better.

Perhaps it was no surprise, then, that we lost that second Test, although the story was pretty similar to the Auckland game. Fifteen minutes from time we were leading, but then they got a late converted try, we had lost by three points and the series was gone.

By the time of the third Test in Christchurch we were on our knees, and they really bashed us, winning 32–12. I only lasted half the game in that one, because I ran into Grant Young, a giant of a prop forward, and felt like my shoulder was coming out of my back, he was that solid. They were a huge bunch of lads, and one tackle that Quentin Pongia put in on me in a subsequent World Cup game is still probably the hardest I've been hit.

Losing my first series as a Great Britain tourist was a huge disappointment, but it was still a memorable trip – and there were loads of laughs along the way. We went out one night in New Zealand and something kicked off in this club, when some of the locals had a go at Dave Bradbury. We were out with a guy called Afi Leuila, who played with Dave at Oldham, and he went absolutely wild. I've never seen anyone fight like Afi did that night.

He was picking up the rope rails where you queue to go in, and launching them at the bouncers, who were keeping well out of it, as he smashed anyone who came in touching distance. The amazing thing was that Afi was usually such a quiet, amiable bloke. I saw him in a different light after that – someone who certainly believed in looking after his mates.

There was another incident in New Zealand, and I'd better not mention the bloke involved for his own sake! Suffice to say that Phil Lowe got a knock on his door and one of the hotel staff told him: 'One of your players is urinating out of the top-floor window – and has thrown an ironing board out as well.' There never seemed to be a dull moment.

Once the Tests were over, we had one day left and the choice of spending it on the beach or going skiing up Mount Hutt. As I'd never been skiing before I thought I'd give that a crack, but doubted the wisdom of it as the coach edged up all these winding roads, with a sheer drop just yards away. Most of the lads came along, as well as three of the press – Phil Thomas, Graham Clay and Dave Hadfield, who I think had decided he fancied a pint up a mountain – and it was a fantastic day. I didn't get much skiing done, as I stayed on the nursery slopes, but me and Kris Radlinski had a whale of a time going up to the top in the ski lift, and just staying on for the ride down again.

I also met Toa Kohe-Love's dad on that trip, and what a great guy he turned out to be. Toa was a team-mate of mine from Warrington, and obviously had loads of friends and family in New Zealand from playing there before he came to England. His dad, Hukka, was a lovely bloke and I got him tickets for the Palmerston North Test. I ended up sending him a Britain shirt and him returning the favour with a Wellington Hurricanes one. He was later killed in a boating accident, a tragedy to lose such a great fellow.

By now my stock was rising back home, and when details were announced of a revolutionary World Club Championship competition whereby all the Aussie teams came to England to play ones from Super League, and vice versa, myself and Bradford's Robbie Paul were chosen to fly out and promote the tournament. It was a real honour to be picked, but it was a hell of a long way to go for a one-day promotion – but at least we were promised business-class flights and £1,500 each.

It was pretty clear, pretty quickly, that maybe things weren't all they were cracked up to be, when we found ourselves stuck in economy both ways. As for the money we'd been promised, well, I am still waiting. It wasn't really about the cash, though, it was more about the flights. I've nothing against kids – I've got two myself – but when you are stuck in the middle seats in the middle aisle, with screaming babies on both legs, it makes it seem an even longer trip than it really is.

We touched down in Sydney at about 8 p.m. and went straight out on the grog. The next morning we did a photo shoot and press conference for an hour or so, almost straight away. That was something of a joke as well, because we were supposed to wear our club shirts, which the Aussies were providing, but they hadn't got a Warrington top so I did mine in a Great Britain kit. I felt rougher than a bear's arse, so you could say I wasn't at my most photogenic, and me and Robbie spent the rest of the day looking around Sydney, before flying back.

As for the competition itself, Warrington acquitted themselves reasonably well, even though we didn't manage to win a game, home or away, against Penrith, Cronulla or Auckland. We did manage to hold Auckland to 16–4 on a shocking day in New Zealand, which wasn't too bad considering they put seventy points on St Helens. It was even better given the fact that we took a young team out, to give fringe players like Chris Causey and Shaun Geritas a taste of the first team.

The thing that really sticks out about that game against Auckland was the conditions. It wasn't just cold, it was really, really wet. In the very first tackle I had my face pushed into the ground, like you do, and it was so bad I thought I was going to drown. So atrocious was it that I'm sure someone ended up getting hypothermia.

We decided that there was no way we could even consider a running game, and I don't think we got past three or four tackles all game when we were in possession, before putting huge kicks up to full-back Matthew Ridge to try and force errors. As I said, they ended up winning, but we had at least come out of it with our pride intact.

A few people seem to think the competition wasn't treated entirely seriously, but nothing could have been further from the truth when Darryl Van De Velde was in charge. He had us training very hard every day, and imposed a drinking ban to make sure no one went off the rails. Unfortunately Tony Tatupu and Nigel Vagana broke it, and we all got flogged in the next session. Darryl said: 'It's the same as a game situation – if one person makes a mistake, you all suffer.' And believe me, we all bloody suffered.

But as far as my own performances over there were concerned, I knew I must have impressed because Shane Richardson, the big cheese at Penrith, spoke to me about going to Australia to play. The Aussies are hardly known for their love of English players, so it was a real pat on the back, even though it was never really on as I was still only making my way in the game over here.

The concept of that competition was great, but really highlighted the gap between their domestic game and ours. We'd only been full-time professionals for just over a year, and that really told as they dished out one beating after another. When you compare the differences now to those days, it really shows how far the English game has come in the past decade.

I had the honour of being named Warrington's man of the match in our game over there against Cronulla. That was something of a feat in itself, because I clashed heads with Chris McKenna after twenty-five minutes and had no idea where I was for the rest of the match. I couldn't even remember the physio's name at half-time, and had to ask the lads if we were winning, and if the game had finished or we had another half to play.

I somehow managed to keep the extent of my concussion from our coaching team, and I carried on – and apparently played really well. I was running around without a care in the world. They must have told me I was Mal Meninga and we were winning 20–0! Going away with Great Britain was fantastic, but with your club it was something else again. You were spending your time with mates you saw every day, and it was a real good trip – even if some of it does remain a blur to this day.

My room-mate was Lee Briers, for the first and last time. We'd got a big bag of prawns from the fish market, which ended up in the bin behind the door for the whole week of the stay. They're probably still trying to get the smell out of the room even now – suffice to say Lee wasn't the cleanest bloke I've ever shared a hotel room with.

At least the competition was memorable for our Dan, because when their teams came to England for that stage of the tournament he had a great night out with all the Kiwi lads after Auckland had played at Wilderspool. A few of the Warrington lads were friendly with their lot, and he tagged along, having a great time with the likes of Stacey Jones. But he didn't have any decent trousers with him to go to a club, and ended up borrowing a pair off Salesi Finau. Sal is about six inches shorter than Dan, so you can imagine how they looked. I can still picture him to this day, with his half-mast kecks, all set to paint the town red.

The funny thing about Salesi and his big mate Mateaki Mafi was that they arrived at Warrington from Down Under and hardly said a word to anyone. In fact Matty only ever drank water back then, but by the time he left the club you couldn't shut him up and he'd drink anything going. Talk about a successful conversion.

My only other international trip abroad – that one-off Test in Australia aside – was the 1999 tour for the Tri-Nations tournament, which proved a total washout and a real personal disappointment as well.

We knew we were up against it anyway, trying to beat the Kangaroos and Kiwis in their own backyard, but things became even worse when we got off to a shocking start. We had a warm-up game against Burleigh Bears, who were the Queensland Cup champions, which was little more than the reserve grade over in Australia.

We weren't helped by a referee who absolutely killed us with the penalty count, but with only a quarter of the game to go we were losing 6–4 and it took a late try and goal from Andy Farrell to save us from complete humiliation. Burleigh weren't exactly up for a free-flowing game, and most of them looked like they'd come straight from the gym. Clearly they wanted to make a name for themselves by bashing a few Poms, which maybe you couldn't blame them for, and we didn't help ourselves when we only won by four points either.

It has to be one of the craziest games I've ever played in, where they were just trying to turn it into one big thugfest, but you can imagine the sort of coverage we got after that. The papers were full of it, both here and over there: how can Britain expect to beat the Aussies and New Zealanders when they can only just scrape home against a semi-professional outfit?

The fact that coach Andy Goodway had fielded a team largely made up of his full-strength Test side merely rubbed salt into the wounds. It's never particularly easy to get yourself up for matches like that, but Andy avoided the flak a bit by saying we'd only just arrived, that it was only a warm-up before the serious business. But the fact that the Kiwis had beaten the Aussies in the first Tri-Nations game a day earlier left us in no doubt that an already uphill task was now looking like a truly mountainous one.

So it proved, unfortunately, when we kicked off our competition by getting steamrollered by the Aussies at Lang Park, in Brisbane. The fans had already voted with their feet after our game against the Bears, because the attendance was the lowest ever for an Anglo-Aussie Test Down Under. Clearly the supporters did not expect a genuine contest, and sadly they were proved correct when we got stuffed 42–6, despite only trailing by four points at half-time.

That was the first game we had ever played with the unlimited substitution rule, which – as it suggests – allows you to make as many replacements as you want. In Britain we are used to playing with a maximum of twelve changes throughout the game, and clearly there is an art in timing them right. This time we were all at sea, and no one knew if they were coming or going.

It was fine for the Aussies: they'd grown up with the rule and played that way all their lives. And I know the system had its supporters among those who said it allowed players to have crucial breaks, which in theory should prevent weary legs at any stage. But you can't just chuck a new operation into play and expect it to click straight off, and it did anything but. I think it was just another instance of us trying to follow the Aussies' lead, because if they did it we always seemed to think that was the right way.

We should have stuck to our normal game, and made the subs accordingly. Personally I thought it was a nightmare. I was used to playing eighty minutes week in, week out, and to find yourself on and off about four or five times meant there was no chance of getting into a rhythm, or adapting to the pace of the game. Internationals are fast enough without being handicapped by a stop–start approach. Fair enough if some of the forwards need a break, but the way we used it was a big, big mistake.

That defeat left us needing to beat New Zealand in Auckland by twenty points if we were to reach the final, and I think in our heart of hearts we knew that was never really on. Mind you, I never even got the chance to have a go because for the first and only time in my career I was dropped – but I was never even told this properly to my face.

I'd picked up a bit of a dead leg against the Aussies, but unless it's a real shocker that is never going to keep you out. A decent rub, or running it off for a while, and you're generally fine. It certainly hadn't stopped me training in the week leading up to the Kiwi game, but Goodway pulled me over, asked me how the injury was then said he wasn't playing me because of my leg.

I told him I was fit, but he stuck to his guns: 'I've decided not to go with you.' I told him: 'What you're saying is I'm dropped.' He replied: 'I want us to play a different way, and you don't play the game that way.' Goodway was going to tell the press that I was out because of an injury, but I don't even know if that was the official story, I was that hacked off about it.

It certainly soured the whole tour for me, made even worse by the fact that he never really did tell me I was dropped, even though we both knew it. Goodway obviously had very strong Wigan links, from his playing days as a member of the side which dominated the game, and his team reflected that.

Ten of the thirteen starters were from either Wigan or Leeds, another of Goodway's old clubs, and he was very close to Denis Betts, who had played alongside him in the glory days at Central Park for years. Denis was by now plying his trade with Auckland Warriors, but clearly had a big input as to how things were run. I had no qualms about Andy Farrell having a huge say.

Faz was captain, for God's sake, so it was only right that he had an influence, but I do still wonder whether Denis played a bigger part in things than maybe he should've done. All in all there were simply too many outside influences in Goodway's team selection. Perhaps the fact that I had no Wigan links did me no favours.

So we went off to Auckland's Ericsson Stadium to face the Kiwis, and by half-time knew that any chance of making the final had been blown away, as we trailed 14–0. It wasn't any easier sitting on the sidelines and watching it, and we ended up crashing 26–4. To rub salt into the wounds, the organisers had decided beforehand that whoever failed to reach the final of the Tri-Nations would have to play the Maoris in a curtain-raiser to the big game.

Whenever we have reached a final against the Aussies since then, that has never even been suggested. Do you honestly think the Kiwis would allow themselves to be put through something like that? No chance. But by then it had been arranged, it was part of the schedule, and we just had to lump it. There was nothing we could do so we really wanted a big performance to at least leave the competition on a high.

I was back in the starting line-up, having not even made the substitutes' bench for the Kiwi match, and had a brilliant game as I set about showing that I hadn't deserved to be dropped in the first place. We all played pretty well in fact and ended up winning 22–12, although at only four points in front with fifteen minutes to go it was in the balance for a bit when Paul Anderson got sin-binned. But I was having a field day, making breaks for fun, and set up Sean Long for a couple of tries too, the second of which sealed victory. Even so, we had been stripped of a lot of dignity in having to play the game in the first place, and rugby-wise it was a fairly dismal trip. The fact that we finished without a single point and that our leading scorer was Iestyn Harris with six – the winner was Australia's Matt Rogers with thirty-six – told its own story.

I know that being dropped meant that, for all the Maori game was meaningless, I was certainly well motivated and Goodway said to me afterwards: 'That's the way I wanted you to play.' I just answered: 'You've only got to tell me and keep me on the field, because I'm not going to do it sitting in the stands.'

All in all I feel that whole tour was a bit too cliquey. All the lads got on well enough together, but I thought people were sitting in club groups a bit too much. Yet while the rugby was a bit of a washout, the organisation itself was awesome and my golf went through the roof. We stayed at the Radisson on the Gold Coast, and – apart from the rugby – it was one of the best trips I've ever been on.

We were actually on the Gold Coast at the same time as the IndyCar Grand Prix was being held, and the place was absolutely mobbed. We all went up to watch the race itself, the chance of a lifetime, and it was fantastic to see the cars scorching around the streets up to Surfers Paradise. And because the hotel was on a golf resort, I think we managed to get eighteen holes in every single day. It was quite something. Unfortunately we didn't come out of the matches themselves with a similar sense of satisfaction.

16
Tough Cookies

I think everyone would accept you've got to be pretty bloody tough simply to set foot on a rugby pitch in the first place. But clearly some are going to stand out as being that bit rougher – or crazier – than most.

I've had my fair share of scrapes over the years, and one bloke I always seemed to have a run-in with, be it for Warrington or St Helens, was Leeds Rhinos prop Barrie McDermott – albeit not as many as Wigan's Stu Fielden. Now, take Barrie away from a rugby field and he is as nice as pie, one of the best guys you could ever meet. In fact we are still very close mates even now – probably especially now – that he's called it a day playing-wise, as he's an Oldham lad too. But for some reason he always set out to give me a good battering whenever we were in opposition, and the same probably applied to me.

During my Warrington days we had an Aussie front-rower called Dave King, who was knocking out these shoulder pads from the boot of his car. Barrie got wind of it and rang me, actually a few hours before we were playing Leeds at Wilderspool, and said: 'Can you get me a set of them and bring them to the game tonight?' I had no problem helping out a mate, so took them along to the match, and he was full of thanks.

Yet as soon as we kicked off, probably in my first touch of the night, he came steaming in and tried to take my head off my shoulders. He got sent off, and I remember thinking what a nice way it was to repay me for a favour. But the good thing with Barrie is that whatever happened on the pitch stayed on the pitch. He would always have a chat and a pint after the game, and whatever had gone on was forgotten, which is obviously the way it should be.

We were constantly having digs at each other throughout matches, although these days everything is picked up on video, whether the ref sees it or not. Mind you, with Barrie you didn't need technology half the time to spot what had gone on – he wasn't the most subtle, shall we say. I always tried to wind him up, and there would invariably be some sort of incident between us.

Needless to say when I intercepted a pass off him in a Challenge Cup semi-final, and went over for a try, his mood didn't exactly improve. It got even worse when I cracked him in one tackle, a real good one, and he was looking for revenge. The only problem was that he had clearly not realised who had hit him in the first place, because he absolutely pole-axed Saints prop Peter Shiels, proper laid him out and made a real mess of him. Barrie got done for that one and ended up getting suspended, Shielsy got a hell of a headache and I got away scot-free.

But with Barrie you knew that if you caught him, however he reacted on the field, he wouldn't spend hours moaning about it afterwards. Yes, he could dish it out, but he could also take it too, and not everyone was like that.

Some people seemed to enjoy whinging as part of their game.

There was one Test match against the Aussies at Old Trafford when I really wound up second-rower Gorden Tallis. He also happens to be one of the best and toughest guys I've ever played against. This time I had taken the ball in, and he was doing the usual pushing and shoving in the tackle, so as I got to my feet I stuck the head in. The next time we were in possession, he came steaming in to try and dish out a real big hit, tried to take out Chris Joynt, but he left a big gap because he was so pumped up, and Andy Farrell promptly shot straight through and scored.

You don't have to be one of the real big blokes to have a reputation as a tough guy, either. Andrew Johns is one of the most skilful I've ever seen, and the Aussie scrum half is rightly in the rugby league hall of fame as a previous Golden Boot winner, given to the world's greatest player.

But what Joey lacked in inches he more than made up for in the tackle, and I remember in that one-off summer Test how he really whacked a few of the British lads with his tackling. I know I felt a few off him that day, while on our own shores Bobbie Goulding was even smaller, but, bloody hell, could he pack a punch.

When I was first coming through at Warrington, they used to revel in their Wilderspool ground being known as 'the Zoo', because it was so tough for visiting teams. Nothing was ever said about roughing sides up – it was just something of an unwritten law at Warrington – and in my early days I was probably a bit too robust myself.

We played Saints in one of my early games, and I remember having a clash with Chris Joynt, who was to become my captain at Knowsley Road. Now that I'm a bit older and wiser, I wouldn't dream of being dirty against a player like that, some-one I respect so much. But back then I was out to make my mark

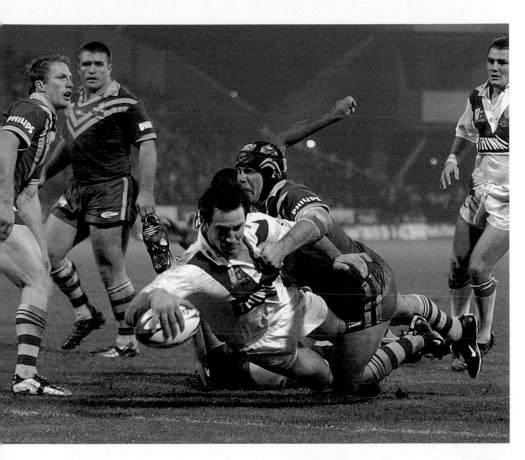

ROO'S A CLEVER BOY...
Reaching out to score for
Great Britain against Australia.

UP TO THE CHALLENGE...
Proudly showing the 2004
Challenge Cup to the Saints fans.

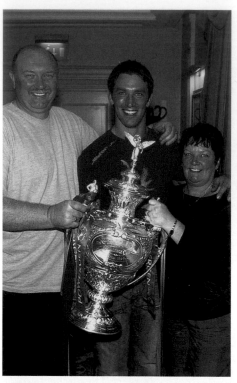

CUPPA CHEER…Mum and Dad get to grips with the Challenge Cup after our 2004 success.

NOBLE GESTURE…Coach Brian Noble made me so proud when he named me as Great Britain captain. Vice captain Jamie Peacock is on the right.

JUST FOR KICKS…Lining up a conversion for St Helens.

KING OF THE WORLD...Scoring a try against Brisbane Broncos in the
2007 World Club Challenge.

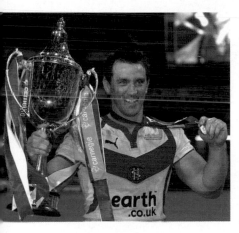

WINNER BY A SMILE...
Our World Club Challenge win
made it a memorable return to
action for yours truly.

SON SHINE...
Jake joins in the celebrations
in the Saints' dressing room.

HAPPY FAMILY…
Me and Lindsay celebrate
our new addition – Jake.

DOUBLE
TOPPER…
proudly showing
off my Man of
Steel trophies.

SUPER HEROES!... Lucy-Jo and Jake proudly show off their Spiderman outfits.

GLAD RAGS…Myself and Lindsay, about to head out for a formal night out.

SITTING PRETTY… Me, Lindsay, Jake and Boss.

SNOOKER LOOPY…Jake doesn't look too impressed with my cueing action.

THE GANG…The Sculthorpes get together. The couples are (from left) myself, Jake, Lucy-Jo and Lindsay, Lee, Lauren and Sally, Mum and Dad, Danny and Natalie.

PERFECT COUPLE...
Mum and Dad, who
gave us all such a great
grounding in life.

HAIR WE GO...
Me and Superwoman
(Lindsay) all set for
one of Saints' famous
fancy dress parties.

HIGH FLIERS…With Flight Sgt. Damien Clayton before the thrill of a lifetime at RAF Marham

FAMILY SUPPORT…The three most important people in my life – Lindsay, Jake and Lucy-Jo

and in that game, whenever he came near me I tried to whack him.

Eventually he had had enough, turned round and said: 'Oy, Sculthorpe. You've been with that fucking Paul Cullen too long.' Cul had a reputation for sailing a bit close to the wind when it came to discipline, and Joynty still reminds me of that game to this day. Fortunately I grew out of it, and the way the game's gone, the dirtier players are picked up the vast majority of the time.

I have to say that's much better for the sport as a whole. The game is so fast now, so much more physical than when I started. Any cheap shots tend to get spotted on video even if the referee doesn't see it, and anyone who persisted with it would end up being drummed out of the game. Fortunately there aren't too many nasty ones around any more. I can only think of one who likes to play the tough guy but he has very little to actually back it up. I'm keeping his name up my sleeve, because he's still playing in Super League, and I don't want to give him any more reason for trying to justify a tough-guy image – he doesn't really need one.

In those days at Wilderspool we used to love the fact that it was such a fearsome place. The atmosphere was always great: the fans must have been some of the noisiest in the game, and that gets the adrenalin pumping to start with. And there is nothing wrong with trying to turn your home ground into a fortress – that's something we want at St Helens. We had one prop called Mark Hilton who, while he was never a dirty player, never gave you less than 100 per cent. He was the sort of bloke who, if you asked him to run at a brick wall, would keep pounding away until he knocked the bloody thing down.

As a kid I did get carried away a bit, and got sent off a couple of times early on in my career with them. There was a big piece in the local paper one week, with the headline 'Bad Boy Paul', and chairman Peter Higham stopped us all talking to the local press for a bit. Mind you, those dismissals had come in successive games, so I could understand why the press were thinking I might be a bit of a loose cannon.

Fortunately those two dismissals remain the only ones of my career – although I have been put on report a few times. One of them came when I was in the Saints side that lost at Warrington the week before we were due at Twickenham for the Challenge Cup final in 2001. We were pretty awful that day, and I wasn't the only one in hot water, as Paul Newlove got a red card for flattening Toa Kohe-Love with a straight arm after being side-stepped.

My own indiscretion came on Warrington prop Danny Nutley, who I caught with a swinging arm when I steamed into a tackle. That incident was referred to the RL's disciplinary panel, and we both had a nervous wait to see if we'd be cleared to play in the final, where we beat Bradford.

I landed in trouble again after one match against Leeds, when I had a run-in with Ryan Bailey. He'd grabbed me after I played the ball and I retaliated by giving him a couple of digs. The referee didn't even see it because he was following play, and his touch judges missed the incident, too.

But Warrington coach Paul Cullen, the same man who had been such a roughhouse in his own playing days, was sum-marising for Sky Sports and made a big fuss about how you couldn't do things like that on a rugby field. He was right, of course, but it was a bit rich coming from him. Yet I suppose you could say he was just being pretty shrewd, because his side played Saints the following week and if he pointed something out that got an opponent ruled out of that match, then it was a job well done.

I got sin-binned on another occasion while on Great Britain duty, playing New Zealand in 1999. They had a giant prop forward called Joe Vagana, who had such a successful career with Bradford Bulls, and he was charging in. In one tackle I speared him into the ground – obviously not a legal tackle – and they weren't too happy about it. Neither was Logan Swann, who cracked me from behind. It all kicked off and I ended up having an all-in with Jarrod McCracken.

Off I went to the sidelines for ten minutes, and I still remember it well – it was worth getting sin-binned because I was so chuffed to have actually lifted Joe, he was such a size. It used not to make any difference who was in the New Zealand side – they always seemed to be bloody huge.

As far as my own big hits are concerned, probably the hardest I ever put on anyone was an Aussie prop called Adam Ross, who came over to play for London Broncos, as they were at the time. It was his very first game, and we hadn't been going that long when I caught him with an absolute pearler of a tackle. He was all over the place, ended up going off and never played for them again.

Dave Rotherham was involved with them at the time, and we ended up working together when he joined the Saints coaching set-up. He hadn't been with us that long when he came over before one game and said: 'I want you to put yourself about like that one you put on Adam Ross at London.' It had been years before, but he'd never forgotten it.

There was another incident with a London player called Mark Carroll, who was a big noise in Australia and a Test forward. He had some frightening run-ins with another giant over there called Paul Harragon, and the pair of them had a pretty awesome reputation. Saints were due to play them not long after Carroll had come to England, and he'd been shouting his mouth off in the newspapers beforehand. I remember the article, with the headline 'Northern Softies', which obviously went down well in our dressing room.

Someone made several copies, and they were stuck up all over the walls. We didn't need any motivation and Carroll himself had been around long enough to realise we'd be targeting him. Myself and Karle Hammond decided between us that straight from the kickoff we were going to smash him, and when he got the ball we made straight for him. Carroll knew what to expect, because as we arrived he ducked. The only thing was that he ducked straight into me, and our heads met with a hell of a collision. Thankfully for me, I was sweet, absolutely no problem at all. Carroll, on the other hand, had his head split open like a melon and I can still picture Karle standing over him and snarling: 'Who's a fucking northern softie now, hey?'

One of the bravest things I ever saw on a rugby field came when I was still only a kid, and one of the ball boys at the 1990 Challenge Cup final. Warrington, ironically, were up against Wigan, and I was running the sideline along with other members of the Oldham Schoolboys Under 13 side.

Not too long had gone when Warrington second-rower Bob Jackson caught stand off Shaun Edwards in the face fairly near the Wigan line. I don't think it was necessarily deliberate, but it left Shaun all over the place. He was a real mess and had fractured his eye socket. No one knew quite how serious it was at the time, but Shaun insisted on staying on, and went on to have a storming game and help his side to the cup.

Fortunately no one has ever caught me with such a bad one

that I've suffered anything similar, even though the problems with my knee and Achilles in recent years have been bad enough. I have suffered a broken jaw and fractured eye socket in the past, although neither of those were as bad as Shaun's. Mind you, it hasn't been for want of trying on our Dan's part. I think every tackle he's ever made on me has been filthy. He tries everything.

In one game against Wigan, he arrived as third man in the tackle and dropped his knees right on to my back. He knew exactly what he was doing, and I certainly never got any favours off him. The annoying thing was that, for all the video technology of recent seasons, he never seemed to get penalised either.

Yet if Shaun's performance at Wembley was the single bravest one I have ever seen on a pitch, the toughest player is definitely hooker Keiron Cunningham – and fortunately I don't have to tackle him too often, given that he plays alongside me at St Helens.

I knew Kez was hard before I joined Saints; I'd come up against him a few times already for Warrington. At half-time in one game before I moved, coach Darryl Van De Velde came into the dressing room absolutely steaming. Saints, as they tended to, were beating us again, and Kez was having a field day – he'd already run right through me on one occasion.

Darryl stormed in, fuming: 'That fucking Cunningham's wearing his underpants over his shorts, and has got a bloody big "S" on his chest. You're making him look like Superman. He's making you all look stupid so sort yourselves out.' In theory they were fine words, but talking about stopping Kez is one thing. Actually managing it is another entirely.

Kez goes out to leave his mark in every single tackle, not in a nasty way, just to let you know you've been hit good and hard.

He usually manages it as well. Mind you, we all want to be as physical as possible in the tackles. You don't go out there with the intention of maiming an opponent, just to get stuck in and try and make them less effective throughout the game.

What makes Keiron's fantastic performances even more incredible is that he, too, has suffered terrible injury problems over the years. He actually had the same micro-fracture operation on his knee, and also had to overcome a long-standing elbow problem which he really struggled with at one stage. When you are battling injuries for so long, you do begin to ask yourself if you'll ever be quite as effective again. Touch wood Kez has managed it so far and long may he do so.

He's someone I think every player would pick in their team – and I include the Aussie sides in that as well. They are never particularly quick out of the traps when it comes to praising British players, so the fact they even accepted him as the world's leading hooker is probably the best indication you can get. He's absolutely solid, but also has great pace in his locker to boot, to go with great vision. I owe many a try to him.

If he comes steaming for the line from close range I can't think of too many players in the world who would fancy trying to stop him – or actually manage to achieve it, either. Put it this way: if you could choose your opponent for tackling practice, Kez would be the last name you'd ever pick. Thank God Saints will never sell him!

17

Jokers Wild

I've lost count of the number of times I'm asked what it takes to make a career in rugby league. Some of the answers are pretty obvious – commitment, the right attitude, dedication, knowing you never stop learning. Plus, of course, a fair smattering of ability and being in the right place at the right time as a kid. Pretty soon after first joining Warrington I realised you needed another – a sense of humour.

If I had a quid for every time I've played a joke or been on the receiving end of someone taking the piss, I'm sure I'd have more money than I know what to do with. It was also obvious very early that if you dished it out, then you had to be prepared to take it as well.

One of the big problems early on at Warrington was killing time in between training sessions. We'd do one in the morning and another in the late afternoon, so you had to pass a good few hours in between. Myself and Jon Roper used to knock about together, and we thought it would be a good idea to buy one of those big water guns that seemed to be all the rage a few years back.

We headed off to Toys 'Я' Us in his little cabriolet, picked up a gun, filled it with water and set about finding some decent targets. He was driving and I'd have it poking out of the little side window, spraying passers-by as we scooted around. The big mistake we made was targeting Mark Jones as one of our victims. Jonesy, a huge prop forward who had joined us from Welsh rugby union, was a lovely bloke, with a great sense of humour. We must have caught him on a bad day.

We gave him a soaking, which the pair of us thought hilarious, but Mark went berserk. He demanded the gun off me and seeing the look in his eyes I meekly handed it over. We were convinced he was just going to get his own back, and got ready for a drenching. Instead he glared as us and snapped the bloody thing over his knee. It cost us £30 as well, so we knew who the winner was that day.

But if Ropes was in the thick of it with me at Warrington, when I went to Saints Chris Smith took over the mantle. Smiggy was a real lunatic, always up for a laugh, and – fair dos to him – on the receiving end of as much as he gave out. There was one game when Super League took the fixtures on the road, to try and spread interest in the sport, and we played Wigan down in Swansea. Afterwards we all went for a few drinks, and ended up having so many that Smiggy was absolutely trashed by the end of the night.

He was so bad that we had to carry him to his room, and that gave us a chance we weren't about to miss. When he was face down on the bed, we pulled his trollies down and filled his undies with all those coffee and chocolate drinks sachets you get in hotels. We even mashed a banana all over his backside, before finishing off by shaving off one of his eyebrows and one of his sideburns.

Come the next morning we were all down for breakfast when Smiggy appeared, looking really sheepish. We were expecting a real volley from him, but he hadn't even seen the damage we'd done to his face. Everyone was taking the mick, and of course the whole story came out. But instead of going mad, he just reacted with total relief. We realised why when he told us: 'Thank Christ for that – I thought I'd shat myself!'

It was clear he would be looking for revenge, and wouldn't stop until he'd got it. I didn't have long to wait, either. We had signed for Saints around the same time, and after going out for a few drinks one night we both stayed over with Damian Smith, an Aussie team-mate.

I had bought a new Peugeot cabriolet, which I left outside Damo's house, and Smiggy wasn't going to miss that chance. Without me knowing, he got my car and went off for a razz around the area. He told me: 'I've just driven your car all the way to Birch Services, on the M62, and back with the top down, going through every speed camera I could find as fast as possible. Oh, and if you're going to hide your keys anywhere, choose somewhere better than your shoes, because that's the first place I looked.'

I knew he was telling the truth because the car was parked in a different place from where I'd left it, and, yes, I know now that I should have been more imaginative in finding a hiding place for the keys, but fortunately I never got a single speeding ticket. I can only think there must have been a hell of a lot of cameras with no film in them, because I know damn well he'd have put his foot down when he saw them.

One of the reasons Saints have been so successful is because the lads are such a close-knit unit, and that stemmed from the fact we were mates away from the club as well as on the pitch.

We socialise together as well as playing together, and there have been countless days out when all we seemed to have done is laugh.

As memorable as any was the Saturday we all went on a pub crawl on bikes to celebrate Adey Gardner's new baby being born. We'd played on the Friday night, and because we had the next day off someone suggested we do something different. First thing in the morning I jumped in the car and shot off to try and find a few cheap bikes, the crappiest ones I could find, and ended up getting half a dozen or so for about £30.

Lindsay dropped them off at the Eagle and Child in Rainford where we were all meeting and it was a case of grabbing what you could. Willie Talau ended up with the best – a woman's bike with the biggest wheels you've ever seen. He only needed to pedal once and he'd shoot about a hundred yards, and he was miles in front of everyone else. The more blind drunk we got, the funnier it was and it just became a free-for-all in the end.

We'd go from pub to pub, and everyone was trying to throw their drink down as quickly as possible, to get outside first and get the pick of the bikes. Not that there was a great deal to choose from in terms of top-quality machines – that was proved when half of them were knackered before we'd gone too far.

Leon Pryce had come along in his car because he had to be somewhere that night – obviously he was leaving off the booze and just coming for the craic – and his wheels came in very handy up one steep hill in Billinge. I grabbed on to the back of his boot and I absolutely flew it. In the end I decided enough was enough and chucked the bike, jumped in with Leon and got a lift the rest of the way.

I'll never forget driving through Crank and seeing James Roby walking along, pushing his bike, covered in blood. He'd really been going for it, come flying off and looked like he'd been ten rounds with Mike Tyson. By the end of the day there were bikes all over the area – people were just chucking them. They were in trees, dumped at the side of the road, everywhere. I drove through Rainford the next day and there seemed to be bikes around every corner.

But perhaps the most comical incident of all happened when I came across a nutritionist called Mick Sutherland, a man I met for the first time in the Great Britain camp in 2002. I don't know who brought him in to start with, but this fellow walked in, introduced himself and started telling us all these tales about how he had worked with the top Great Britain athletes. He was going to oversee all our nutritional needs and, to be honest, what he told us did seem to make sense and he did seem to help all the guys.

When we got back to Saints, all the lads from international duty were talking about Mick in glowing terms, and Basil ended up bringing him into Knowsley Road to work with us at club level. He had us giving urine samples, the whole works, and would come in and tell each of us which particular food disagreed with us. He told us he had his own lab at home – in hindsight I think he probably meant his pet dog.

He was a real mystery man, but seemed to know his stuff and I got on a treat with him. We got supplements – all legal – off him, and looking back now maybe some of it was psychological on his part. But we were all taken in, especially by his tales of working with such great athletes.

The only one who was a bit suspicious was Stan Wall, the Saints kitman, following a conversation he had as we headed off for warm-weather training one pre-season in La Santa, in Lanzarote. Mick told him he'd been there thirty-seven times with the athletics team, and when we checked into our rooms Stan told him we were all going to meet up in the Green Bar. Mick said he didn't know where it was, but there were only two bloody bars in the whole place and everyone met in that one. Stan said: 'You've been here thirty-seven times and you don't know where the Green Bar is? You can't know this place.'

Mick insisted it was only because the athletes were never allowed into the bar, but that was crap – every sports team gets at least one night out, so Stan was a bit wary; but we were all none the wiser. The lads who didn't live in St Helens used to get the coach to away games at Birch Services and Mick came along with us. One day he was telling me about how much money he'd made from the athletes being so successful, claiming he'd been given £87,000 in bonuses. I had no reason to disbelieve him at the time, and thought that was bloody good going.

He told us that he was also brought in to try and get Scottish skier Alain Baxter's Olympic medal back as well, when he was stripped of it for taking a banned substance at the 2002 Salt Lake City Winter Olympics. Mick said he had to fly to Paris for the hearing, and he was that credible that none of us suspected a thing.

It only came to light a couple of days after the end of the 2003 season, when all the players were out on their traditional 'Mad Monday', which is exactly what the name suggests – a day when the whole squad basically goes out and gets bladdered. We were sitting in the Black Bull pub, near Knowsley Road, when my mobile went and it was a very worked-up Basil on the other end.

He said: 'Scully, you will never believe this, but Sean McGuire's had Mick in and sacked him. The British Olympic Association have never heard of him, and it turns out he's a fireman from Bolton.' When Mick, who was only working part-time for Saints, couldn't get in, he'd said it was because he was shooting all over the place with his work for other organisations. In truth it was because he was working bloody shifts at the fire station – it was pure comedy; you couldn't have made it up. Anyway, he'd ended up getting rumbled, and he was out. The funny thing was that we played Castleford in our next game and got beaten – everyone in the dressing room was saying we should bring back the fireman. As cons go, it has to be up there with the best ever, because every one of us fell for it hook, line and sinker.

That was my second example of how things can work for you psychologically, after a previous experience with a guy called Dave Berry. He was assistant coach at Rose Bridge when I went there, and is actually a very close friend of the family. Dave was really into his psychology, and spent thousands going on courses.

As he was just beginning, he asked if I'd be prepared to help him with a bit of practice, which obviously couldn't do me any harm either. He was obsessed with imagery, where you visualise being successful, or whatever, and he certainly seemed to be good. The first year I worked with him was in 2001 – and I ended the season winning the Man of Steel award. At the start of the next year, he told me I had to visualise winning it again – and once again I did. I couldn't knock his results, though.

Psychology is something you cannot really do in a team environment; it's much better with a one-on-one situation. We tried it twice with Great Britain, but that was just never going to happen with James Lowes in the room. Jimmy was a top hooker, who always had an answer or a quick witticism. So when we were all lying on our backs with our eyes closed, trying to picture this or that, he was chirping away and cracking one-liners. Needless to say it wasn't something we tried after those two attempts.

But as much as rugby league can put a smile on your face, it can just as easily leave it stained with tears. Obviously there are going to be injuries along the way; everyone expects that from a collision sport like this. Unfortunately there are certain times when things go beyond the norm, and sadly I have seen that happen far too often for my liking.

One of the finest full backs in the Super League era has been Steve Prescott, who was within a whisker of winning £10,000 for the first hat-trick in a Wembley final in the 1996 Challenge Cup final, before Robbie Paul did so later in the same game. I played with Prekky for Great Britain Academy and then England, and he was always a really good bloke. Tragically he has been suffering from stomach cancer, which was absolutely devastating news and put everything in perspective.

Another who was rocked by something totally unconnected with anything on a rugby field was Mike Gregory, the former Warrington and Great Britain skipper. Greg was assistant coach to Shaun McRae when I joined Saints, and a top, top fellow. As a player he had been an absolute legend, and every rugby fan can remember him charging half the length of the field to clinch a famous Test win for Britain in Australia in 1988. Greg's coaching career in charge of Wigan was cut short when he was struck down with a debilitating disease after working abroad, and he has been fighting a hell of a battle since. He's another who is never far from my thoughts.

But perhaps the one which was closest to home was my good mate Ian Knott, who I first played with in the Under Nines at Oldham Juniors. We both went to Warrington and used to travel in together, along with other lads from our area like Iestyn

Harris, Chris Eckersley and John Hough. In those days even the journey in was a real laugh, all of us larking about down the M62 as we headed to Wilderspool for training.

Knotty moved on to Wakefield and Leigh, but was eventually forced to retire through injury. He ended up having his three bottom vertebrae fused together, and he has to spend most of his time on his back, so obviously can't work. That's clearly terrible news for anyone, but I think it probably hits you even harder when you've been so active and earned your living in sport. So for as many laughs in the game, there are plenty of tears as well. It's at times like that when you realise what the really important things in life are. Good luck to all of you, lads.

18

Nearest and Dearest

When you consider the massive part rugby league has played in my life, perhaps it should come as no surprise that I first met Lindsay through the sport. Never mind any of the team or individual honours I have won since – that was the day I really struck it lucky.

I was only fifteen at the time and had just signed for Wigan Rose Bridge, who were coached by her dad, Ian McCulloch. It was near the end of the season, and I got talking to Lindsay at the club's presentation night. Nothing deep, just a quick hello and a smile, but I had seen enough to know she was someone special.

At the time I was still living at home with Mum and Dad, and became a regular visitor to Ian's house. We used to train on a Saturday, with a game on the Sunday, so rather than making two trips Ian would put me up for the night.

Over the months I got to know Lindsay really well, together with her mum, Eileen, and sister Lisa. I'd had girlfriends going through school, but nothing too serious. I think I was going out with someone when I first met her, to be honest. But despite getting to know her more and more, and fancying her more and more as well, we still hadn't actually gone out. In fact she was the one who asked me out in the end – or at least she tried to.

Lindsay phoned me at Mum and Dad's but I wasn't there. She told me later that she'd spent ages plucking up courage to ask, but as soon as my parents said she'd called, I was straight on the phone. She invited me to a party for her grandma and grand-dad's wedding anniversary, and it was a great night. Obviously I knew her family really well, and me and Lindsay got along like a house on fire.

I was hooked, and we went out regularly after that. I was at Warrington by now, but still living in Oldham, and would drive over, collect her from where she worked as a pharmaceutical assistant, and we'd go for meals, to the pictures or just stay in at her folks'. We never really went to pubs – well, strictly speaking we were both still too young – and would have a whale of a time together.

When I decided I would buy a house, Lindsay played a big role in coming to view them with me, and had a major input into what I'd get. In fact she was the one who eventually picked the keys up for me in February 1996, because I was away at the World Nines with England. I was only eighteen and Lindsay a year younger, but we had discussed her moving in, and that just seemed to be the next natural step in our relationship. I know we were still only teenagers, but we were the best of mates, and because I'd spent so much time with her family, I knew what I was getting!

When I got selected for Great Britain's Oceania tour at the end of '96, we decided that Lindsay would move in as soon as I got back. It wouldn't have been fair to expect her to do so earlier. It would have meant her being stuck in Oldham for six weeks on her own while I was away on international duty. Obviously she knew my mum and dad really well, but it would still have meant her being away from friends and family as she couldn't drive, so we decided to wait. As much as I loved getting that first chance of a Great Britain tour, I couldn't get home quickly enough to begin my new life with Linds.

As young as we were, we had both been brought up really well, and we slotted into life together straight away. We could both look after ourselves, because her parents were like mine – we could both work a washing machine, cook, iron, the works, and life couldn't have been better. It was wonderful, and no man could ever wish for a better wife or mother to their kids. If anything she's over the top now, because she's always on the go. I end up having a dig at her sometimes, saying: 'Just come and sit down with me for a bit', when I get back from training or wherever. But she's always doing something, either around the house or, more usually, for the kids. She's just awesome.

The only thing she doesn't excel at is drinking – she's rubbish! Even now if we go to a do, she'll have three or four and that's enough. Maybe I shouldn't complain, because it's a lot cheaper than if she got through a whole bottle.

We had spoken about having children at some stage, and when she became pregnant with Jake the feeling was like nothing I'd ever experienced. I came home from training one day and could see straight away that something was on her mind. She didn't know how to tell me because she wasn't sure how I'd react, but I was absolutely buzzing; it was just the best. When Jake was born that was just unbelievable – I never even knew emotions like that existed.

He arrived at the end of a week which had seen Ian Millward take over as Saints coach, on the night of his first game since being appointed, at Hull on a Friday evening. Lindsay had started having pains two days earlier, and when we went to the hospital the midwife told us they thought the baby would be born that night. The pains were coming and going, so they decided to keep her in because things were about to happen. Friday came, and still nothing, and in the end the doctor told me I'd be okay to play – it's murder getting Lindsay to part with these babies.

I dashed straight back from the match and at just gone midnight I got a call at home saying that she had started. Myself and Eileen, who was staying at my house, raced over and both went in for the birth. Jake eventually arrived at 10.18 a.m. on 18 March 2000, and I cried my eyes out. The fact we'd had a boy was even better. Don't get me wrong, I was just delighted that they were both fit and healthy. But I think if you asked any bloke what sex he would choose for his first-born, and 99 per cent would go for a lad. I've got two brothers, so it was all I'd really known, and having my own son to play with was brilliant.

Me and Eileen were both in bits in the delivery room; we were all over each other sobbing buckets. I managed to get it back together, but then fell apart again when I went outside to tell Mum and Dad. I tell you what – I could win Man of Steel every year for the rest of my life, win the double every season, win the Ashes with Great Britain, but lump them all together and they still wouldn't come remotely close to how I felt then. I had a beautiful girlfriend and now a gorgeous baby boy as well. Surely life couldn't get any better than this.

I suppose no one knows how they'll adapt to being a parent until it actually happens, but we both loved it straight away. Lindsay was absolutely brilliant with him, and the fact the pair of us are so close to our families made life easier too. We all get on really well, to the point that if anyone ever kicked one of us, the whole lot would limp.

I had known for ages that I wanted to marry Lindsay – it was something we both knew – and this was the right time. Jake had a different surname from his mum, and we wanted that to change. Mind you, I don't think I ever really proposed to her, certainly not the old asking permission of her dad, and going down on one knee. I gave her the engagement ring on Christmas Day in 2001, as we were unwrapping the presents.

I'd wrapped everything up, put them in a big Christmas sack and she'd opened the lot. Then I reached in and said: 'Oh, I've forgotten this, there's one left in the bottom', and chucked it at her. She burst into tears, and I had to ask: 'Is that a yes, then?' I know we'd spoken about marriage before, but it was still a fantastic moment when she agreed. I left most of the preparations to Lindsay and the women, but helped out when I was asked – or told. We had always said we'd have the full hit, because Linds is a real girly girl and had wanted that sort of wedding since she was a kid.

We set the date for 4 January 2003, at Park Hall, in Charnock Richard, and it was everything we'd both dreamed of. The night before we decided to go out for a couple in Wigan. There was myself, our Lee and Danny, Lisa's fiancé Paul, Lindsay's dad Ian and his mate Terry, plus Longy from Saints. We were staying at the hotel that night, but just thought we'd have a quiet one before the big day – some hope. It turned into a crazy evening. Something happened to one of them which turned into a full-on brawl and the night eventually finished at 4 a.m.

Fortunately I didn't have too much of a banging head the next morning – or should I say later that morning – and after a swim and a decent breakfast I was all set. A couple of early beers helped settle the nerves, although they didn't exactly help me to hold it together at the reception. The one thing I had been dreading ever since I proposed was making the groom's speech, and in the end it was pretty non-existent. I knew I couldn't talk about my family, say all the relevant thank yous and talk about how beautiful Lindsay looked without my lower lip going, and so it proved. It must be one of the shortest wedding speeches on record, because my arse went and I got a bit emotional.

Danny and Lee shared the best man's role, and their speeches were the exact opposite of mine. They just bounced off each other, one saying something and the other coming in with his own bits. It really was unbelievable and when they'd finished everyone was trying to get them to do it again, it was so good. From there it was on to the night do, also at Park Hall, and the next day me, Lindsay and Jake flew out to Gran Canaria for a week. I couldn't get any longer off, because of St Helens' pre-season training, so it wasn't the longest honeymoon ever, but it was still really memorable.

As soon as we were back I was off for warm-weather training, which was rough. Even now I don't like going away and leaving the family, but then it was even harder. Whereas once I'd be off with Saints or Great Britain, and see it as just part of the job, since Jake's birth it was a nightmare. I still remember how low I felt when Britain had ten days in America before the 2000 World Cup. That was the first time I'd really been away from him, and I found it incredibly tough.

We knew Jake wasn't going to be an only child, and on 11 November 2003, at 5.27 p.m., he had a sister when Lucy-Jo was born – and it was just as incredible a feeling as before. I was actually in camp with Great Britain at the time, at the Worsley Marriott hotel, preparing for the series against New Zealand,

and had spent the day in bed because I felt like I was dying with a really bad throat infection. Dr Chris Brooks was up and down from my room all day, and had me on a drip trying to get me right in time for the Tests.

Then the phone call came that Lindsay needed to go into hospital because things were starting to happen, so I bombed it home. It was lucky that I'd actually been given the day off from training, because it was just a case of jumping straight in the car and racing back. Once again there was no need to rush, because it was another long labour – what was it I said about Lindsay being a bugger for parting with these babies? It must have been a weird scene in her room: she was lying on the bed and I spent most of my time lying on the floor because I felt so rough.

Once again Eileen was in with us and once again we were both in pieces when Lucy arrived. Me and Lindsay didn't know what we were having for either child – we wanted the surprise – but this time I did want a girl. I think everyone wants one of each and we were lucky enough to get it – and what a star Lucy is.

We actually spent the first six months of her life living in rented accommodation in Hindley, in Longy's old house. We'd sold the place in Oldham and bought the new property, but they hadn't finished building the house. Longy had bought one down the same road, and his was ready, so he was in. He'd part-exchanged his old place, and because our builders were running a bit late, we moved in there for a while. It was fine, but there's nothing like your own home, and it was a great day when we were eventually able to move in.

So now we were a family complete, and no man could have had more. Gorgeous wife, two fantastic kids, and a really, really close relationship with both sets of relations. Jake and Lucy are both growing up into lovely children and money couldn't buy what I had.

Jake is really getting into his sport now; it's all he wants to do when he gets back each day. He's doing very well at school, but the minute he's home on goes the football or rugby kit, including the boots, and he's into the back garden kicking or throwing a ball around. He's playing rugby for Orrell St James, and football for the school. In fact he's already picked up his first trophy, when they won the Wigan Schools Year Two Cup in a five-a-side tournament at the JJB.

I say it myself, but he's a lovely lad, so pleasant to everyone. I think sport does help give you a sense of values, sharing, teamwork and the like, but Lindsay deserves so much praise for how the children have turned out. Obviously we both have a big input, but Linds is different class.

Jake's so good with Lucy-Jo and it really pulls on your heartstrings when you see the way he looks out for her. He is so protective towards his sister, and she is so advanced because of what she learns from him. He's taught her so much, but I think it's probably true that everyone's second child is more advanced because of what they pick up off their older brother or sister. Jake is fantastic, though, in terms of how he looks after her. There are four years between them, but you never hear him saying he doesn't want to play with her because she's a baby.

For her part, Lucy-Jo is a real character, comical and independent. There was one time at Asda when we turned our backs for two minutes and lost sight of them. They were only in the next aisle but Jake was in tears, because he thought he'd lost us. Lucy-Jo was just standing there with her bag of sweets, without a care in the world. She wants to do everything herself, rather than have it done for her. She's already into her bags and shoes, and is forever putting on Lindsay's make-up.

They have both reached the stage where they know what I do for a living, even though they still find a few things confusing. If we're in the players' bar after a game, and fans are coming up asking for autographs, Jake will say to Lindsay: 'Mummy, why do all those people want my dad to write things for them all the time', or 'What's my dad doing on television?'

But that's exactly how I want it. I'm just Dad, not Paul Sculthorpe, rugby league player, and that's how it will always be. Jake has started to come to training with me whenever he can, in the holidays and suchlike, and knows all the players. I think half the lads are waiting for him now when they know he's off school, and they are always off kicking a ball around or playing darts with them. So all in all, parenthood is everything I imagined it would be, and then more beyond. I realise I'm a bloody lucky bloke. I really couldn't have wished for anyone better than Lindsay, she is absolutely brilliant. I've never known anyone with a bad word against her. When I was laid up recovering from my knee injury, she really looked after me and put up with loads. And it was the same when I damaged my Achilles in June – it must have been like having three kids for her at times. She's had to put up with a lot from me, but always stood by me. Don't I know how much she really does mean to me.

Someone once said to me that you know how good your home life is from how you feel when you're walking up to the front door to go home. Well, I can't get my key in the lock quickly enough, because it means everything to me and that will never change.

I've mentioned all those who have influenced and helped my

career since I was a kid, but none of them come close to Mum and Dad. As a child, I was never simply packed off to play: they always came everywhere with me – in fact Dad still does. He's been really closely involved in everything I've done throughout my career, and was in again at Saints the last time I was holding contract talks. I go to him for advice on everything, whether it's looking at a business opportunity, buying property, anything. As far as I'm concerned, if I could only ever go to one person for help and advice again, it would be him.

Mum and Dad gave all three of us the perfect upbringing, and – just as we've tried to instil into Jake and Lucy-Jo – we all knew right from wrong. Of course there would be the usual little falling outs that every family experiences, and there were times we'd be stomping upstairs to our room and cursing under our breath. But none of us would have ever dreamt of swearing in front of Mum and Dad because we had so much respect for them as kids, and that's true to this day.

They have given us all so much love and we never wanted for anything. I'm not suggesting we were spoiled, because we all had to work for what we got, but we couldn't have asked for a better upbringing. I got my tellings off the same as every kid, but never fell out with them once. We all got a great grounding in life, and Lindsay had the same from her folks. I only hope we can bring our children up the same way.

Growing up as the middle one of three brothers, there was always going to be the occasional scrap or argument. But when it came to anyone from outside the family, myself, Lee and Danny would always be together. If anyone had a go at one of us, they'd have another two to contend with. That happened once with three brothers from another family, funnily enough the same age and difference between them as us. I can't remem-

ber which one of us they had offended; I can't even remember
their real names. What I can remember is that they only did it
the once.

They were dead legs. They weren't interested in sport, they
weren't bothered about getting good grades and a decent job
from school, and they were only keen on causing trouble. They
lived on the same street as us in Royton, went to the same school
as well, but were never going to be mates.

They were a real bunch of scruffs, and we knew them as the
'duffel-coat gang' because they always wore these horrible
brown things. Anyway, they'd done something to one of us, so
we all headed off to find them. I was about eleven, Lee three
years older and our Danny just nine. Not that that had any
affect on anything, because, knowing Dan, he'd have been the
first one in. He's always been able to look after himself, and has
never needed me or Lee to act as his minder. These three lads
were hanging around outside when we arrived, and we knocked
seven bells out of them. Not surprisingly, we never heard a peep
out of them again.

Of the three of us, Lee was always the craziest, while I am the
most laid back by a mile. Anyone who ever saw Lee play rugby
league would tell you the same; he's a total madman. But he was
also the most skilful of the three by a long way, and if you ask
anyone around Waterhead they still say the same. If he had had
a mind for it, he could have gone right to the top.

He came through at a slightly different time to me, and
although he played a lot of rugby for the school and Waterhead,
I think it was more of a social thing for Lee, to be with his mates.
I have no doubt that if he had taken it more seriously, he would
have had a brilliant career in the game. I never ever played
against him – in fact I never played on the same side either – and,

seeing how he was, I thank God he was never an opponent. He was a stand off, and not one for charging the ball in like me and our Dan. He had too many brains for that. Half back isn't a position you usually associate with the real scrappers, but, bloody hell, he could fight.

Lee was actually offered a full-time deal by Halifax, just as the sport was really taking off, but declined the chance. But by then he was already progressing in his job, and stuck with that. He works with air-conditioning units, he's a sheet-metal worker, and has risen up with his company to the point where he's doing really well now. I've never known anyone to work harder, whether it is in his job or doing stuff at home – he's got an attitude second to none.

Unfortunately he works away a lot of the time in the week, so I don't see as much of him as I would like, but we still speak regularly on the phone and we're still incredibly close. He still lives in Oldham and is married, to Sally, and has two lovely girls in Lauren and Lily. His days off fall at the weekend, when we usually have a game, while I get time off in the week, which makes it a little more awkward to link up, because obviously his free time is spent with Sally and the girls. I have known her for over ten years and she's a great girl – another who's like a sister to me.

With our Dan, though, it's a bit different. I see him virtually every day, because he only lives five hundred yards from my house, and as kids we did play in the same side. For a long time I always seemed to be playing a year above my age, but when I dropped down to lads the same as me at Under 15, Dan was a team-mate. He, like me, tended to play in a higher age group, and when the chance finally arose it was great to line up alongside him.

It was certainly a lot safer than playing *against* him, because he always likes to let me know he's around – that's as nice a way of putting it as I can. I couldn't be closer to our Dan, but anyone who saw us playing on opposite teams would never think we were brothers. He always goes looking for me, and it's probably the same with me. I don't think anyone whacks me harder than Dan, and I do try to give him a big one myself. The only difference is that I do it legally, while he bends the rules now and again – but whatever happens on the pitch stays there when the final whistle goes, and nothing is ever carried into home life.

We had plenty of run-ins when we were growing up, and I always seemed to come off worst, even when I was the innocent one – which was most of the time. There was an occasion, during one of our many fights, when he'd pissed me off and I went to stick one on him. Unfortunately he ducked and I hit the wall full on. It was the week before a big Under 15 county game, and I ended up having a pot stuck on my hand. I'd depressed my knuckle, and it looked doubtful if I'd make the game at one stage. In the end I took it off myself beforehand, so I didn't miss out. I've been trying to get our Dan back ever since, but not managed it.

I seemed to spend much of my childhood collecting various bangs and scrapes, and that incident with Danny was just one of them. When we were young, there was a chippy in a row of shops in a little courtyard. There was a little flagged area in the middle, and we used to ride our bikes around the outside, timing ourselves to see who was the fastest. I was absolutely bombing around when Lee came out of the chip shop and I crashed straight into him. I came flying off, hit my head on the corner of the flagging and split my head like a melon. The Chinese owner came running out of the shop, took me home with a tea towel over my head, and it was straight off to hospital for twenty stitches.

On another occasion my mate was giving me a 'fronty' on his bike – you sit on the crossbar while he pedals – and we were racing down the road when his wheel went straight into a grid. The wheels jammed and the bike stopped dead, but I went sailing over and smashed my face into the handlebars, losing my two front teeth in the process. Dad was in the bath when we got home, and they just plonked me in with him – turning the water bright red.

Then there was the day we decided on a change, and had a game of British bulldog, instead of the usual football or rugby. The streets were a bit quieter then, so there was no risk of being run over, but that still didn't prevent me from making another trip to hospital. I was legging it across the road, but tripped over the kerb and went head first into the wall. Another cut head, blood everywhere, and another set of stitches promptly inserted.

If our Dan had connected with half the shots he's swung at me as a professional, I'd probably have had more stitches in me than the underwear in the knicker factory on *Coronation Street*. It started the first time we played against each other – in fact I think it was actually his debut for Wigan. He was still living in Oldham with Mum and Dad at the time, and I went round to pick him up and drive him to the JJB Stadium. I parked up and he headed in to join the Wigan lads, while I waited for the Saints bus to arrive – and Dan then seemed to take every opportunity looking to stick one on me. Nothing's changed much over the years as far as that goes, either.

We made a pact very early in our careers that we would never speak about the game beforehand when we were playing against each other. He wouldn't ask anything about what the St Helens team would be, and I wouldn't try and get any information about Wigan from him. I think our dad absolutely hated those weeks, because he lives and breathes rugby league, but on the occasions his sons were in opposition he couldn't discuss it with anyone.

When people ask me what the greatest memories are from my career, I always say that picking up the Challenge Cup as Saints captain at the Millennium Stadium in 2004 is up there with any of them. If our Dan is in the same room I always make sure I give him a little smile. It was his first final as a professional, but not the greatest moment of his career, even though I maintain to this day that he turned in such a great performance that he didn't deserve to be on the losing side.

Maybe my more laid-back attitude comes from the people I was coached by as a youngster. Lindsay's dad Ian really helped me in the two years I played under him at Rose Bridge. He has always been like a best mate, rather than simply my father-in-law, and I know I can talk to him about any subject under the sun. He was helped out by a guy called Billy Halliwell, whose son Martin became a really close friend, too. Me and Martin came through the ranks together and still keep in touch to this day.

For all I had decided I wanted to be a professional rugby player at a very early age, my schooling never really suffered because of it. I wasn't one of those who would spend the whole lesson staring out of the window and daydreaming about the time I could get a ball in my hands, however much I loved it. I was pretty easy-going and never in trouble that much, but I really used to look forward to break and lunchtimes when I would charge around playing football with my mates. You can do a bit too much rugby, probably could even at that age, so it was good to do something different – even though I never stood out at football that much. There was plenty of time for rugby league in PE, in the school team and with the various other clubs I played for over the years.

That was how plenty of my spare time was spent after school as well. I was never one for knocking around the streets at night; it was sport first, second and third for me. The others could hang about on the corners if they wanted; I was more interested in getting down to Waterhead Park to have a game.

It was the same story when some of the other lads started to discover beer. I already knew what I wanted from life and knew what would help get me there – and what wouldn't – so in that respect I never really saw it as a case of missing out or making a sacrifice.

I wasn't one of those who would go around preaching to his mates, or acting the martyr, though, because I've always had the opinion that whatever they want to get involved in is up to them – it would never stop me being their friend. There was a time when a couple of them started using drugs, nothing really heavy, just a bit of weed now and again. I remember walking home from school with some mates when I was about fifteen, and one of them had a joint. I still recall saying to him: 'Don't blow any of that shit near me', and I still feel the same way now. That's why becoming Rugby League Ambassador for UK Sport means so much to me, because of its close links with the anti-drugs campaign. In fact all the things I'm involved in, like being Merseyside's ambassador against racial hatred, are close to my heart.

Anyway, all my mates knew that I would never touch drugs even then, so it was never really an issue. Having said that, there was one day when one mate, just arsing around, did blow smoke in my direction. He had a block of weed and was saying to me: 'Go on, Scully – just try this.' It was only a joke, but he didn't find it funny when I grabbed it off him and chucked it down the grid. He'd probably spent a month's pocket money on it, but although I wasn't bothered about what they were getting into, I wasn't having it forced on me.

I know you hear about plenty of sportsmen getting dragged into the drugs culture when they are at the top of their profession, but it has never cropped up in my life. No one has ever suggested it – I think they know they'd be wasting their time – and because I moved over to the Wigan area I tend to knock about with other rugby league lads. None of them is into drugs, and no one would be crazy enough to come up to a gang of professional rugby players and try and force that stuff on them.

I was never a trouble-maker, just a fairly quiet kid who got on with it, and I ended up coming out of school with six grade Cs and two grade Ds in my GCSEs. Maybe I could have done better, who knows, but I wasn't into spending hours studying. Whenever I had tests or exams, the revision would always be done at the last minute, but I still did okay.

Of all the subjects maths was probably my best, I just seemed to click with that particular one. I must have got it from Dad, because he is good at it, too. It's the same even now when Jake does his homework. I can do it straight away – although seeing he's only seven, maybe that's not something to boast about! I always had a decent amount of common sense, and I think that's half the battle with your school work. But I established my goals very early, and they all involved rugby league – probably a bit too much, if I'm honest. If I had a really tough game on the Sunday, I probably wouldn't be at my best on a Monday morning.

I had no particular fall-outs with the teachers (apart from the odd one with Mr Broadfoot, as mentioned earlier) and – as you would probably expect – was closer to the ones who taught PE than the rest. There was one called Bill Ainsworth who got me out of a couple of sticky situations with other teachers when my rugby took over at times. He's still a huge rugby league fan and, even when I was a kid, he could see that I had a decent amount of ability and wanted me to go on to better things.

When he left, Steve Craythorne took over, and I actually bumped into him a few years after I'd left, when I was out in Oldham. The funny thing is that even though I'm heading into my thirties now, I still call them all sir whenever our paths cross.

It was exactly the same with the old town team teachers, Fred Laughton and Iain MacCorquodale, who had a successful career with the likes of Whitehaven and Workington, where he became their record points and goal scorer. Iain went on to work as a travel agent with a guy called Dave Whitehead, and actually sorted out mine and Lindsay's holiday last year. He was on the phone saying he'd got this and that for us, and I was at the other end replying: 'Yes, sir, thanks, sir.' Iain got to know Mum and Dad well, too, and them and Danny met him in Barcelona, when they were over for a Super League game against Catalans Dragons. Until he died, Fred also kept a very close eye on my career as it developed.

Most of the boozy nights out I have tend to involve the lads from St Helens, and there have been quite a few over the years. There's nothing better than sitting in a beer garden in the sun with all the lads, then kicking on for a night out. Then there have been the countless fancy-dress parties that Basil would organise to welcome the new guys.

Me and Lindsay still love going to clubs, too, but that is a lot less frequent than it used to be when we were kids. To be honest, we probably don't go out as much as we should, but then again we both love being at home. We both hate being away from Jake and Lucy-Jo, Lindsay especially, and we love just going for meals or family days out – usually to the zoo when it's left to the kids.

I still keep in touch with a few of the mates I had as a youngster, too, especially a guy called Wes Rogers. I first met him through rugby league, when I was about ten, and we've been as thick as thieves ever since. He was very dedicated to the sport even as a kid, and we really helped each other out training-wise in the early days of our careers. We'd constantly be in the gym, pushing each other to the limit, and he went on to play for Widnes in the old First Division, before the days of Super League. There was no one more dedicated than Wes, and if success in rugby was basely purely on effort and commitment, he would have gone right to the top.

His mum and dad, Pauline and Alan, became good family friends and Alan loves nothing better than talking rugby league whenever we catch up – which admittedly isn't nearly often enough. They took me on holiday with them as a kid, and the time we spent in Portugal when I was fourteen is still a very warm memory for me.

Probably my closest friend at school itself was a guy called Christian Wheeler, who I first met at the age of nine or ten at Watersheddings Junior School. We moved to Counthill together, and we played in the same school and county teams, usually as captain and vice-captain. We even went to college together, but then I gave it up after six months because I was going full time at Warrington and putting everything into my rugby league. He's another who still lives in Oldham, but we haven't caught up for ages.

At St Helens we are fortunate in that all the lads get on superbly, and there has never really been a problem with cliques. Keiron Cunningham, who came into the pro ranks around the same time, has been my weights partner for years and we're obviously very close. I also see a lot of Sean Long, who lives a couple of houses away. Jason Hooper, Paul Wellens and Jon Willkin are others I'm close to.

Jon Roper was the one I linked up with more than any other when I was finding my way at Warrington, and we still keep in touch, now he's back in Cumbria, on the coaching staff at Workington. Craig Barker was another close pal from that neck of the woods. I met him when I was fifteen, and in the BARLA Under 18 team that played the Junior Kiwis. Butch, as everyone has always called him, is a real character and it was an honour when he invited me to open his rugby league shop, Tryzone, in Workington last year.

These days I'm lucky enough to have various sponsors, but when I first started out it wasn't something that was even considered. I used to get my stuff from a rugby league shop run by Malcolm Brown in Ashton-in-Makerfield, and he was another who really looked after me. He got me my first ever sponsorship deal with Mizuno, and kept me kitted out in gear for ages. I just happened to call in to his shop one day and he surprised me with the news that they wanted to take me on.

In fact when I broke through at Warrington, and got sparked by Bernard Dwyer, I started wearing Malcolm's headguards after that. He's a huge St Helens fan and has looked after a lot of the young lads at Knowsley Road over the years. When you are a kid coming through the ranks, getting a pair of boots, trainers or some sports gear is a big thing and Malcolm really is one of the good guys – I've been fortunate to come across a lot of such people throughout the years.

19

Under the Influence

Over the years I have lost count of the number of people who have gone out of their way to help me, and I could probably fill a book just listing those I owe thanks to. Rugby league makes a big play of the sport being one big family, and in many cases that's definitely true.

Of those who have helped and supported me over the years, no one comes close to Mum, Dad and Lindsay. But those aside, I'd have to say that one particular man I met when I was still a kid played a massive part in my development.

That guy was Ken Wilson – or Tug, as everyone called him – in my early days at Waterhead, when I was not even in my teens. Tug ran the club gym – in fact everyone referred to it as his place – and he quickly instilled in us the value of discipline.

Tug always said that if you were going to train then make sure you gave it 100 per cent, or there was no point. The man had a certain aura about him, and there was certainly never any danger of him being talked back to – you just daren't – and I include the open-age players in that as well. He always got the maximum out of you, and I was lucky in that he took me under his wing and always showed a lot of interest as he felt I had a decent amount of ability.

Tug always told me: 'If you want to do anything in this game, you have to prepare right.' At that age all you really want to do is play, but he instilled in us the virtues of the correct training and generally how to look after yourself in the right way. Funnily enough, although he coached the open-age team, he never really saw me play many matches. But training-wise few people have had as big an impact on me. He absolutely hated what he termed soft lads, those who didn't put everything into their work. If you were one of those, you didn't hang around his gym for too long – he'd have you out.

Tug, who has sadly since passed away, and Howard Leach before him gave me the perfect grounding in rugby league, and I will always think of the pair of them as top, top men. Howard was my first real coach when I was at Mayfield, and a true gent. He never seemed to raise his voice, and when you're dealing with a bunch of kids that really is a rarity. Even when we were young he commanded total and utter respect, and he taught me an expression that has stuck with me since I was ten. He said: 'Never mind practice makes perfect – perfect practice makes perfect.' In other words, if your practice is shite and you keep dropping the ball and stuff, then it won't be any different come the game. How right he was.

Professionally I have worked with some great, great men as well – the first of whom was Brian Johnson, who gave me my big break at Warrington. I'll always be grateful to Jonno for giving me my chance in the first team, and he was a big believer in keeping everyone involved, whatever level they were at. He used to have a Saturday morning training session for the full club, from Academy to first team, which was brilliant for the younger ones.

He'd split the positions, so you'd have the Academy hooker working with the first team one, and so on. Even the parents were involved in loads, and there would be hotpot evenings, nights out and stuff where everyone was there. It fostered a fantastic team spirit and really helped us to become a very close unit.

The players were a great bunch, too, and probably the best of the lot in terms of helping me settle in was a guy called Gary Sanderson. He went out of his way to make me feel comfortable and a part of things. That's something I have never forgotten. Sandy was a first team regular, and could have been awkward because I was this young kid who wanted his position. But he wasn't like that at all, helped me out tremendously, and is a superb bloke.

We also had a fitness trainer called Phil Chadwick, who looked like an old-school groupie for a rock group, with his long hair and gaucho moustache. Chaddy played a massive part in helping me develop my fitness to the standard you needed at a professional level, and always managed to do it with a smile on his face as well. He made gang training so much fun, and would never ask you to do anything he couldn't manage himself. I've still never seen anyone take him when it comes to chins and dips.

It really was one big happy family at Wilderspool back then, and it was there that I first came into contact with Bernie Lenihan and his wife Jan. In those days Bernie was the bar manager, but virtually ran the whole of the club away from the rugby side. Both him and Jan were really, really good to me and I was delighted when he was named stadium manager when Warrington got their new Halliwell Jones ground. The pair of them still look after me and the family whenever Saints are in town.

Clive Griffiths was the coach I worked with probably more than Jonno when I first arrived. Clive was in charge of the reserves when I was making my way, and I got along great with him. There's no doubt he was a massive influence on me in those early days.

After those two John Dorahy arrived as our new coach. JD had his fair share of critics both as coach of Wigan and also Warrington, but I can't speak highly enough of the guy. He took over when we were going through a pretty rough patch, but had some great, innovative ideas, and I think we all benefited from his knowledge. JD had been very skilful in his playing days, and was always looking to break new ground with his tactics.

I can still picture his face when one move worked a treat against Saints, the time I gave the ball to Richard Henare on the blind side from the base of a scrum and he went the length of the field to score. JD had been working on it all week, and to see it fall into place so perfectly was fantastic. They don't always work like that!

Ironically it was the fact that John was so innovative that probably cost him his chance at Wigan. He had started to change a few things in the way they trained and prepared, and that didn't go down too well with some of the old guard. Most of his changes were probably for the better, but it was different from how they'd done things in the past, and player power clearly counted for a lot at Central Park, as he was the one who paid the price. But I thought he had loads of good ideas about the game and he was another who helped my own reach a different level.

It wasn't always sweetness and light with JD, though, and there was one game when he ended up acting as peacemaker at half-time. Once again it was against Saints, and once again it involved Henare – only this time it was memorable for the wrong reasons. Richard had gone over for a try and was running under the posts to make the conversion easier, when St Helens winger Anthony Sullivan flew in from behind, Henare dropped the ball before he could ground it, and we had blown a try.

Fair enough, it was a pretty basic mistake – and everyone's made them – but obviously when it costs you a try it's a lot more noticeable. At the time Alex Murphy, one of the real legends of the game, was director of rugby at Wilderspool and a real old-school guy. He stormed into the dressing room at half-time and started screaming at Richard. Henare was a bit of a barn-pot anyway, as much as he was a great bloke, and blew up. He was on his feet, telling Murph exactly what he thought of his advice, and JD ended up having to step in and calm the situation.

But while that may not have been the most creative advice Murphy ever dished out, it was great to work with such a legend, and he made sure I had a lot of input into things at Warrington. He was very good at seeing how things were going personally, and made you feel a really important part of everything.

Darryl Van De Velde, the man who replaced Dorahy, was another who had his fair share of critics, but I found him great to deal with. He arrived with a reputation among outsiders as being a bit intense and serious. But to those who knew him there was much more to the bloke. He hadn't been in charge at Warrington for too long when the club found itself with a bit of a financial problem. Actually it was a pretty big one, because at times they were struggling to pay people on time, or in some cases at all. For some of the younger ones with bills and mortgages to pay, that was obviously a hell of a problem, but the money just wasn't there.

Darryl wasn't about to see his players go short, and I know that at times he actually dug into his own pocket to help them out. That was a real touch of class from him and proved what a top bloke he was. True, he could have his moments when things weren't going well, but he had his fun side as well and was another big advocate of bonding sessions. When he had his rugby head on he was totally focused, but he knew the value of team spirit, too, and certainly left his mark on me by the time I moved on.

One of the main reasons I joined Saints was coach Shaun McRae, a man I also worked closely with when he was part of the Great Britain coaching team. Shaun was an absolute gent, one of the nicest men I've ever come across, but that amiable exterior hid a huge knowledge of the game.

He'd worked as conditioner for the Australian Test team, so was used to handling big personalities. You've got to have a bloody strong character yourself to coach a club like St Helens, and throughout his stay Shaun proved himself more than capable.

Ellery Hanley did likewise, and I've already said how big a part he played in my career, while Ian Millward enjoyed huge success during his reign. Basil was very, very big on bonding, and made sure all the wives and girlfriends were involved as much as possible. That's a hugely important part that can often be overlooked, but the fact is that if a player is happy at home, then it has a knock-on effect in his game. Basil was particularly good whenever a new signing arrived, especially from overseas.

It can be really tough for a player's partner when they move somewhere else, especially the other side of the world, because more often than not they have to start from scratch, without really knowing a soul. It's not usually a problem for players, because obviously they are surrounded by new mates at the club, but if things are unsettled at home, it can lead to problems. Ian used to organise these fancy-dress nights, where everyone would mix and have a great time. The only problem was that because everyone was in costume, half the time you wouldn't know who you were talking to!

Basil brought in a guy called Harry Bryant as his assistant, and what a bloke he turned out to be. Harry was a really funny character, a complete eccentric, and the first time we saw him we were all wondering where he had parked his horse. He had these big pointed boots, and looked like he had come straight from the sticks.

But you couldn't fault his knowledge of the game, and he was really, really good for us all. Ian knew Harry was very much an unknown to us all, but assured us that he knew rugby league inside out, and he was right. Harry had an incredible wealth of information about every aspect, and the fact that he was drafted into the Great Britain set-up under David Waite, for the one-off Test against the Aussies in 2002, was proof of his ability.

Jon Sharp also had a successful spell as Saints' assistant, before he became a coach in his own right at Huddersfield – and took them to the Challenge Cup final. Sharpy had a huge input and I got on a treat with him. He had spent a lot of time with Brian Smith, who had great success in Australia and over here with Bradford, and Sharpy obviously learned well from him.

When Basil got the boot, Daniel Anderson came over as our new coach, and we all knew what a top man we were getting because his record Down Under was second to none. We'd heard only good things about him and when he arrived we weren't disappointed. Everyone we asked about him said he really knew his stuff, and so it proved. He was in charge of New Zealand at the time we got him, and to land one of the best international coaches in the world was a real coup for the club.

He'd worked wonders with the Kiwis, and had also been a real success with New Zealand Warriors, in the Aussie competition. He took the Warriors to a Grand Final Down Under, and to the semi-finals the next season and when Eamonn McManus told us he was joining, it sent a huge buzz through the entire place.

I've already said that there was a bit of a split among the lads when it came to Basil, but he had won so much that he left huge boots to fill. But Ando had been around too long to start worrying about that, and immediately proved that he was his own man, with his own ideas, and total belief in what he was doing. And while Basil would come up with some suggestions that were right off the wall, Ando quickly emphasised that he saw rugby league as a simple game, and had us concentrating on doing the basics well.

He is very big on a solid defence, and I remember very early into his reign how he told us: 'Just make the tackle.' That sounds pretty obvious, but it's surprising how much else you can find yourself concentrating on when you're in the defensive line. Ando just wanted the man tackled, back into position, and take it from there.

We have seen flashes of his temper at times – when we've deserved it – and he can shout with the best of them. But that hasn't happened too often and it isn't a case of everyone listening when he raises his voice, because he doesn't have to.

Like Ellery before him, Ando commands so much respect among the lads that as soon as he speaks, you listen anyway. He's one of those guys who just has a real presence, and I think that's been proved by our results and the trophies which have come our way since he took over.

You can tell his grounding has been in the Australian competition, because the foundations of their success have always been built around solid defence, and he was no different, just like his assistant coach, Alan Wilson. That was a bit of a swing from St Helens' reputation as a team which pinged the ball around, with the attitude that, however many the opponents scored, we'd just make sure we scored more than them. But Ando wasn't one for winning a game 50–36 – he'd sooner make sure we limited their points, because scoring was never going to be a problem with all the flair players and great finishers in the side.

On the Great Britain stage, David Waite was a fantastic guy to work for, incredibly thorough and a top man. But I will always owe special thanks to Brian Noble, the man who gave me the captain's armband. I've a lot of respect for Nobby, and had a great relationship with him. Unfortunately I didn't play as many games for Britain as I'd have like when he was in charge, because of those two years of injuries, but his influence on the way things were done was superb. Nobby brought a lot of stability to the Great Britain scene, keeping the same management structure in place, whereas in previous years it had changed too much. He tried to do the same things every year, which helped a hell of a lot, and off the field things became a lot more professional when he was in command than at certain times in the past.

I've also been lucky enough to play alongside some of the greatest names in the modern era, but if I had to pick one who has had the biggest influence on me, it would have to be my old Saints skipper Chris Joynt – the man whose head I tried to knock off when I came up against him as a Warrington youngster. Joynty helped me develop so much as a player and as a person over the years, and he is probably the greatest captain of the Super League era.

The man has been there and done it all, but you would never guess it if you spent an evening in his company. He is modesty personified, yet if anyone has plenty to brag about it's Chris. One of the major things I learned from him was how to treat others. His attitude to everyone, whether it was a youngster breaking through the ranks or a big-name signing from the other side of the world, was to treat them as you'd expect them to treat you. That's something I have always tried to do, and I thank him for the lessons he gave me.

When I was his vice-captain at Saints, Joynty made sure I was involved as much as possible. He would always ask my opinion, which was a compliment in itself given his standing in the game, and, all in all, he taught me so much. When you retire, you can be quickly forgotten in this business, but I still see a lot of Joynty and will be forever grateful for all the help he's given.

Another player who proved a real guiding light to me was Mike Ford, the captain of the Oldham team when I used to ball-boy for them as a kid. I've already told you of the time I jumped the wall behind the stands to retrieve one stray kick, only to land on a load of rubble and get a nail through my trainer. Fordy, together with team-mates Richard Russell and John Henderson, came round with a get-well card signed by the whole team, and the club sent physio John Watkins to take me into town for some new trainers.

But my association with Fordy went way, way beyond that, and I was delighted when Warrington signed him after he decided to return from North Queensland Crushers, the Aussie side he'd been playing for. The local Warrington paper ran the story again, complete with pictures, and he was really embarrassed by it all. Obviously I knew all about Fordy before he became my team-mate, and on his return to England we used to travel over together all the time.

Back then he was living with his in-laws until his own house became available again, because it still had tenants in it. It never dawned on me he lived in the same road as me when I ended up buying a place – in fact he was next door but one. That was fantastic, having one of your idols as a neighbour. The fact that he was a team-mate as well was an added bonus.

We became really, really close mates with the whole family, and Sally-Anne – Fordy's wife – and Lindsay got on a treat. They have three cracking lads, Joe, George and Jacob, who are all into their rugby league, and we had some great games of tick and pass in the street.

You could see in Fordy's eyes that he was a real winner, and that attitude rubbed off even more on me. When he eventually ended up as Oldham coach, he'd always be picking my brains after training about what we'd done and why, trying to get an edge wherever he could. A couple of times he even came down and watched our sessions at Saints and he clearly took a lot in, because he has gone on to become England's defensive coach in the Union code.

I'd go round to his house and he would be sitting in front of his computer, either studying videos or working on stats, constantly trying to improve. His lads have clearly inherited his ability, too, because Joe and George are both fantastic prospects who are doing really well. Keep an eye out for their names: I reckon the pair of them could go right to the top.

20

Places to Go, People to Meet

As much as I love rugby league, and owe my lifestyle to it, I have always had plenty of interests outside the sport. I couldn't be one of those who trains, plays and when I'm doing neither, simply reads books and watches tapes on it. Cooking, for example, has always interested me and I can be a dab hand in the kitchen – although I'm not so sure Lindsay would always agree. Having a house at eighteen certainly helped push me in that direction, because it was a case of learn to cook or starve.

I like turning my hand to a spot of DIY at times as well and I've learned a lot from Lindsay's dad, Ian. He did loads to the house when I first got it, although the day we decided to build a snooker room turned into a job far bigger than first imagined.

Myself and a few friends and family all mucked in when it came to digging out the foundations, and it took bloody ages. Obviously we had to meet building regulations, and we must have got rid of enough soil to fill the bloody Albert Hall by the time we'd finished. Then we had to lay two feet of concrete all the way through, so it would take the weight of the snooker table. I had mates in doing the bricklaying work, plastering, loads of us labouring and Mick Slicker, the former Huddersfield player, sorting the floor.

It was satisfying when the whole thing was done, but I think there were times when I was wondering if it would have been a damned sight easier just to go for a game at the local British Legion instead. But I must admit that I get a real buzz out of achieving anything DIY-related, and I suppose the good thing in my favour is the fact that I don't give up very easily.

I've always been a huge dog lover as well, and had wanted a British bulldog from the day I saw the one my mate, Wes Rogers, had. I'll never forget the moment I walked through the door of my house in Oldham, after Great Britain's 1996 tour. We'd got the house in February, but Lindsay was only moving in when I got back, so she wouldn't be spending six weeks there on her own.

Unknown to me, Lindsay and my parents had spent ages looking for a bulldog to surprise me when I got back – they certainly did that. In the end they found a breeder in Oldham itself, through the Kennel Club, and they hid the dog in the hall when I arrived home. It was an awesome present, the best, and we've still got Boss now.

We bred Boss with my mate Roy's dog and the stud fee was that I got the pick of the litter, so I chose a gorgeous all-white bulldog. We called him Junior, and he got on a treat with Boss at first – until he grew bigger. That's when they suddenly turned on each other and it was clear that we couldn't keep them both, especially because we'd had Jake by then.

It wasn't fair on the dogs either, and because Boss had been there first, we decided to get rid of Junior, provided we could find a good, caring home for him, so we knew he'd be properly looked after. I couldn't believe my luck when Tommy Martyn, one of my Saints team-mates, said he'd love him, so we thought that was the problem solved at once.

Unfortunately his girlfriend had a dog which didn't take to Junior, so he was back with us that same night. We decided that if we couldn't find a decent home, he would have to stay with us. But Rob Smyth, who was with Warrington at the time, heard about it and loved bulldogs too. The fact he lived next door to Lindsay's mum and dad made it perfect, because it meant we could still see him – Junior, not Rob – as much as we wanted too.

Bikes have also been a great passion of mine, ever since I used to go watching speedway and grass track stuff with my dad, Lee and Danny when we were younger. Mum and Dad bought me a little 50cc Yamaha for my seventh birthday, and I used to love razzing around on that. That eventually stopped when I had to make a choice between that and rugby league. But I have always been very keen, and a while ago myself and Sean Long decided we'd go in for our Compulsory Basic Training, and get a bike each.

Your CBT is basically four hours in a car park on a Sunday morning, getting used to working the gears, brakes and stuff, which allows you to get your 'L' plates, and ride a 125cc machine. All Longy had been going on about was getting a Vespa scooter, and he actually ordered it before he'd even done his CBT. I told him I was going to carry on with my lessons so I could get a full licence, because I wanted to get a superbike.

As I'd ridden a bit as a kid, I knew how to ride one, but Longy was absolutely hopeless. Somehow he managed to convince the instructor he knew what he was doing, which meant we could go out on their 125s. The first time we took them out, us two in the front and the instructor behind, you can imagine what we did – opened them up as much as we could, and went as fast as possible. That was a big mistake because we'd only gone about half a mile when we came to a corner and both nearly hit the kerb. We only just managed to stay on and feared the worst when the instructor arrived. The first thing he said was: 'I had someone go through a bush here last week', so maybe we weren't as bad as we thought.

We stuck at it, blitzed our lessons, so much so that within nine weeks we'd done our tests, the theory and everything, and were qualified. We had both already bought bikes, Longy having scrubbed the idea of a scooter in favour of a Honda, while I got myself a lovely Suzuki, and we'd go flying down the Rainford bypass, really opening them out.

They have these meets up at the Hen and Chicken in Ormskirk, and Southport was also very popular with a lot of the bikers. We would go up and watch them all doing their wheelies and various stunts, which was great fun. There was one occasion when myself, Longy and a couple of mates went, and we were roaring down the M58 at full throttle. All four of us were going full whack. I was doing just under 165mph, really caning it, and sailing a bit close to the wind, to be honest.

I used to have two visors for going out on the bike, one tinted for the daytime, and a clear one for night. When we set off it was a fine day, so obviously I put the tinted one on. The problem was that we didn't come back until it was dark, and I couldn't see a bloody thing through it. I had to ride with my visor up and swallowed more flies than I could count. In the end I'd had enough, and when the others flew past me, I went shooting up the slip road and took it steady heading for home.

There were a lot of rumours that Wigan had actually stopped Greg Florimo, one of their Aussie players who was keen on bikes, from having one, so we decided to check out the situation with St Helens. We asked Sean McGuire, the chief executive, if there was anything in rugby league contracts banning you from riding them. He said no, but obviously had no idea how fast we were going. We didn't keep the fact we had bikes a secret, and would arrive for training on them, so everyone at the club knew about it.

In the end, though, I ended up selling it. The way I was riding it, I knew I was chancing my arm each time I went out. I couldn't ride it any other way, so I decided to get rid and have now just got a little 110cc midi-chopper, which me and Jake fly up and down the road on. Mum, Dad and Lindsay were all pretty chuffed when I sold the Suzuki, and Lucy-Jo clearly was because she used to hate it every time I started it up. My insurance was also costing me a fortune because of my job, so it had to go, and it was probably a pretty wise decision too.

I've also been hugely fortunate that, through rugby league, I've done things I could otherwise have only dreamed of, and met some really memorable people along the way. One which sticks in the mind was the day I was invited down to 31 Squadron at RAF Marham in Norfolk, to have a go in a Tornado. Graham Clay, who was doing some work for Gillette in the Tri-Nations, organised it, and I couldn't wait as we headed down there.

All the lads there were great. Wing commander Dean Andrew was a huge follower of Hull, also in charge of the RAF Rugby League set-up, and the man who initially invited me to have a go. My pilot was actually the main man, Group Captain Greg Bagwell, who took me out on a full sortie with a few of the others. A guy called Damian Clayton was also with us. Damian was the Flight Sergeant, and skipper of the RAF's Rugby League side, and it was an experience I'll never forget. We flew from Norfolk to Scotland in forty-five minutes, and they treated me to the full works. They had the full after burners on, simulated a bomb drop in Scotland, did a mock airfield attack at Marham on the way back, dropping to 100 feet and everything. I got the fly by, the barrel roll, everything – it was bloody amazing.

I don't know if I'd have been quite so quick to have a big night out beforehand if I'd realised what I was in for. Me, Graham, Damian and a couple of the Sky TV guys who'd come to cover it, were taken into the sergeants' mess, where we were told to have a couple of drinks and get an early night. As me and Damo were walking past the barracks bar to turn in, one of us suggested having just one more for the road. Ten pints of Guinness later we made it to bed, and when I woke up I could remember everyone in there telling me: 'You've no idea what's in store tomorrow, take it easy.' Fortunately we were up early, had a full breakfast, and – despite a couple of queasy moments – managed to keep it down as well.

To cap it all they gave me the whole uniform as well, and that's how I turned up at home, after a journey back which seemed a hell of a lot slower than the one down. I knocked on the door, wearing the full hit, ray bans and everything, and Lindsay's face was a picture when she answered it.

I also got to have a ride on a Royal Navy Sea King helicopter at one event at Jake's school. His headmaster, Gerald McArdle, had arranged it because his son was in the navy, and all the kids loved having a look around it. The next thing he had invited me up to have a go, and I was there in a shot. I was flown all over the place, and they fitted this harness thing to me, so I actually spent the entire flight leaning right out of the door. I got some pictures from above my house, and some great shots of

Knowsley Road when he took us over the Saints ground. Then they winched up the headmaster, simulating a helicopter rescue, and all in all that was another great experience.

I've also been lucky enough to be invited to Oulton Park as the guest of Team RAC for the British Touring Car Championship, along with Lindsay and Jake, who absolutely loved it. So much so that he's already got his own little quad bike at home. Unfortunately they didn't let him in the pits, but I nipped in and even got interviewed by Vicky Butler-Henderson on Granada when I had a look at the starting grid, too.

A more sedate invite came from Jonathan Neill, a big mate of mine who works in PR for Lexis. Jon got us tickets to the semi-finals of the 888.com darts tournament at the G-Mex in Manchester, and a few of us from the club went down. There was myself, Paul Wellens and Jon Wilkin from Saints, while our Dan, Terry Newton and Danny Tickle came along from Wigan. What a laugh that turned out to be, and we got to meet Phil Taylor and Colin Lloyd as well.

We all went upstairs and had a little throw of the darts with the players, too, and that Taylor's not too bad you know! But the best laugh came in the tournament itself, because we'd all made our own cards to hold up, like you see at all the big darts events. The only thing was, ours didn't have anything like '180' written on them – they were a bit more abusive than that. We'd warned the others what we were going to do, so God knows what Martin Gleeson thought when the camera focused on one of our placards that read 'Glees Is a Tranny'.

I've said earlier that I am a huge fan of boxing, and couldn't get to his Phoenix Camp in Hyde quick enough when I was asked if I fancied a sparring session with Ricky 'The Hitman' Hatton. It was a promotional thing for Tetleys, and it was pretty bloody obvious that he wouldn't be going full out when I got in the ring with him, but it was still a real eye-opener.

First up I watched him go through a full-on training session, which was just awesome. When I got in the ring with him, it was something else beyond. I'd always done a lot of boxing training since I was a kid, and it was fantastic meeting his trainer, Billy Graham, and assistant Bobby Rimmer as well. Myself and Ricky did some knockabout stuff for promo pictures, and I certainly wouldn't fancy taking a serious hit off him.

When they gave us ringside tickets for his WBU light welter-weight title fight against Ben Tackie as well, that just put the icing on the cake. I just love the way Ricky conducts himself, for someone who is so high up in his profession. He is incredibly dignified, a genuinely lovely bloke, who puts himself across so well. What you see on TV is what he's like in real life, and the fact he celebrates all his wins at his local boozer says a lot about him. He'd certainly fit in well in any rugby league team, because he's so down to earth and has a great sense of humour – and of course no one would ever start on him.

Ricky certainly made a much better impression on me than another boxing legend, in George Foreman. I've been lucky enough to get invited onto *Question of Sport* five times, and each occasion has been absolutely brilliant. It's just as it comes across on the telly, dead laid back and real good fun. Everyone gets in the Green Room beforehand for a few drinks and something to eat, and generally just has a really good laugh.

When I was told that Foreman was one of the guests I was buzzing, because he'd always been a hero of mine. Unfortunately the Foreman in the flesh wasn't quite the man I imagined. Instead of mucking in with everyone else, he arrived with an entourage of about forty, demanded his own Green Room, and wouldn't talk to anyone else. He even refused to sign the guest book, which is always auctioned off at the end of the series for charity. He really couldn't be arsed with the whole thing, and I wonder why he decided to go on in the first place. Foreman just sat there through the whole show, I don't think he even answered a question – although that helped our team win – and that was that.

Former Liverpool footballer Jason McAteer, who I'd met a few times, was on the same show and we were having a bit of a giggle about it all after the programme. He came over and said: 'Hey Scully, I was going to ask him for one of his grills, but I don't think I'll bother now.'

Each time I've been on the show I have been on Ally McCoist's team, and on each occasion I have loved it. Ally is a top fella, just like Frankie Dettori, and the pair of them couldn't do enough to make you feel relaxed. The second time I went down I was barely through the door when Frankie jumped on my back and tried to strangle me. He always has a couple of Geordie guys with him, and when Longy was on the show after me on one visit, we got stuck into a few in the Green Room. Frankie invited me out with him afterwards, but we were training early the next day, or we'd have gone into Manchester with him and probably ended up in a right state. Me and Longy made provisional arrangements to go along and meet Frankie again the next time he was riding at Haydock Park, but unfortunately we've not managed it yet.

I've been a team-mate of Stephen Hendry, Paula Radcliffe, Jason Crump and Matthew Upson twice, and every show has been a real laugh. We were in the middle of one, when a lad got up out of the crowd, threw his hat onto the table and said: 'Here you go, sign that for us Ally, I'm just going for a piss.' The whole place fell apart and I think that particular show took even longer than usual to film.

They had Ted Robbins doing the audience warm-up beforehand, and because he's a big RL fan, he came straight over when I walked in. I told him that my dad was a huge fan of *Phoenix Nights*, which he starred in as Den Perry, and he immediately asked for his address. It ended up with Dad getting an official-looking letter on headed notepaper, asking if he fancied doing a set on stage at the Banana Grove, Den's club. It was absolutely priceless.

Yet if they make you totally relaxed and at home when you're on the show, they leave you feeling anything but when they rope you in to be the mystery guest – and that's something I've let myself get talked into five times. On one occasion they asked me to get to the Hard Rock Café, in the Printworks in Manchester. I obviously thought that if the place itself wasn't closed while we filmed, at least they would have a section cordoned off. That was my first mistake.

The second was agreeing to wear a Bruce Springsteen wig and bandana, wearing the old leather jacket with the sleeves rolled up. That was bad enough, but then they had me dancing through the place, pretending to play the guitar and miming to 'Glory Days'. It wasn't as though I was so well disguised that no one could recognise me. Everyone seemed to and had a bloody good laugh about it – total nightmare.

Another time they had me as a lifeguard who ended up getting in trouble when he dived into the pool to save a girl who was struggling, and needed rescuing himself. Then I was dressed up as a vicar, with the big cape and hat on. I had to go into an old church in Manchester that had been converted into a rock-climbing centre, and scale the wall. I've also been David

Dickinson, doing my 'cheap as chips' *Bargain Hunt* impression with an orange face, and I was Boy George for a Live Aid multiple mystery guest round.

That was some bloody make-up job, but it was brilliant. Lee Sharpe, Gary Speed, Mark Cueto and Longy were all in there as well, as Simon Le Bon, George Michael and the like. To be honest I never get tired of going on the programme, it's fantastic fun, and you get a real true-to-life impression on the box.

I found myself rubbing shoulders with the stars once again when I was one of the St Helens contingent invited down to the BBC Sports Personality of the Year awards, together with Longy, Kez, Jon Wilkin and Paul Wellens. Daniel Anderson had won the Coach of the Year, but because he had gone back home as it was in the close season, I was chosen to collect it on his behalf. They had tipped me off about that beforehand, so I could think about what I'd say up there, but I had no idea who had won the Team of the Year.

Obviously there were some pretty strong candidates – the Ryder Cup winners and Chelsea's Premiership champions to name but two. But when they read out the winner it was us, and I was up there again. That one really was nerve-wracking because they don't actually interview you as such, just hand you the microphone and expect you to make a speech. Considering I didn't have anything planned, I don't suppose it went too badly.

Apparently Ian Woosnam, the Ryder Cup captain, was kicking off a bit that his team hadn't won, and he wasn't too impressed when Wilko told him to chill out after the show. What Woosnam didn't realise was that we had received over 70 per cent of the viewers' votes, and the Ryder Cup team weren't even second, that place had gone to Surrey cricket club.

All in all that completed a pretty impressive for Saints, because we cleaned up in just about everything going. We'd already won the Challenge Cup and Grand Final, we were the world champions, and mopped up every individual award at the end-of-season Man of Steel presentation night. In fact the only thing we didn't win was the BBC's North West award, which went to Sale Sharks rugby union boys.

The first individual award I received came back in my days at Wilderspool, when I was named the 1997 Warrington Sports Personality of the Year. That was a great night in the town hall, and apparently I was the first rugby league player to win it. I don't know how many sponsors they had, but from all the stuff I took home it was a fair few. As well as the trophy I got a television, loads of New Balance gear, and a year's membership to The Village hotel and leisure club . . . plus a huge box of crisps.

The first individual award is always memorable, but the Scouseology trophy I received in 2005 went down just as well. It's given to those who have made a big contribution to sport in the Merseyside area, and because Liverpool had just won the Champions League, it made it extra special when they read my name out. I was in exalted company as well, given that the previous winners were Steven Gerrard and Michael Owen. I even got nominated for their international award, which eventually went to a worthy winner in Jamie Carragher. I must have been up for it because of my off-field stuff, because I'd not been on the pitch that much because of my injuries.

I had an idea I might be close to winning the Scouseology one when I arrived to find I was sitting in a table right in the middle of the room. You get an impression of whether you're in the running from where they seat you, and if they've placed you where everyone can get a good glimpse as you get up, you know you're on the short list. But I found out for certain when one of the organisers who was on our table said to me: 'Have you got your speech ready?' The look on her face was marvellous when I told her I hadn't got a clue what she was on about, and she realised she'd let the cat out of the bag. It still didn't help me with the speech much, though, because that was another one when they just give you the mike, rather than asking you questions.

At least I didn't have to make one when I was named in Lancashire Life's Fifty Greatest Living Lancastrians. Andrew Flintoff won it, from Peter Kay, but I was in there at number 21, one place behind Steve Coogan – and 28 ahead of my Saints team-mate Kez. There were some other big, big names behind me, like Cilla Black, Ringo Starr, Caroline Aherne and Liam and Noel Gallagher, so that was a real honour.

Obviously over the years I have grown well used to seeing myself on television, but 99 per cent of the time it involves something to do with rugby league. Yet I still cringe when I think of the first TV appearance I made – strutting across a studio wearing nothing but a pair of lime green boxer shorts. It came when I was still with Warrington, and I went down to London with Longy and Wes Cotton – who were both playing for Wigan back then – for the Richard and Judy show.

None of us had a real idea of what we'd be doing – I think they realised they may have struggled to get us there if we had – and when we arrived we were stunned when they said we'd be modelling male underwear. They just chucked all these undies in the middle and we grabbed what we wanted. I think I went for the boxers because they were the safer option. They were certainly a lot safer than the red G-string which Wes ended up with, as we paraded up and down while Davina McCall passed comment. At the time Wes was a real sunbed king, so I stuck out a mile with my white body and my lime green undies – I felt a million dollars!

But if that was just hugely embarrassing, we do get some things that are the chance of a lifetime – like the time we got the chance to walk the Sydney Harbour Bridge on Great Britain's visit to Australia for that one-off Test a couple of years ago. You go up and along halfway, cut across and then back down, but you're all strapped into a harness and there's no chance of you falling.

The most frightening bit is actually climbing up from the road in the first place. You don't realise how high it really is until you set off. Most of the British lads had gone, but Hull forward Paul King saw his arse when he realised the height. That's when he decided the best option would be to head back to base. So while we were stepping out over one of Sydney's greatest sights, he was probably back in his room having a sly ciggie. You could say it was a bridge too far for Kingy – I've crossed a few of those in my time, too.

21

Heroes and Heartbreakers

If I had to pick one man above all others who made me even more determined to make a career of rugby league, it would have to be the Aussie legend Ray Price. The game was still a total mystery to me when Mick Slicker, the father of the old Huddersfield star who was big mates with my dad, dropped a video of Australian clips round at our house in Oldham.

They called him Mr Perpetual Motion – Ray, that is, not Mick or my dad – because he was constantly on the move, absolutely tireless. Throw in more than his fair share of natural ability, too, and it's easy to see why a young lad on the other side of the world was so impressed. The fact that he played in the same position as me, at loose forward, was an added bonus.

At the time I was taking my first steps in the game, and would sit in the lounge open-mouthed at Price's toughness. He was that hard I'm sure our telly used to shake with some of his tackles. Back in those days there wasn't any Australian rugby league on the TV, and I had to quench my thirst for the game with those old Micron videos – but I still saw enough to get me even more hooked on a sport that was quickly becoming such a massive part of my life. I've met loads of the old greats over the years, but if I have any regrets about the one that got away, it would be never having had the honour of meeting Ray.

I suppose you can't have everything, but that would have been nice. But as I grew up, my heroes weren't just confined to the sport I play. Everyone knows I am a huge fan of boxing, and Mike Tyson in his prime was a particular hero. Before everyone starts thinking I'm some sort of monster, I don't for one second condone all the things he has done out of the ring. Inside it, however, was another matter. The man was an absolute animal, the epitome of aggression and toughness.

I used to sit there amazed, as the bell went and he'd go storming into his opponent and batter him to a pulp. The man was totally unstoppable and the last person you'd want in the opposite corner. Not the sort of bloke whose pint you'd want to knock over in the pub.

When I got in the ring for a promotional photo-shoot with Ricky Hatton, and we ended with a bit of sparring, it was hard enough. If the offer had been there with Tyson at his peak, you'd have needed the entire Saints front row to drag me up there. Mind you, I might fancy my chances against him now. Then again, maybe not.

Ricky is another boxer for whom I have a lot of time. What you see is what you get with him, and I think he's a great example to all the youngsters of how fame and fortune doesn't have to change you. He still has the same mates he's had for years, and I love the way he celebrates his title wins with a bad-taste shirt day down at his local boozer. It's a little bit like Saints on a Mad Monday! They say you should never meet your heroes, because so often they turn out to be a disappointment, but it certainly wasn't the case with Ricky. He was a genuinely nice, down-to-earth guy, and what struck me was how humble, polite and dignified he was. There are a few in other sports – my own included – who could do worse than follow his lead about how to conduct themselves.

Motor-cycling is another sport I have loved ever since my dad used to take me, Danny and Lee to see scrambling and grass-track racing as kids. As I've said, I even had my own bike and loved nothing better than razzing around on my Suzuki before I sold it. For a long time I didn't have anyone in particular I'd follow closely, but then Valentino Rossi came on to the scene and blew me away. I've been to a few race days at the World Superbikes and the moto GP, and the way he handles his machine is breathtaking. I just love way he goes at such speed yet is still in total control. For them to ride them in that way is just unbelievable, and some of my best days out have been at Brands Hatch, Mallory Park and similar places to see the bikes in action.

Golf is a world away from the noise and speed of motor cycling, but I find that relaxing and frustrating in equal measures. It couldn't be further removed from rugby league, but it's no less impressive. I've been to the Open at Sandwich and Hoylake, and the control those guys have is fantastic. I think the way they handle the pressure of a crucial putt with all that money riding on it is unreal, and of course Tiger Woods is in a class of his own when it comes to the big occasion. The man's just a freak – his timing, coordination and ability are phenomenal.

I play a bit myself, too, even though I had to take a break for a couple of years while my knee was sorted out. There is no more frustrating game in the world. You can be having the round of your life, but play one bad hole and it finishes you.

Quite a few of the Saints lads are keen golfers, and I used to play a lot with Darren Albert, before he went back to Australia. Albie was pretty useful, and I was getting up there myself until I had to put it on hold.

I think that if you play one sport, it definitely gives you an advantage in certain others, and I found that hand–eye co-ordination came quite naturally when I took it up. It's the same with snooker and pool – I love relaxing with a frame or two, and I'm actually pretty decent at both. Having said that, I have had a snooker room in the house for ten years, so I should be able to hold my own.

I used to play quite a lot of pool with Sean Long, Glees and the boys, and we're always round at Longy's house knocking the balls about. Wello won't thank me for saying it, but I've given him a couple of hidings on the green baize as well over the years.

In fact away from rugby league, snooker gave me one of my greatest sporting moments, when I got invited on to 'The Yellow to Black Challenge' on Sky Sports' *Soccer AM* programme a few years ago. As you may guess from the title, you have to pot all the coloured balls, in order, from their spots in as quick a time as possible. I was really psyched up for that, although they only gave me a couple of shots to warm up and get my eye in.

That didn't seem to matter, though, because I cleaned up first time and didn't miss a shot. I managed to pot the lot in thirty seconds, and was at the top of the leader board for a while. Sam Torrance, the former golfer, was on another programme and it took him something like three minutes! I was right up there among the non-snooker players who had a go, but then they asked a few of the professionals, which I thought was a bit unfair. Even then Stephen Hendry only managed to beat me by one second, but then Mark Williams did it in twenty-four, so my moment of glory was snatched away. In the end I think the top three were Williams, Hendry and Ronnie O'Sullivan, but I was still dead chuffed at the way I'd held my own. I'll have to suggest to Sky Sports that we get some of the snooker players in a goal-kicking competition and see how they do at our sport . . .

I was telling someone the story the other day, and they were saying how great it must have been to play at The Crucible. For some reason they just assumed that we'd gone to a professional venue to film it. Unfortunately it wasn't quite as glamorous as that, because we all trotted down to Rainford Labour Club – really plush.

Sky had a similar challenge in darts, where you had to get as big a score as possible in thirty seconds. Me and Jamie Lyon, St Helens' Aussie centre, were chosen for that one but I never threatened the leaders there. I can't even remember how many I managed, but I do know I was crap. Perhaps that hand–eye coordination doesn't always work after all.

I was lucky enough to be on Hendry's team when I was on *A Question of Sport* and he was a top, top bloke. We had a great chat and there was really no side to him. To the general public he had a reputation of being very serious, very dour, but he was a great guy, yet utterly dedicated – he'd have to be, to stay at the top for so long. I love nothing better than relaxing with a game of snooker, but once I've had about four frames, that's enough for me. These guys practise for hours and hours, frame after frame, and I find their concentration and commitment unbelievable.

Another hero of mine, whose name probably wouldn't mean a thing to the majority of people, is Andrew Williams, who I first mentioned in Chapter 1. He's the surgeon who carried out my knee operation and basically the key figure behind getting me back on to the field in tiptop shape for that World Club Challenge win once again. When I first met Andrew, who works down in Chelsea, I was surprised how young he is. You always imagine people in his position to be getting on, but he put paid to that myth. Saints had told me they'd get me the best possible treatment, and when they sorted me out with Andrew they were true to their word. Fair play to the club, and especially Eamonn McManus, who has never wavered in his support and help. When I damaged my Achilles he promised again to get me the best help possible, and once more he came up trumps for me.

One sport I've got into quite heavily recently is the Ultimate Fighting that's come over from America. It's been on the telly quite a lot over the past few years and I've become a huge fan, especially of Chuck 'The Iceman' Liddell. Quite a few of the lads are big followers, especially Ade Gardner and Scott Moore.

Ultimate Fighting is like street fighting in the ring, with a few rules thrown in for good measure. Lindsay's not too keen on it, but my dad is a fan and my mum loves it. I was all set to go and watch it when it came to Manchester a while ago, but we were playing at Leeds Rhinos on the same night, so that put the kibosh on it.

Music is another big passion of mine, although no one group in particular. I'm into all sorts, modern, the old stuff, everything, and it has always been that way since I was a youngster. I used to listen to a lot of music before games, to help with motivation and stuff, but not so much now. I'd have M People or the like blasting through the headphones, more for the inspiring lyrics than anything else, but these days I just tend to chill out beforehand.

To be honest, I try not to think about the matches themselves too much. Obviously I know what's expected, what the game plan is, and the rest, but it's not something that eats away at me all week. Fortunately I don't tend to suffer with nerves, either; I just get really excited about what lies ahead. For me the bigger the match, the bigger the buzz and there is no better feeling than walking out of the tunnel to a packed stadium with the greatest prizes in rugby league up for grabs.

You've got to have the right amount of self-belief, but not arrogance, and there have been a few times when I've led the team out thinking 'this is what I play this game for'. I have turned in some of my best performances in the big games for St Helens and Great Britain, and you can't describe how good it feels to come off at the end, with the cup under your arm, knowing you've performed your best.

Not all the lads are 100 per cent relaxed before matches, though, and Keiron Cunningham is probably the worst. He always throws up beforehand, always has since he was coming through the ranks as a youngster. I don't know if it's down to nerves or it has simply become psychological now, but it wouldn't matter if we were playing a bunch of amateurs in the Challenge Cup or the Aussies in an Ashes decider at Sydney Football Stadium, he'd be off to the toilet while we were getting ready. That's the other thing with Kez – he leaves everything right until the last second.

Ten minutes before we are due to go out for the warm-up, he'll still be sitting there in his tracksuit, and will then rush to get changed just as we're heading on to the pitch. I think it comes down to the fact that he must hate sitting around and waiting to go out there, and I must admit that once you're stripped and ready to go, all you want to do is play the game.

It's no secret that I rate our sport as the toughest in the world, and I've got nothing but admiration for everyone who goes out there. But while no one would ever question the courage of anyone lucky enough – or mad enough – to play rugby league, I've been reduced to tears by the bravery and heroics of some people I've come across who have never picked up a ball in their life.

One of the off-field things we do quite a lot is visiting kids in local hospitals, and I can honestly say that that's something the lads do without a quibble. If ever we needed bringing down to earth, or getting things into perspective, then an afternoon spent in the children's ward certainly does so. Devastatingly, heart-breakingly so on numerous occasions.

Saints are regular visitors to Whiston Hospital around Christmas time, while I have also visited the children's cancer ward at the Royal Manchester Children's Hospital too. No one likes to see the kids suffering, but it pulls even more on your heartstrings when you have young ones of your own. I know it certainly did with me.

The kiddies' ward is always packed with smiling faces, they are so delighted to see some of their heroes. Well, let me say here and now that we're not the heroes in all this – they are, without a shadow of a doubt. The kids are so sharp, so bright and so full of life, and that is the real tragedy, because you know some of them aren't going to walk out of there.

The first time I went I don't think I let Jake off my knee for the rest of the night once I got home. It really touched me and it has stayed with me ever since. They are suffering so much but are so cheerful and happy just to share a few words or get an autograph or the like. It certainly makes you feel very humble, and I know I can speak for the rest of the lads when I say it's exactly the same for them all.

There was one young St Helens fan we went to see who was suffering from cancer, and me and Longy went over one day to give him a signed shirt and stuff for his birthday. He was undergoing chemotherapy, but you couldn't get the smile off his face, and he was a lovely, lovely kid. We got to know him pretty well over the months, and it was a privilege and honour for me when we led Saints out together when he was mascot for one game.

They were trying to raise money for him to go to Disneyland for a holiday, but unfortunately it had to be cancelled because he became so ill again, and I was so sad to learn that he had passed away. He was only eleven and we went to his funeral – it was terrible, and you could only imagine the agonies his family suffered.

Anyone with a heart would have been devastated to see what they went through, and you just want to do what you can to help – even though you know it can never be enough. Visits like that, to see the sick children, cannot be described as work. It is just a chance to give something back, maybe leave a smile on their faces, and if it helps for them to meet their heroes then that's fantastic.

I tell you one thing, the conversation in the car on the journey to and from the hospital could not be more different. On the way you will be moaning about the usual things, complaining about something or other that's gone on in a game or training, and generally feeling you could always have a better deal than the one you've got. A few hours with the kids, and the chat is incredibly subdued as you head home. If reaching the top in rugby league has helped any youngsters over the years, then it is a career well spent.

22

The Times They Are A Changing

Over the past two years I have spent many hours wondering what the future holds for me. When you're unable to do even the simplest of tasks like go upstairs or nip out for a paper, there's not a great deal to do other than think – there's only so much daytime telly a man can take.

So no one could ever accuse me of making a snap judgement when I decided to call time on my international career this season. Plenty of people will have their own theories about the reasoning involved, but if they are anything like the rumours which went around during my injuries, I can guarantee there won't be a word of truth in them.

Quite simply, I have decided to retire from the Great Britain scene because I want to play for as long as possible, and that is the best way to squeeze a few more seasons out of the game. My priority is, and always has been, St Helens. They stood by me through thick and thin when I was struggling with my knee, and were as good as their word when they promised to find me the best possible treatment. If they hadn't been quite so understanding, tried to rush me back, or whatever, then who knows what I would be doing now.

They turn up trumps for me, once again, when I suffered my horrible Achilles injury in training in June, and I owe it to them, as much as myself, to make sure they see the best of me – and will continue to do so for the foreseeable future.

Since I first became a regular in the Warrington side as a teenager, I have never had a full, 'normal' pre-season. There has always been some tournament or another before you go into a break, which has the knock-on effect of seeing you return to training later than the non-internationals in the squad. By the end of the season, when you hope to be slugging it out for Grand Finals and the like, you are shattered, probably in more of a mental than a physical sense.

So you can rest assured that plenty of thought and consideration had gone into the decision when I informed the Rugby League authorities that I no longer wanted to be considered for international selection. The fact that I was Great Britain captain made it an even tougher one to take. One of the greatest regrets I have in my career is the fact that I only actually skippered the side for eighteen minutes, in that game against New Zealand in 2006.

There is no greater honour than captaining your country, whether it's a game of dominoes or in a World Cup final, and I will always be grateful to former British coach Brian Noble for giving me that opportunity. But there comes a time when tough decisions have to be made, and in my eyes that time had approached. In a nutshell, if I want to carry on for a few years at the top level, then I had to take a step back and listen to what my body was telling me.

Saints pay my wages, Saints are my employers and Saints are the ones who have to come first when considering my career. So it was with them in mind that I called a halt to things. Don't get me wrong: the family obviously came into the equation as well, and there's no doubt that getting the chance to spend more time with them, when in the past I would have been jetting off to Papua New Guinea, Australia or New Zealand, is an added bonus. But don't forget that Lindsay has grown up with me being away from home for lengthy periods, and while she may not have been jumping through hoops about it, she knew it was part of the job and that there are plenty of benefits to compensate for the absences.

I had found being away in camp to be an even bigger wrench after Jake and Lucy-Jo arrived, but I think if I had to put my finger on one single factor, it would be the demands placed on you. People wouldn't realise, but when you are in camp, preparing for a high-profile, high-pressure set of matches, it is incredibly draining. There weren't too many benefits from being out injured, but one of them was the fact that I could really refresh my mind while I was sitting there in a leg brace.

I know some people will have their own theories about me quitting the international scene, but I can say with hand on heart that it was a decision I had already reached way before I damaged my Achilles before a Challenge Cup quarter-final against Warrington Wolves.

They say that bad luck has a nasty habit of biting you on the backside when you least expect it, and I can certainly vouch for that. It came during Saints' last session before the Warrington game, and there was no hint of what lay around the next corner, as we went through our paces.

Ironically I was absolutely flying at the time, and the session had gone really, really well. I was looking forward to hopefully helping St Helens into the last four, and this time playing a major role in them picking up another trophy when bang, I was on the floor in absolute agony.

I have suffered hamstring injuries in the past and they are bad enough, while obviously breaking my jaw and fracturing my eye socket at various times in the past were very painful. But this was something way, way beyond anything I had ever experienced in my life.

I was literally just running along when it felt as though someone had shot me in the back of the leg. I went down immediately and even the other lads said they had heard the crack. It was just unbearable, and the boys rushed over to see what the problem was. I was helped off the training ground by Apollo Perelini and Maurie Fa'asavalu, and at one point they had to put me down as I felt sick and light-headed with the pain. I was hoping for the best but knew it was a pretty serious one because I'd done my hamstring in the past, and this was a lot worse.

Mike Bennett had just returned from snapping his calf muscle, and the symptoms he described over that seemed similar to mine. That was a six-week lay-off, so I had my fingers crossed over the weekend – which I spent on crutches – that I'd done the same. Unfortunately, as soon as I went for a scan the following morning, they confirmed that I had ruptured the Achilles tendon in my left foot and my season was in bits, just as it was really clicking into gear.

That Saturday morning I felt as low as I have done in a long time, and I don't think too many would be too surprised at that. After all I'd been through, the long road back, I was suddenly facing months on the sidelines again. The lads were really good to me, everyone texting to see how I was. Martin Gleeson came around on the Saturday afternoon to cheer me up, and did such a good job that he didn't leave until the Sunday night. Glees has had a rough deal off the press at times, but he's a bloody good mate, and you couldn't wish to meet a nicer bloke.

Obviously my family were all as gutted as me, and Mum and Dad were round straight away. But the one who was once more really supportive was Lindsay. She has never flinched in her help and support, and yet again she excelled herself in aiding my recovery. It can't have been easy for her, especially because it meant a short holiday we'd booked for the following week was looking ominous if I required surgery.

Come the Monday I was beginning to look on the positive side of things again, and went into Saints to do some upper body work while waiting for the date to see the specialist. It came sooner than I thought, as I got the call to be in Harley Street for 5 p.m. that afternoon, so down I went with Dad. I actually drove – it wasn't a problem because the car's an automatic – because I'm a terrible passenger and it made for a more stress-free trip!

Dad was doing his best to keep my spirits up and I must admit that I was already trying to use what positives I could from the situation by the time we were approaching London – not least proving all those doubters – who were questioning my future – wrong once again. There was a spot of good news as well, when the specialist told me that while the Achilles was ruptured, it was actually a little further up the heel, rather than right in the middle. The big bonus of his diagnosis was that I didn't need surgery, which had looked certain two days earlier, even though the recovery period was still a few months.

I had to wear an aircast, which kept the foot pointing downwards to keep the strain off the Achilles, and was laid up for the best part of two months unable to do much at all. Cue

Lindsay for her Florence Nightingale impression once again! But even that was better than the prospect of being incapacitated for God knows how long, and there was even the slight chance that I could return for the back end of the season – assuming Saints made the Grand Final again.

So reports of my demise were, once again, grossly exaggerated, and I was champing at the bit once more, determined to come back fitter and stronger than ever. There was no reason why not, either – after all, I had come back from a far more serious injury at the start of the season, so I knew I could do it again. It also gave me time to plan a few things for the future.

And at least I knew I would be able to have a full and proper pre-season for the next campaign, whether I made it back for the season's finale or not – and the fact I knew I wouldn't be rushing back to try and make an international series meant there was no chance of me attempting to come back too soon.

It was also a time for reflection on what had gone before, and I know I will look back in years to come and wonder if we could have done more to bring the Ashes back to Britain. Then again, I don't suppose I will be the only one. I must admit, though, that the biggest regret of all is not having played in an Ashes-winning series – to do so as captain would have been the pinnacle. We have got closer and closer to them throughout my career, without managing to finish the job, but sadly it has never been quite enough.

Again, that's something plenty have their own theories about, and I know many of them put it down to the fact that the Aussies are simply too skilful and talented for us, and there is no doubt they have proved that they're number one in the world. How many times over recent seasons have we beaten them in one game, but we have not done it consistently. But that isn't down to the fact we are not good enough – one of the major factors must be the season we go through over here.

We have a longer season than the Australians, fewer breaks and shorter time between many of the games in the regular campaign – and when it comes to the Test matches or Tri-Nations, we go straight into a high-pressure tournament without really having time to draw breath. I'm not saying changing all that would bring back the Ashes, but give us a fair crack. It's something we need to address, and we should be on a level playing field when it comes to that.

Another regret is the fact that I never got to play in the same team as our Dan at a professional level. We did it a few times as youngsters, but only came close once as pros. We were both in the Lancashire side for a Wars of the Roses clash with Yorkshire, but I picked up a hamstring injury and had to pull out. Lancashire ended up getting a towelling that day, so in hindsight it probably wasn't a bad game to miss.

When I first came into the game, Wigan were totally dominant, the outstanding club side in either code, in either hemisphere. They were greatly helped by the fact that they were the only full-time outfit at the time, and, generally speaking, I think it was a lot easier to predict the results each week. Well, no one could label Super League a predictable competition any more, especially after what we have seen this season alone.

Who, for example, would have predicted anything but a season of struggling for newly promoted Hull KR? I doubt if even their supporters could have dreamed of some of the results they pulled off, like going to the JJB and completing the double over Wigan, for example. Wakefield, too, were tipped to be at the bottom from the off, but they shook everyone with their flying start. And before the doom and gloom merchants say that games are tighter because standards have dropped, well that's just crap!

Standards all over the sport have improved steadily over the years and that in turn has made rugby league an even more attractive spectacle. No one wants to see one-sided contests like maybe we had at times in the past. We don't want to go along to see what is effectively little more than an exhibition match, with one side running away with it.

But when it comes to facing Australia, I would have loved the chance to do so on a level playing field. You only have to look at the respective schedules for the various Tri-Nations tournaments we've played over the seasons to prove that one. Great Britain would find themselves having to play five matches on the bounce, with no break in between; the Aussies, on the other hand, would have a couple of games and then a week off before they go back into action. When you are talking about such a high-impact collision sport as ours, believe me that makes one hell of a difference. I'd love to see things made a little fairer in that respect.

There are a few other changes I'd like to see introduced as well. Like, for example, the number of overseas players in the English game. Don't get me wrong, it's not as bad as the situation a few years ago, when players who were little more than ageing journeymen or even reserves back home would come to England to finish their careers and line their pockets. It wouldn't have been so bad if they'd had the good of our game at heart, but plenty of them couldn't have given a toss and probably never gave it a second thought once they had returned home.

It stands to reason that if your club is flooded with overseas players it is obviously going to limit the openings available to home-produced talent. I was delighted when the Rugby League announced that they were cutting the import quota in 2009, because that can only benefit the development of British youngsters. I wouldn't have a total ban on overseas players, as some have bizarrely suggested. When you look at some of the talents who have played over here in recent seasons alone, think how poorer our game would have been without them.

The legacy of players like Trent Barrett and Jamie Lyon, to name but two, will live on long after they have played their last. I think the attitude of Aussies and Kiwis to our game has changed quite dramatically over the years, and some of the players have been huge successes for their respective clubs. And, personally speaking, playing alongside Jamie will remain one of the great honours I have had. But speaking with my Great Britain hat on – if not the shirt to go with it any more – then a restriction in the numbers can only benefit our chances in future Ashes series.

You just have to keep a lid on things and stop the market being flooded. And I must say that the ruling about players from the Pacific Islands only muddies the waters even more for some people, as they are not counted on the overseas player register.

Another huge bugbear of mine has been the low profile that the international game suffers from in England. I know football is the be all and end all to many people, and I guess that will always be the case, as much as I'd love to see it differently. But you only have to look at rugby union to see how the game can be projected, regardless of the obvious bias it enjoys from many quarters and media outlets. Maybe overhauling union in terms of international interest is something we will never manage, and it's certainly not something that will change dramatically in the immediate future.

But to people outside of the rugby league heartland it must seem at times as if our international game is almost something of an afterthought. It simply never seems to be pushed heavily enough to those outside the M62 corridor – and, let's be honest, most of those fans know about it anyway. The governing bodies in our sport have got to do more to get the message out to as many as possible, because I'm sure some Test matches have been played without those in 'alien' territory even knowing they have ever taken place.

The incredible thing is that I've met so many people over the years who have stumbled across rugby league almost by accident, and have subsequently become hooked. They alone are proof that the product is good enough – it just seems to be a major problem in selling the idea to them in the first place.

I know the sentiment behind taking an entire weekend of Super League fixtures on the road to Wales this season was fantastic, but the real aim must surely be to target children and get them interested, both in playing and watching. One solution could possibly be more Rugby League coaching in schools and organising camps for the kids. You will always get supporters of one team or another travelling far and wide to watch their heroes, and it's great to see such a strong base of support for so many clubs these days. But my interest in rugby league didn't originate from watching a game on *Grandstand* on a Saturday afternoon – it came from getting out there and playing it. I was no different from the majority of sports-mad youngsters all over the country, so why shouldn't there be a similar result when others give it a go?

Look at the success Soccer Schools have enjoyed over the years. You probably couldn't name all the clubs who get out into the community, working with the kids, and getting their reward when those youngsters become regular football players. Why couldn't something similar work in rugby league?

In times to come I would love to play a part in helping to establish RL Schools, Summer Camps or the like. But I don't mean simply by doing it in Lancashire, Yorkshire and Cumbria. The idea would have to be taken all over the country, and organised on a serious and professional basis, to make sure those youngsters get the maximum enjoyment from it. I've spoken to various people about the idea, and it's something I'd love to be involved in. I've had a bee in my bonnet about that for a long time, and it would be great to put something back into the sport which has treated me so well.

I think the difference these days is that youngsters can look at RL players and realise that you can make a serious, successful career out of it. There was a time, not too long ago either, when playing the sport, as an amateur, could only be done around a full-time career. Now you can go into it knowing that's what you are employed solely to do, and the benefits for everyone are obvious. I simply cannot see any losers.

The biggest change in the contemporary era has obviously been the introduction of the big screen to determine whether a try has been scored or not, in the shape of the video official – even though at times I do feel it is overused. In theory every time the match referee goes to the big screen, we should get the correct ruling. Unfortunately that isn't always the case, as Leeds and Bradford will testify after a controversial (wrong) decision decided their game in the Millennium Magic weekend earlier this season. But by and large the video ref gets it right, and if that helps take some of the controversy and argument out of the game, it has to be a good thing.

In the main, though, I'm happy with it, and I know from speaking to fans that they are in favour of it. Cricket took the hint and introduced a third umpire for iffy run-outs, leg-before-wicket decisions and suchlike, and the debate over whether football should follow our lead to see if the ball has crossed the line continues to rage. Mind you, if we'd had it in 1966, would we have ended up winning the World Cup?

But when it's a tight game, and everything depends on the video ref's decision, the tension is fantastic – especially when you're all looking at the big screen and the ruling comes up in your favour. The most satisfying thing to arise from its introduction is when you know, as a player, that there's been a knock on in the run-up to a try, for example, but the referee out there in the middle has missed it. When that happens, and they go to the video, it does ensure that justice is done in the end.

And I don't suppose there will be too many Saints fans who would disagree with that, because it helped us to win the 1999 Grand Final against Bradford. Bradford thought they'd scored, but video evidence proved that there had been a slight knock on from Michael Withers. No doubt Bulls fans will disagree but as far as we are concerned the video ref definitely got it right. Having said that, we had one ruled out for an infringement from Freddie Tuilagi, so it worked both ways on that occasion.

Speaking of referees, when you talk to former players, it seems there were a few more characters among the officials of the past than there are now. Stan Wall, now one of our backroom team at Saints, used to be a ref, and he is always telling us stories of the banter that would go on with players in his day. If they were all like Stan, I can imagine it as well. I mean, what other kitman would get a standing ovation from his team's supporters? I can't think of any, but to a man everyone got to his feet to applaud Stan on to the field when he was putting the tackling bags out for our pre-match warm-up at the JJB Stadium last season. It was an amazing sight, and we were all delighted for him – he's really looked after me, as has his assistant Alan Clarke, or Gibbsy as we call him. The man is a legend.

The first taste I got of a top-level international referee came when I was still at Counthill Secondary School, in the shape of a retired teacher who used to come in on a supply basis, called Sam Shepherd. He was there to teach us French, supposedly, but would end up spending virtually the entire lesson talking rugby league with me, and always in English as well. No wonder I ended up getting a D!

In my early days as a player at Warrington, I remember a referee called Colin Morris who was a real joker. Whenever Jonathan Davies was lining up a shot at goal, Colin would be on his shoulder as he placed the ball, having a few quid with him on each kick. I'm not sure who finished in front by the time he eventually retired, but knowing how accurate Jiffy could be I wouldn't have thought it was Col. Mind you, getting the money out of him would have been another story entirely, certainly tougher than any tackle Jonathan may have suffered in the game itself.

Colin has become a good friend of ours over the years and the game was a lot poorer when he whistled his last. He was actually employed as a financial adviser and helped me a lot in that direction when I first got into the team. There was one time when he came round to the house the same week that he had sent off our Dan, who was with Rochdale at the time, in a game against Keighley. I would imagine the rest of his appointments that day were running well late, because my dad was grilling him for the best part of an hour and getting him to explain the decision.

The good thing with Col was that you could talk to him during a game. You'd be able to ask him something rugby wise – or simply have the craic – and it wasn't always complimentary. In fact I can't remember it ever being complimentary! Of course he would get decisions wrong, they all do at times, but at least he would talk to the players and they knew where they stood. I think the officials prefer to talk less these days.

Ian McGregor was another who was always willing to have a bit of banter with the lads out there in the middle. And the one thing with Ian, a Scotsman who lived in Yorkshire – is there a tighter possible combination? – was that you knew he could never send you off for bad language, because his was worse than anyone's. But it wasn't just mindless abuse from him; he would do it in such a funny way that you'd have to smile, even if a decision had gone against your side.

He actually refereed a few schools games I played in for Counthill, in the Lancashire and English Schools Cup, after Sam Shepherd pulled a few strings to get him in. At least he toned down his swearing then. If he still refereed these days, they'd have to get the matches kicking off after the nine o'clock watershed in case the microphones picked up his colourful language.

You couldn't have wished to meet a nicer bloke, and you still see him knocking around the game these days, as he's working as a match commissioner for Super League, and he hasn't changed a bit. Every other word is 'f-ing this, or f-ing that'. In fact, when I come to think of it, he abuses me even more now than when he did out there in the middle of the pitch – but what a laugh he was.

The highest-profile official in the English game of recent times is probably Russell Smith, who took the bold step of upping sticks and moving to Australia to referee. You have to admire his balls for doing that, because the Aussies aren't too receptive to British players in their game, let alone officials. Russell made his mistakes from time to time, but at least he was another you could talk to, occasionally with your tongue in your cheek.

When you get someone like Russell, Colin or the like there does tend to be a lot more mutual respect, even if you still disagree when things go against you. But I don't suppose you can ever win when you are the man with the whistle. During the game you always find that both sets of supporters are against you, and spend as much time questioning your parentage as cheering for their side. Then, when one team has lost, you can guarantee at least half the fans in the ground will go home cursing you. So fair play to Russell for trying his luck Down Under – I'm sure he has developed a thicker skin and broader shoulders over the past few years than he ever needed when he was officiating in England.

They've introduced professional referees in Super League these days, but obviously you are never going to stop all the mistakes. If that was the case no player would have dropped a clanger since they went full time a few years ago. The full-time thing for players came in at the back end of the 1994–5 season, and it was a massive change for everyone. The great thing for a youngster like me just coming into the game was the fact that you could suddenly earn a decent living from playing rugby league, rather than simply picking up a few quid extra on top of your normal wage away from the game.

It did lead to some casualties, because the older guys, or those with good careers, were left with a very difficult decision to make. Our Lee, as I've already indicated, was a prime example of that: Halifax wanted to offer him a full-time contract, but he had a well-paid job and it was simply too big a risk to give it all up. For someone like me, though, it was a dream come true. I could play the sport I loved, knowing that and that alone was my living, and I could give my all to it. Previously you would be training part-time, usually after a full day's work, and no one can be in the best of shape under those circumstances. Even now, there are times when I have to pinch myself to remind myself how lucky I am. If timing is indeed everything in sport, then it couldn't have been much better as far as I am concerned. It was a case of right time, right age, when I knew that even if I came out of college with top qualifications there was still no guarantee I'd get a job – certainly not one which gave me this much satisfaction.

One of our players at Warrington called Chris Rudd was a prime example of how it could work the other way. Ruddy had a good job, and couldn't afford to walk away, especially because he was coming to the last few years of his playing career. He was a regular in the first team, but suddenly found himself competing for a slot against people who were training day in, day out. They'd be at the club every day, while the likes of Ruddy would have to come in at night and found themselves playing catch-up with the rest of the squad. He would be there at all hours, working on the weights or whatever, but it was very difficult when it came to stuff concerning the team.

Ruddy was a bloody good player as well, who was constantly spoken of as a Great Britain centre earlier in his career, but suddenly the whole thing was blown away, and in his case full-time rugby league was actually more of a hindrance than a help. So for those approaching the back end of their career, there was no chance they could go full time, especially when they had a young family to think of. You simply couldn't take the risk of walking away from your profession, where you might have another thirty years in work, but only another couple as a player. In those circumstances it is a decision you know you have to take, even though it is emotionally very tough because you love playing the game.

Becoming a full-time professional also opened avenues to me that I could otherwise never even have dreamed of. It has given me a great standard of living, and helped me look at business opportunities I didn't even know existed beforehand. As time went on, I set up Paul Sculthorpe Rights Limited, for my off-field interests, like media work and image rights. I've also moved into property rentals, working with a guy who owns David Spencer International. Basically, David has a company concerned with overseas properties for sports people.

He had a few clients who were involved in cricket and rugby union, plus a few Premiership footballers, too, so it was a good opportunity for me. The more I discussed it with him, the more it became clear it was a good proposition, and I was actually the first rugby league player to get involved. We had a few meetings to discuss the finer details and I ended up buying some properties with him.

I have put David in touch with a few of the other RL players over the years, and quite a few have subsequently got involved. He offered me the chance to go in with him as part of the business and, because of my sporting contacts, things have really taken off. A lot of the lads have bought overseas property through David since, and I personally have purchased ones abroad.

In terms of rugby league moving forward, obviously the decision to switch to the summer made a huge impact on the sport as well, although I know there are probably still a few die-hards out there who think we should have continued to play in the winter. But if we want to bring new fans to the sport, it has to be more attractive if you can sit there in nice weather, watching a flowing game on a fast surface, rather than getting drenched and frozen while you're watching two teams slogging it out on a pitch that resembles a ploughed field.

Rugby league as a whole has become a lot more professional, both on and off the field, and a far better spectacle for the supporters. The huge clampdown on bad discipline over the past few seasons has also been a massive benefit, too. Every cough and spit is picked up by the cameras these days, whether the match is screened live on television or not, and no one can get away with a thing. As a player, safety has to be paramount, and while there were certain ones who made a career out of being little more than enforcers, nowadays they have to stay within the rules, knowing they will ultimately be forced out if they carry on trying to bend the rules.

By and large the whole approach to the game is a world away from my first taste of it. Back then you would be training on a Tuesday and Thursday night, after coming straight from a shift or college, and obviously things had to be crammed into a much shorter space of time. And if you've got a load of fit, young lads finishing work, then more often than not they would head out for a pint or two afterwards. It was before my time, but I remember Chris Joynt telling me how they would all go to the pub after a couple of hours' training, which would undo much of the good work they'd just done. These days you will be working at the club in the morning, say, and then have the rest of the day to yourself. That allows you to spend more time with your families and everyone benefits.

There is also a lot more thought given to how you look after yourself away from the game as well. When I was a kid, the thought of employing a nutritionist, someone who would concentrate on your dietary needs, would have been laughed at. You don't just have to be on the ball in the match itself, but every single day in training. Obviously some of the lads will go for a drink after a game, but nothing like it was, because you can't do it with the intense demands of the game these days.

One thing that could still do with improving, however, is how injured players are cared for. If you look at other sports, I think they do a lot more for their casualties than rugby league. Horse racing, for example, has the Injured Jockeys' Fund, and the PFA do a lot for footballers who are forced out of the game.

Rugby league does the odd thing, but by and large it is an area which could do with improving. I know quite a few lads who have had to retire through injuries, and in many cases they have struggled to find work, or are simply unable to because of their injury. My old mate Ian Knott – who is virtually housebound due to a back injury he suffered playing the game – is a prime example, but too often it is merely left to the club to look after them. I know there is a benevolent fund, but when your living has been suddenly snatched away it can be very hard to make ends meet.

One of my old St Helens team-mates, John Stankevitch, was forced to retire and I remember him telling me: 'It doesn't half hit you hard when you have to finish, Scully.' You are going from a full-time wage to not even picking up half of that, and it can put incredible stress on things at home, on top of having to give up the game you love.

The situation is just as bad on the international stage as well. In fact, being injured while I was on Great Britain duty actually ended up costing me money. When you play for your country, you sign an insurance policy. But little did we know that only covers the club for the loss of your services. When that means you are effectively paying for the privilege of representing your country, it does become something of a farce.

The number of games we play is another hot potato, and there are some who feel we should actually increase the number – but obviously none of those are players. I know money will always be a controversial topic, and clubs want as much revenue as possible from their home games, but there is simply no way you could have more matches, or the standard of the product will quickly fall away. There have also been suggestions that if we reduce the number of games, the players' wages should be reduced accordingly, but that is just ridiculous, a real insult to those who are putting their bodies on the line every week.

Everyone can see how great this game is, and it deserves a hell of a lot more publicity than it currently receives. But increasing the number of games would lead to more injuries and a poorer quality of performance. Everyone is looking for that little edge, that extra something to give them an advantage in the modern game. Training methods are constantly changing for the better, even down to the equipment used. The players themselves are getting bigger, stronger and faster, and the impact from the tackles is harder than it has ever been. If you want to maintain the quality, you have to look after the players, and putting more demands on them is definitely not the way to do that.

I think that's something which has always affected us when it comes to an international series at the end of a season. Half the time you end up going into the games missing a handful of your best players – I've missed the last two series myself because of injury. And you find that the ones who are out there are fatigued from going through a brutal domestic campaign. I did ten years of, effectively, back-to-back rugby, and injuries will always take their toll in the end.

But as much as you find yourself living with aches and pains every day of your life, I wouldn't swap for the world. Rugby league is justifiably proud of its reputation as a family sport, and I know I am in a hugely fortunate position.

It's a great way of life for any youngster who manages to make it, and I have lost count of the number of kids who've asked me for advice over the seasons. I always tell them it comes down to dedication, commitment, attitude, discipline and training – but more than anything else, enjoyment. As Howard Leach, my old coach at Mayfield, would drum into us: 'Perfect practice makes perfect.' Rugby league is, indeed, the greatest game of all – if I've helped anyone over the years then it has all been worthwhile. I still wish I'd managed to win the Ashes against those bloody Aussies, though . . .